Helen
Vibe
Prog

C000229435

With a tender hand
A resource book for eldership and oversight

Zélie Gross

Leone Hayward.

First published May 2015

Quaker Books, Friends House, 173 Euston Road, London NW1 2BJ

www.quaker.org.uk

© Zélie Gross

The moral rights of the author are asserted in accordance with the Copyright, Designs and Patents Act 1988. All rights reserved. No part of this book may be reproduced or utilised, in any form or by any means, electronic or mechanical, without permission in writing from the publisher. Reviewers may quote brief passages. Enquiries should be addressed to the Publications Manager, Quaker Books, Friends House, 173 Euston Road, London NW1 2BJ.

ISBN: 978-1-907123-71-9

eISBN: 978-1-907123-75-7

Book designed and typeset by Becky Pickard (www.zebedeedesign.co.uk)

Printed by Henry Ling, Dorchester, UK

Cover image: *Unfolding landscape* by Zélie Gross

While every effort has been made to contact copyright holders of material reproduced in this book, the publisher would be glad to rectify in future editions any errors or omissions.

MIX

FSC   FSC™ C013985

Preface

~

Quaker Life's purpose is to support and strengthen the life of Quaker meetings throughout Britain Yearly Meeting. This includes offering specific support to Friends taking responsibility for eldership and oversight. Quaker meeting communities depend on good eldership and oversight to help deepen their spiritual lives and refresh their sense of vitality.

The nine volumes in the Eldership and Oversight handbook series have been much valued by Friends for a number of years and most volumes are expected to remain in print. However, in 2012 a review by Quaker Life came to a clear recommendation that the time had come for a single publication to meet the needs of contemporary Quakerism. The publication, together with a linked online resource, would aim to provide an early point of reference on all eldership and oversight matters, to explain eldership and oversight in an accessible way and to offer inspiration and encouragement to elders, overseers and other Friends undertaking these responsibilities.

This book, *With a tender hand,* is the result. We were fortunate to be able to commission Zélie Gross to write what we believe is an important new venture for the yearly meeting – a wide-ranging and refreshingly forward-looking resource for strengthening Quaker worshipping communities. When it was previewed at Quaker Life Representative Council, and at Britain Yearly Meeting Gathering in the summer of 2014, the prospect of this publication was greeted by a real sense of anticipation and delight.

Clearly, a printed book or online resource is not the whole answer to providing everything that people might need to serve in eldership and oversight with confidence. We all have much to learn from the wisdom and experience of Friends within our meetings, and through attending workshops, courses and conferences.

With a tender hand is intended to support all the ways Friends learn about and grow into the service of eldership and oversight; we are confident that this book will help Quakers today to strengthen and nurture each other with love, and to become true communities of the spirit.

Our life is love, and peace, and tenderness; and bearing one with another, and forgiving one another, and not laying accusations one against another; but praying one for another, and helping one another up with a tender hand.

(Isaac Penington, *Quaker faith & practice* 10.01)

Contents

Acknowledgments

~

I would like to thank Quaker Life for commissioning me to write this book and for entrusting me with such a responsible task on behalf of Britain Yearly Meeting – a responsibility that felt increasingly significant as the project progressed. It has been a privilege to be able to offer this service. My particular thanks go to the commissioning group of six Friends who supported me throughout: Rosie Bailey, Simon Best, Michael Booth, Judith Thompson, Marion Wells and Louisa Wright gave unstintingly of their time and patience and their good advice and upholding when I needed it most.

My thanks also go to Jane Muers for sharing with me her ideas on the structure of eldership and oversight and for guidance on writing about mental health issues; to Dr Carolyn Crippen (University of Victoria) for her encouragement and advice on the first draft of a chapter on servant-leadership; to Howard Nurden and the Quaker Life CYP staff team for careful attention to the chapter **All age community**; to Ginny Wall for doing the same with **Being in touch in a modern world**; to Vic Grainger and Mike Golby for reading the first almost-complete draft and offering timely and helpful comments; to Peter Daniels for his editorial expertise; to Diana and John Lampen for reading draft material and taking a keen and supportive interest at every stage; to Alex Wildwood for suggesting the title that turned out to be absolutely right; and to Philip Gross for reading everything at some point, and whose way with words brought freshness each time I got stuck.

Above all I am grateful for the generous responses I received from Friends to research questionnaires and to being approached personally at conferences and courses, in between sessions at Yearly Meeting and every other opportune moment when I was in the company of Quakers gathered together. *With a tender hand* couldn't have been written without the help of these many Friends, who contributed information, ideas, advice and especially their experience. Their influence permeates this book – anonymously in every case as a means of ensuring confidentiality wherever necessary or requested. This is a resource built on the shared wisdom and insights of Friends across Britain Yearly Meeting. My warm thanks go to everyone who played a part in that essential pooling of Quaker gifts and goodwill.

Introduction

~

In early 2012 Quaker Life Central Committee discerned the need for a resource to fill a significant gap in what was then available for eldership and oversight. As the author subsequently commissioned to the task I researched and wrote this book over some 18 months – accompanied along the way by an appointed group of Friends who read and commented on successive drafts. Together we made sure that the writing would fulfil its intended purpose of supporting the work of eldership and oversight in local and area meetings throughout Britain Yearly Meeting.

Concentrating on the local meeting community as the main focus of Friends' service, *With a tender hand* aims to help Friends develop the skills and understanding they need to address current concerns, respond positively in times of change and plan for future development. It recognises and celebrates the wide variety of eldership and oversight practice in local meeting communities, encouraging each participating Friend to have confidence in their role. Eldership and oversight practice in any meeting will be a blend of what is possible and what a community aspires to; this book invites Friends and meetings to broaden their awareness of possibilities and to be ambitious in their aspirations.

Part of the book's approach is to augment and expand on guidance in *Quaker faith & practice*, making it more accessible. *Qf&p* Chapter 12 contains some key guidance – notably the lists of eldership and oversight responsibilities in sections 12.12

and 12.13. Along with immediate issues that arise these responsibilities are where Friends' attention is mostly directed; but we must also engage with the wider principles of eldership and oversight and consider how they find expression in our practice.

The way I looked at this was to imagine searching the depths of the sea for solid ground unaffected by tides and currents, eventually making out the shapes of a group of enduring boulders. Above them, constantly moving around on the surface and very visible, I pictured a flotilla of corks. This unlikely pair of images helped me see that in order to write about the pressing and changing concerns of eldership and oversight, I needed to seek out their links with underlying purposes and essential processes.

Finding the links entailed 'questioning' everything that informed the book's content to discover the fundamentals of eldership and oversight as practised today. As well as *Quaker faith & practice* these sources included many other publications, responses to research queries from a broad spectrum of Friends, my own experience of service, and the insights of liberal Friends elsewhere in the world. I looked at every responsibility, issue or task that presented itself to ask:

So – what's underpinning that?

What's essential here?

Where's the life in this?

And what am I *failing* to see?

Out of this process of research and questioning emerged six 'Themes' that became the basic structure of *With a tender hand*. Together they encompass everything addressed in *Qf&p* Chapter 12, much related guidance elsewhere in *Quaker faith & practice* and some things that appear nowhere, or scarcely, in our current book of discipline. Groups of chapters look at various matters through the lens of a particular Theme, with topics often appearing in more than one Theme, sometimes several. For instance, while conflict has a chapter to itself in **Theme 4: Caring**, other Themes also examine its causes, and worship crops up throughout the book as Friends might expect.

Eldership and oversight in relationship

The first feature of eldership and oversight to become clear was how much common ground they share. *Quaker faith & practice* Chapter 12 recognises this by referring to these two areas of responsibility together as 'pastoral care' – a term which helps us identify 'care' as the first concern of eldership as well as oversight and facilitates addressing matters relevant to both. The opening Theme explores pastoral care as a unifying concept as well as an approach to caring for Quaker worshipping communities through the practices of eldership and oversight. Readers more used to equating pastoral care with oversight alone may need to remind themselves of the intentionally inclusive use of the term in this publication.

How the relationship between eldership and oversight works can very a lot between different meetings; it is no longer the case that a certain way of working is the norm and other ways exceptions to be referenced against it. So when the text refers to eldership, oversight or pastoral meetings, groups, teams or committees, each reader should take this to mean the convened group of Friends *in their own meeting* – which in some meetings will be the whole community. Similarly, where I refer to elders, overseers and their respective or joint responsibilities I trust Friends will translate this in terms of their own meeting's arrangements.

Drawing on the whole of *Quaker faith & practice,* not only Chapter 12, *With a tender hand* guides readers both to look closely at the fertile ground Friends stand on and to explore the unfolding landscape. While directly addressing Friends serving in eldership and oversight, with those appointed for the first time especially in mind, the book anticipates that readers might include anyone interested in how the worship and community life of a Quaker meeting is nurtured and sustained.

Which is surely all of us in Quaker meetings. Whatever our involvement in eldership and oversight, this book can help us recognise and build on what Friends are good at and develop new skills for fresh challenges: we all have things to learn. While not designed as a how-to-do-it manual it *will* help us to do it. *With a tender hand* is better seen as a discernment tool, or rather a toolkit – of information, searching questions, ideas, insights, guidance and examples of good practice – to aid our discernment on how best to serve our unique Quaker worshipping community.

Ways of using *With a tender hand*

1. The contents are sequenced to make sense of reading this book from beginning to end, but its structure enables Themes, and chapters within these, to be read in any order – much as Friends tend to use *Quaker faith & practice*. A first approach might be to look through the Theme introductions for one that seems the most useful or interesting place to start.

2. The layout of text and other material is designed to make the book easy to skim and riffle through, to be visually inviting and to be accessible to any style of reading. Readers should be able to find where they left off last time without having to refer to the index. This feature is achieved partly through frequent use of text boxes of various kinds for different purposes, some of which are self explanatory, others less so:

> Two or several together
> to mark linked examples

"Comments – in quote marks – by contributors to the research. These are often edited to be briefer or to anonymise details, and occasionally combine the words of more than one person commenting on the same subject."

Speech bubbles without quote marks indicate imaginary comments or conversations...

Highlighting a significant point

Occasionally: an experience offered by the author

3. *With a tender hand* is essentially a learning resource that can be used by individuals and meetings in a number of ways to develop understanding of eldership and oversight, including for induction or training of newly appointed Friends. Readers may decide to select certain chapters relating to issues in their meeting, or to consider concepts in a chosen Theme. Queries for reflection, discussion and learning at the end of each chapter are offered as guides to further exploration in a meeting, an eldership/oversight group or by individual Friends. These queries are available to download from the linked online resource – see **5.** below.

4. This is also a reference book supported by a comprehensive index, with much cross-referencing between chapters and notes on further resources. As a new resource, not a compilation of previously published material, *With a tender hand* doesn't repeat what is readily available elsewhere, such as leaflets published by Quaker Life or volumes in the Eldership and Oversight handbook series. Those handbooks

are quoted and referenced where relevant along with a number of other essential publications, many of which will be in meeting libraries or available from the Quaker Centre Bookshop or at Woodbrooke Quaker Study Centre.

5. A book with such a broad compass cannot go into all the detail Friends might require on specific subjects. A linked **online resource**, referenced throughout the text: **www.quaker. org.uk/tender-hand**, provides access to a range of extension materials, further resources and links to other useful sites, and will be regularly updated and added to. The online resource is worth checking for new material not referenced in this volume, including new or revised publications on relevant topics. While certain information here will naturally become out of date over time, the online resource will ensure that at least some of the immediate relevance of *With a tender hand* can be sustained for a good few years to come. Readers without easy access to the Web are encouraged to ask other Friends to download the additional resources they would like to use.

A brief glossary

Abbreviations: On the whole these are explained in the text: CYP stands for children and young people; LM and AM are used in some places as shorthand for local meeting and area meeting respectively: in this book the acronyms usually refer to the local and area meetings for business unless otherwise explained in the text; BYM stands for Britain Yearly Meeting.

Friend: Throughout the book I use Friend for any regular attender of a Quaker meeting, whether or not in membership of the Religious Society of Friends.

THEME 1: Pastoral care

The term 'pastoral care' occurs frequently in *Quaker faith & practice*, though not always carrying the same meaning. While British Friends sometimes use it interchangeably with 'oversight', throughout *Qf&p* Chapter 12 pastoral care occurs as an umbrella term for both oversight *and* eldership. Where it refers to oversight practice, this is further qualified, for instance as the more practical or the more outward aspects of pastoral care.

> *Qf&p* **12.11** Traditionally the first concern of elders is for the nurture of the spiritual life of the group as a whole and of its individual members so that all may be brought closer to God and therefore to one another, thus enabling them to be more sensitive and obedient to the will of God. So the right holding of our meetings for worship will be their particular care. The chief concern of overseers is with the more outward aspects of pastoral care, with building a community in which all members find acceptance, loving care and opportunities for service.
>
> Though there is a difference of function, much of the work of elders and overseers is of the same nature...

This passage guides us towards an understanding of eldership and oversight as the means by which Friends care for their meeting's spiritual purpose – encompassing worship, the people and the community, and implicitly ministry. Distinguishing between two chief concerns for pastoral care helps to identify the separate attention a meeting needs to give to each. But the ways of carrying out these responsibilities are much the same: care, nurture, guidance, encouragement, advice, listening, leading by example, etc. are all aspects of both eldership and oversight.

'Pastoral care' is used in that inclusive sense throughout this book to preserve the meaning intended in *Qf&p* Chapter 12 – and largely elsewhere in *Quaker faith & practice*. It reminds us that 'care' is as relevant to eldership as to oversight and that the two areas of responsibility have more in common than may be apparent. Whether separate, joint or shared more widely, eldership and oversight contribute together to the meeting's care for its members and the community as a whole.

A further point about the term 'pastoral' influences the way British Friends understand this differently from many churches, where it applies to the work of clergy having care of a 'flock' or congregation. In Britain Yearly Meeting we don't appoint pastors, nor do overseers or elders serve their communities in that way. We can trace this difference back to early Friends, who witnessed not only *against* any intermediary between the individual and God, but also *for* communities of equals who actively cared for one another. And they incurred wrath, ridicule, injury and even death for defying the accepted norms of respect for social status and for political and religious hierarchies.

Each chapter in this Theme explores aspects of pastoral care from a perspective that reflects that early – and our continuing – witness to equality: Friends see it as the ministry of us all in the service of our meeting community.

Chapter 1: Quaker pastoral practice
considers what pastoral care is for in 21st century British Quakerism, reflecting on Friends' perceptions and expectations and looking at ways to address misconceptions.

Chapter 2: Ways of working together

examines the principles behind various patterns of pastoral care, laying out the pros and cons of different systems to aid our understanding of how pastoral care is organised in our own meeting.

Chapter 3: Grounding our practice

looks at the purposes of pastoral meetings, building community in our groups, the use we make of area meeting pastoral committees, and how we prepare for and develop our skills including reviewing our practice.

Chapter 1: Quaker pastoral practice

~

1. Why do Quaker meetings need eldership and oversight?

Writing in 2010 for the Quaker website (**www.quaker.org.uk/ religious-society-friends-quakers**) Harvey Gillman produced a thoughtful exploration of what our name 'The Religious Society of Friends (Quakers)' says about us. Any name an organisation chooses to be known by is meant to convey something of its essence. Ours is significant to how Quakers are recognised in the world as a distinct faith group with something unique to offer, and to Friends it speaks of who we are and what binds us together as a Society. For both these reasons it is a good reminder too of the purpose of pastoral care. The same idea that Harvey Gillman offered us, of taking a close look at each word of our name in turn, illustrates here how embedded pastoral care is in the essentials of Quakerism:

Religious
We exist as a faith group to practise our way of religion by pursuing a distinctive spiritual path. A chief concern of eldership is to support worship and to nurture the spiritual life of the community. It provides leadership to ensure that what Friends practise is Quaker and not something else.

Society

All societies have a structure of some kind and ours is no exception. As key functions in a religious organisation that has evolved to embody and witness to our Quaker identity, eldership and oversight seek to sustain the life of the Society. This includes fostering understanding of our structures and encouraging involvement in how these work.

of Friends

Quakers hope to relate to one another as friends do – in the everyday sense of the word. So meetings need to build community that will encourage and nurture friendship and mutual care. Oversight especially supports the growth of community and of caring relationships.

Quakers

Our history and tradition provide the context for recognising how Quakerism has become what it is today. Our spiritual path and core testimony – of putting faith into action in response to leadings of the Spirit – are less well understood than we often hope, not just by non-Quakers but also by many in local meetings who for various reasons have limited experience of Quaker practice. Eldership and oversight serve meetings by their own example of the Quaker way, by helping people learn about and experience Quaker faith and practice, and through encouraging and supporting Friends in their witness to our vision as a Society.

Dissecting our name like this is more than an engaging exercise; it shows eldership and oversight permeating every aspect of who we are as Friends. All the ways we seek to nurture the Spirit, care for one another, build community, encourage learning and enable ministry, are how our meetings both express and underpin the spiritual purpose of the Religious Society of Friends. It helps put the details of our long lists of responsibilities into perspective to be reminded that this is why our service matters.

2. How it appears to Friends

> **Qf&p 12.18** Nor would we limit the performance of these duties to those who occupy such stations; we are all to watch over one another for good and to be mutually interested one for another, being united together as lively stones in the spiritual building of which the Lord Jesus Christ is the chief corner-stone.
>
> (Yearly Meeting in London, 1851)

Eldership and oversight work with and through everyone in the meeting; they *depend* on involvement and participation. How well Friends understand the purpose of pastoral care will therefore influence what we are able to achieve through our practice. So it is important that we are aware of Friends' perceptions of eldership and oversight and their assumptions about how pastoral care practice affects them. We need to be alert especially to misconceptions and unrealistic expectations among Friends.

i. Assumptions that are 'transferred in'

Since the middle of the last century most people attending Quaker meetings have not been born into Quaker families or brought up as Quakers. The lifelong Friend is now a rarity; increasingly Friends have found the Society in adulthood, often having been members of other faith groups in some period before they first attend a Quaker meeting. These Friends (and that includes many of us) unsurprisingly bring ideas and experience that affect their understanding of what may appear to be familiar terms and approaches to pastoral care. And these effects can endure, even though many leave a previous church because they are attracted to the difference of the Quaker way.

> Differences in how people understand the purpose of pastoral care often centre on what some view as paternalistic or intrusive and others find reassuringly welcoming and supportive. If a number of people in a meeting see pastoral care as something certain Friends appointed to the task 'do' for others, while others understand it as a more reciprocal arrangement that everyone can be part of, we have a mismatch of perception that will affect the meeting.

Because everyone attending meeting goes through a process of becoming more Quaker over time, eldership and oversight have an ongoing task that comes with a steady (and welcome) stream of newcomers. How do meetings assimilate and address the influence of people who bring from a previous faith experience a concept of pastoral care still settled in their minds as 'natural'? On the one hand they may idealise this concept, feeling critical of their old church for not living up to the ideal and hoping to find it done better or more authentically in this very different 'church'. On the other hand they may struggle with anything at all that reminds them of what they have chosen to leave behind. In either case, people who have left previous churches can bring a backwash of reactions to Quaker ways that seem to move in both these directions, and which take time to become resolved.

ii. Perceptions of hierarchy and 'status'

We may also note differences in how eldership and oversight are understood by Friends in the following (and other) dissimilar or contrasting circumstances in a meeting:

Friends appointed to roles	Friends not currently serving
Friends very active in the meeting and/or the Society	Friends who only come to meeting for worship
Friends in membership	Friends not in membership
Friends who attend regularly	Friends who attend infrequently
Friends with time to spare	Friends in full time work or occupied with family responsibilities

This is not to suggest it is possible, or helpful, to presume we know about people from these facts alone – we are all aware of the Friend in full-time work who gives huge service to the meeting, and the attender who is far more involved than many members. But differences in perception between Friends in different circumstances *can* be associated with how connected they feel to the meeting and how immersed in Quaker ways.

The more engaged Friends are in the life of the meeting, the more likely they are to identify with the reasons for having eldership and oversight and to see the point in participating. The less engaged they are, the more Friends will tend to see others as being 'in charge' and either to resist this or to be happy to let them get on with it.

"We send a letter to each person saying who overseers are and that we are all available but need everyone to help and to bring matters to our attention. We also remind them that everyone in the meeting is responsible for care."

"We notice what helps friendships get going and who is being left out, and we make sure they aren't that way for long – if it's what they want. We do a lot to support friendships, and new people seem to strike up friendships with each other very early on."

Another complication that can lead people to perceive a division of 'status' in the meeting stems from tensions between our need for organisation, which ensures things get done effectively, and our need for community, which helps us get along together and encourages commitment and involvement.

Friends are often less accepting of organisation in Quaker meetings than in previous generations, and less comprehending of why a degree of organisation and structure might be essential for our community to work. Many coming to Quakers see our non-hierarchical structures as a significant attraction and may expect to find few similarities, if any, with their secular experience or to the practices of a church they have chosen to leave behind. Appointing Friends to roles that bring authority to act, or to engage in discernment and decision-making separately from the whole group (e.g. pastoral meetings), can be seen from such a perspective as creating a hierarchy in the meeting.

> "Appointing people to offices makes the appointees more responsible and others less responsible – and possibly somewhat alienated. It might be better if we relied more on rotas of all and less on roles for a designated few."

> "I have had misgivings about eldership and oversight for some time. Having elders and overseers seems unnatural to a Society of Friends with equality as a testimony. Those who need or desire support are in a better position to know whom they would like to provide it than are members of nominations committees."

Whether hierarchy in our meeting is real or only a perception among some, it can lead to a sense of *them and us*. Not everyone is unhappy with an apparent division between people appointed to roles and those the roles serve: some might be glad of the benefits, including feeling relieved of responsibility. For others, seeing divisions in the meeting (real or imagined) can lead them to feel put out, critical of how Friends carry out their roles, or discouraged from contributing. A Friend might consider that it isn't their job to visit a sick Friend they aren't especially close to, or even to thank someone for their helpful ministry.

When people assume they are expected to defer to those they see as being in authority they may also believe they are not entitled to speak about their unease, so we can miss the signs. If we do spot a problem of this kind we should first check that eldership and oversight practice is not encouraging deferential attitudes in some way, perhaps inadvertently.

There may be a need for occasions when people can share their thinking and their feelings on the subject and say the things that are difficult to say. The practical arrangements will only be part of this; more important will be a commitment to establishing a climate of listening without judgment.

Qf&p 12.01 Careful listening is fundamental to helping each other; it goes beyond finding out about needs and becomes part of meeting them. Some would say that it is the single most useful thing that we can do. Those churches that have formal confession understand its value, but confession does not have to be formal to bring benefits. Speaking the unspeakable, admitting the shameful, to someone who can be trusted and who will accept you in love as you are, is enormously helpful.

❖ **Chapter 9:** *Belonging and commitment* looks at issues to do with inclusion and exclusion in meeting communities, offering suggestions for how they might be addressed.

❖ **Chapter 14:** *Conflict and difficulty in the meeting* and **Chapter 19:** *Making connections* each address the subject of sharing and listening practice in eldership and oversight.

❖ **Chapter 21:** *Leadership among equals* offers insights and practical approaches to making leadership a more accessible and less distancing idea to Friends.

3. Addressing misconceptions

Most meetings will need to clarify Quaker practice from time to time, be patient with people who appear neither to listen nor observe and sometimes challenge a misconception. Occasionally misconceptions hold sway to a degree that distorts accepted Quaker practice. For example, a meeting may arrive at a settled belief that elders should prepare suitable spoken ministry in advance; that Friends should respect elders as their spiritual superiors; that overseers have a duty to attend personally to each person's needs – and that people have a right to expect this.

i. Ways to promote understanding

If we feel there is a lack of understanding of eldership and oversight among Friends there are several approaches we could take:

- opportunities for Friends to share and discuss their perceptions, expectations and/or their concerns about eldership or oversight
- an invited speaker or facilitator to lead the meeting in learning about eldership/oversight
- holding eldership/oversight meetings that are open to everyone – sometimes or more regularly. With careful clerking, open discernment is possible for most pastoral care matters
- ensuring all Friends appointed to pastoral care roles receive training
- a rolling programme of Quaker learning in the meeting
- encouragement and support for Friends to attend courses, conferences, area meetings for business and Yearly Meeting.

ii. Making our practice visible

It makes a big difference to Friends' assumptions about Quaker practice if arrangements for eldership and oversight are clearly visible, or at least easy to discover. Being able to 'see the wheels go round' helps everyone recognise why eldership and oversight matter, and how they can play their part. We need to see things through other people's eyes, especially those who are less involved. Are there unwritten rules that only some of us understand or know the reasons for? Are some Friends getting on with things so efficiently that no one else is even aware there is a job to be done? Further chapters look at these and other questions on the importance of knowing why and how we do things – in eldership and oversight practice, in the meeting generally, and simply as Friends.

❖ **Chapter 3:** *Grounding our practice* includes discussion of transparency in how pastoral care business is conducted.

❖ There may be more we can do to provide information, explain things and invite involvement that doesn't compromise confidentiality. **Chapter 18:** *Keeping people informed* includes useful ideas for how to go about this.

❖ **Chapter 9:** *Belonging and commitment* looks at possibilities for engaging with questions that could help with understanding how our meeting works.

❖ We may not even know why our meeting does things in certain ways apart from this being how they are always done. **Chapter 2:** *Ways of working together* takes a close look at different kinds of eldership and oversight provision to help us reflect on the system of pastoral care in our own meeting and ask the questions that enable us to work within it more effectively.

❖ **Chapter 21**: *Leadership among equals* and **Chapter 22** *Leading with discernment* explore the visible and invisible processes that enable our meeting to *be* a Quaker community.

Queries for reflection, discussion and learning

Chapter 1: Quaker pastoral practice

Queries for individual reflection

1. What do I understand to be the underlying purpose of pastoral care (including both eldership and oversight)? How does this underlying purpose affect me as a person and as a Quaker?
2. What am I bringing from my previous faith or non-faith experience that influences what I hope to find in my Quaker meeting?
3. Who do I see as being 'in charge' in my meeting? How do I feel about that? Does it make a difference to how I feel if I am one of the people in a significant role?

Queries for pastoral groups

1. Do some people have a better understanding of the aims of eldership and oversight than others? Why might that be? Why might Friends not really understand what we are here for and what we are trying to do? How can we address that?
2. In what ways might we be encouraging unhelpful assumptions among Friends about our service?
3. How might we create opportunities for people to share their thoughts and feelings about the way things are done or organised in the meeting? How might such opportunities also be part of the thinking that could lead to changes?

Queries for meetings

1. What do we hope or expect eldership and oversight will achieve for our community?

2. Are we aware of tensions to do with perceptions of hierarchy? Where do they come from? Might the way things happen or are organised in the meeting be encouraging this view? How might we together address both the tensions and the perceptions?

3. What are the unwritten rules in our meeting? Do we need to clarify Quaker practice, and if so in which areas? How should we go about that?

❖ These pages can be downloaded from the online resource: **www.quaker.org.uk/tender-hand**

Chapter 2: Ways of working together

~

Quaker faith & practice Chapter 12 begins with eleven passages on aspects of pastoral care followed by two sections listing the responsibilities of eldership (12.12) and of oversight (12.13). Reading these lists we could perhaps be forgiven for assuming that after all, only one of them is concerned with 'care', and that there are just a couple of items in each list for which eldership and oversight share responsibility. But we need to read on:

> **Qf&p 12.14** However pastoral care is organised, it is essential that the responsibilities for spiritual, intellectual, emotional, material and physical care for each member of the Quaker community, as listed above, should be given prayerful consideration. As the responsibilities of eldership and oversight overlap in many instances, there should be close co-operation between elders and overseers at all times.

The differences between eldership and oversight, and what they have in common, are both significant to 'close co-operation'. Looking in detail at the principles behind various systems for providing pastoral care, this chapter is an opportunity to gain a clearer picture of whatever system our own meeting has so that we can consider the implications of doing things in one way rather than another.

❖ *Patterns of eldership and oversight*: *Volume 1 of the Eldership and Oversight handbook series* discusses a range of variations in how eldership and oversight are provided in meetings; it will be very useful reading for any meeting considering changing or developing its system.

1. Pastoral care systems and organisation

In this investigation of pastoral care organisation eldership and oversight systems are pictured as differing from one another along two axes of a square grid – or matrix – encompassing any number of variations in how pastoral care is provided in different meetings:

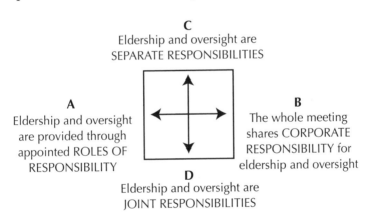

C
Eldership and oversight are
SEPARATE RESPONSIBILITIES

A
Eldership and oversight
are provided through
appointed ROLES OF
RESPONSIBILITY

B
The whole meeting
shares CORPORATE
RESPONSIBILITY for
eldership and oversight

D
Eldership and oversight are
JOINT RESPONSIBILITIES

Looking along the horizontal axis

➢ At one end (**A**), only Friends appointed to roles provide eldership and oversight.
➢ At the other end (**B**), everyone in the meeting is equally responsible and involved.
➢ In between we will find varying degrees of

involvement in eldership and oversight of people not appointed to roles, in conjunction with some appointments.

Looking up and down the vertical axis

➤ At one end (**C**), eldership and oversight are distinctly separate responsibilities with minimal overlap.
➤ At the other end (**D**), eldership and oversight responsibilities are fully combined.
➤ In between there will be varying degrees of joint/separate working of eldership and oversight.

Some pastoral care systems are easy to place in the matrix. Very traditional systems with elders and overseers working almost entirely separately will occupy the top left corner. Fully corporate systems will be somewhere on the right-hand edge – further up or down depending on how far eldership and oversight are seen as separate or joint responsibilities.

Most meetings fit somewhere in the body of the matrix rather than on the edges because however clearly defined we believe our system is, in practice all meetings tailor their provision to their meeting's needs. For example, our elders and overseers may work together more closely than is apparent to people generally, or others in the meeting may be more involved in the sharing of responsibility than might appear from the fact that elders and overseers are appointed. The following are some of the more explicit ways of organising eldership and oversight provision that are neither exactly one thing nor exactly the other:

• appointed elders with corporate oversight
• appointed 'elderseers' and some degree of corporate sharing of responsibility
• appointed elders and overseers who meet and work closely together

- an appointed pastoral team jointly responsible for eldership and oversight
- a fully corporate system with separate conveners for eldership and oversight
- linked elders and overseers working in pairs.

How conscious are we of the way eldership and oversight work in our own meeting, and does everybody in the meeting know? Plotting its place in the matrix can tell us a lot about our system of pastoral care:

- It helps us see that we have a choice – which could be our choice as a local meeting or perhaps as agreed in our area meeting. Our system could have been inherited, we may have designed it, or perhaps it evolved; but it is the way it is now because we agree to work with it, until we agree to change it.
- It gives us a way of recognising how much or how little we have changed over time and in what directions.
- It can clarify how we accommodate different needs and wants in our meeting, and what is possible in our circumstances.

A closer look at the matrix can tell us more about the possible implications of choices we make as a meeting. All systems have advantages and drawbacks and it is useful to understand how these are balanced in our own way of doing things.

> What follows indicates *possible* advantages and drawbacks. There is no implication that a particular system will inevitably gain or suffer in any of these ways.

Comparing each end of the horizontal axis:

A ←――――――――→ B

Eldership and oversight are provided through appointed ROLES OF RESPONSIBILITY	The whole meeting shares CORPORATE RESPONSIBILITY for eldership and oversight

A. *Left-hand end*: Eldership and oversight through roles of responsibility

The pastoral care structure in most meetings is based on triennial appointments by the area meeting of Friends to key roles such as elder and overseer, or perhaps 'elderseer' for a joint role. Rarely do meetings intend these appointments to be seen as the sole means of providing guidance and care, even if – as can happen – others come to see it that way. More usually the aim is for appointed Friends to serve as 'enablers' of a mutually caring and resourceful community, while encouraging others to prepare for the possibility of being appointed to eldership and oversight roles in due course.

A: ROLES OF RESPONSIBILITY

Possible advantages

- Efficient and simple organisation; a clearly understood system
- Opportunity to train and develop skills in a few individuals at a time
- Clarity about record keeping
- Good discernment through appointed Friends meeting together regularly
- Clarity about issues of confidentiality.

Possible drawbacks

- Inequitable sharing of responsibility and work in the meeting
- Appointed Friends feel over-burdened; others feel disempowered or beholden
- A perception that the system creates a hierarchy; a feeling of them and us
- Too few in membership to appoint; the same serving Friends recycled
- A risk of misjudged exercise of authority

B. *Right-hand end*: Eldership and oversight through corporate responsibility

Systems based on this approach acknowledge that all Friends are capable of contributing and that everyone in the community will benefit if we each do what we can. Corporate systems also seek to address assumptions that certain groups, such as children and the frail or elderly, have little to offer. A fully corporate system may still include some appointments, perhaps as conveners of committees, but in any event leadership will be needed for many purposes and can arise naturally rather than necessarily through appointments.

B: CORPORATE RESPONSIBILITY

Possible advantages

- Strengthened relationships in the meeting
- An enhanced sense of community and belonging; a sense of equality
- More people acquiring skills and understanding
- Release of potential and initiative in the meeting
- Individuals feeling less burdened because many more share the load

Possible drawbacks

- More complex arrangements needing high maintenance
- Lack of clarity about who does what
- Eldership weakened through no one feeling they have the authority to act
- Difficult issues or particular needs not being adequately addressed
- Dependency on relatively few committed and active people; some individuals don't want involvement (it feels like work)

Comparing each end of the vertical axis:

C
Eldership and oversight are
SEPARATE RESPONSIBILITIES

↑

↓

D
Eldership and oversight are
JOINT RESPONSIBILITIES

C. *Top end:* Eldership and oversight through separate responsibilities

This approach emphasises two main functions of pastoral care from a perspective that each needs particular and separate attention. It may also reflect a view that eldership and oversight draw on different skills and experience in the meeting, which contribute differently to natural links between the two areas of responsibility. Whether the separate focuses are maintained through appointed roles or some form of corporate provision, the intention is not to lose sight of one in concentrating on the other, nor to neglect the specific responsibilities of each.

C: SEPARATE RESPONSIBILITIES

Possible ...
- Clarity about the purposes of eldership and oversight
- Opportunity for utilising / developing different gifts in the meeting
- Efficiency through division of tasks

... advantages
- Enabling different emphasis of approach, e.g. modelling by example; being practical
- Focused development of eldership or oversight practice

Possible ...
- Lack of awareness of the connections between eldership and oversight
- Oversight carrying a heavier burden and responsibility for more tasks

... drawbacks
- A perception of eldership as higher 'status' than oversight
- Lack of consultation or mutual understanding between the two
- A male (eldership) / female (oversight) divide

D. *Bottom end*: Eldership and oversight through joint responsibilities

Joint provision – through joint roles, shared responsibilities or a jointly corporate system – recognises eldership and oversight as mutually dependent, each working through the other. It emphasises that the spiritual dimension is present in everything we do as Friends to care for our meeting and each other, and that caring for one another includes care of the spiritual dimension – in our lives and in our meeting. This perspective sees no clear dividing line and finds good reasons to build on natural connections.

D: JOINT RESPONSIBILITIES

Possible advantages

- Pooling of gifts and resources
- Coherence and wholeness in pastoral care provision
- Mutual support and co-operation among all those involved in eldership and oversight
- Shared discernment on complex issues, e.g. affecting worship and community
- Flexibility and adaptability

Possible drawbacks

- Lack of clarity about who does what
- Oversight neglected through being experienced as burdensome
- Eldership neglected among pressing concerns of oversight
- Practical matters taking priority over reflection and worship
- Lack of clarity / confidence / experience concerning exercise of authority

2. It's all about people

Examining different approaches to pastoral care won't reveal the whole story. In every line of the discussion in this chapter are real people just being themselves in diverse life circumstances, and each bringing different gifts and lacks – all of which significantly affect whatever is planned. Eldership and oversight in any meeting necessarily reflect the people who make up that unique community, for example in respect of:

- the size of the meeting – and how many attend and how often
- the presence and numbers of children and young people
- the age profile of people attending
- the meeting's location – and how near or far away people live
- whether the meeting is well-established or more recently formed
- the proportion of members to attenders
- any marked increase or decrease in attendance
- recent experience of conflict or major disruption in the life of the meeting.

And further details of Friends' practice will influence the effectiveness of any system. Two aspects in particular can make a significant difference: how active or inactive eldership and oversight are in the life of the community; and how much Friends generally contribute and participate.

i. Activity or inactivity in eldership and oversight
This is often less to do with how pastoral care is structured than with the people who make up the meeting during any particular phase of its corporate life:

- Very active eldership and oversight might include provision of many organised opportunities for groups, close

engagement with individuals and involvement of elders/
overseers in most meeting initiatives and business.
- Low activity is sometimes characterised by a hands-off
approach (they know where we are if they need us) or
laissez faire (if something needs doing, someone will see to
it eventually).

Most meetings will be somewhere in between these extremes.
Our ways of going about things may be an intentional
feature of our pastoral care system, or might come about
through the appointment of certain Friends rather than others,
but in either case we should be aware of how active or inactive
pastoral care practice appears to Friends. One way or the
other, it can often be a cause for concern in the meeting.

Having lots of opportunities and very engaged pastoral care
might sound ideal, but to some it can feel intrusive, bossy or
demanding. Very detached eldership and oversight might
encourage people to recognise that they too have responsibility
for making things happen and for caring for one another, but
it can also lead to neglect and discontent. The degrees to which
eldership and oversight are active/proactive or sensitively
backstage hold important clues to how acknowledged, included
or supported by the meeting Friends feel. When we spot
responses to our practice that don't fit with our intentions,
some of the causes might be found here.

ii. Participation and contribution in eldership and oversight

A test of the effectiveness of eldership and oversight practice
is how well it expresses the intention in this passage from
Quaker faith & practice Chapter 11 – Membership:

> **Qf&p 11.12** ...Pastoral care, which in many other
> churches is given in part by a separated ministry, is in
> our yearly meeting a responsibility shared by all members.

Whatever the pattern of eldership and oversight in a meeting, it is still everyone's responsibility to be part of ensuring the right holding of meeting for worship, for caring for one another and for nurturing community. Every system of pastoral care – no matter where it appears in our matrix – aims to encourage people to contribute to the life of their meeting community. In practice, sharing responsibility also rests on the available skills, experience and commitment in the meeting. Clearly some people will be able or expected to offer more than others, but where meetings nevertheless preserve a sense of 'everyone in it together' Friends are more likely to participate if they possibly can.

Being included and being involved are the two basic building blocks of community. The responsibilities outlined in *Qf&p* 12.12 and 12.13 indicate how Friends appointed to roles can maintain this focus, and others contributing to the aims of eldership and oversight will find the way these responsibilities are described a useful guide. Corporate systems of pastoral care are just one approach to inclusion and involvement in meetings; there are many others and all of them can work well when Friends are clear about this as their aim.

- ❖ **Chapter 3:** *Grounding our practice* looks at practical arrangements for enabling eldership and oversight to 'share their common commitment to the service of their meetings' (*Qf&p* 12.11).
- ❖ **Chapter 8:** *The meaning of community* explores ways of building community through promoting active participation in the life of the meeting.
- ❖ **Chapter 11:** *Addressing need* considers how we approach our responsibilities with the intention of involving Friends within our own meeting's system of eldership and oversight.

Queries for reflection, discussion and learning

Chapter 2: Ways of working together

Queries for individual reflection
1. How do I understand the distinction between eldership and oversight? Which feels more important or less important to me, and why is that?
2. Where do I think my meeting's system of pastoral care fits in the grid? Do other Friends agree with me? (Consider asking a few.)
3. 'It is the responsibility of everyone to be part of ensuring the right holding of worship, for caring for one another and for building community.' How far do I agree with this? What is my part? What is the part of Friends not appointed to eldership or oversight roles?

Queries for pastoral groups
1. Where do we see overlap between eldership and oversight, and where differences? How do we achieve 'close co-operation' in practice?
2. Where does our system of pastoral care fit in the grid? Has this changed over time? Does it need to change in any way?
3. 'Being included and being involved are the two basic building blocks of community.' How actively do we encourage Friends' involvement in the provision of eldership and oversight?

Queries for meetings

1. Why is pastoral care structured in a certain way in our meeting? What are the advantages of our way of providing eldership and oversight, and what are the disadvantages?

2. How active are eldership and oversight in the life of our meeting? Do we want it to be more or less active? What else would we like to see happening that isn't happening now?

3. 'Pastoral care, which in many other churches is given in part by a separated ministry, is in our yearly meeting a responsibility shared by all members.' (*Qf&p* 11.12). How far is this true in our meeting?

❖ These pages can be downloaded from the online resource: **www.quaker.org.uk/tender-hand**

Chapter 3: Grounding our practice

~

Whatever system of pastoral care our meeting has, Friends with responsibilities for eldership and oversight need a means of coordinating and developing their work. This chapter assumes that it is usual practice for a group to meet for this purpose, and that Friends will agree an approach that ensures their service will be responsive to the meeting's needs for eldership and/or oversight. In most meetings this group will be a certain number of Friends appointed to the task. The larger part of what follows can also be applied to whole-meeting groups undertaking corporate responsibility for eldership and oversight, and/or to the smaller group of conveners in a corporate system.

How our pastoral group goes about its task can be usefully divided into three linked areas:

- eldership and oversight group meetings
- connections with other groups
- developing and reviewing our practice.

Before looking at each of these perhaps we should ask why any of this structural detail matters. Surely it is simple enough to know that our task is to make sure worship and community are nurtured and Friends cared for, and then to get on with it? In fact it is that simple; the structures we work within and the processes and practices we employ are only the ways and means of achieving those aims, and the overriding purpose is to free the Spirit. If we find our structures and processes obstruct the Spirit, impede creativity and initiative, or become rods for our own backs, we are getting something wrong and may need to review our arrangements.

1. Eldership and oversight group meetings

Qf&p **12.12 a.** to meet regularly to uphold the meeting and its members in prayer.

Qf&p **12.13 e.** to meet regularly to ensure that the pastoral needs of everyone associated with the meeting are being noticed; to check the membership list frequently, not only for accuracy but also in order to cover unmet needs – each child and young person should be considered as an individual and not solely as a member of a family group.

Local pastoral groups, whether separate or joint, need regular occasions to meet for a number of purposes in addition to these. For example, we need to:

- discuss the scope of our work and agree on practice
- make decisions on action
- build community as a team and support one another.

Elders meeting separately may have periods when they can focus largely on the duty of upholding the meeting in prayer, whereas oversight asks for more constant attention to the changing needs of individuals and the community as a whole. If we meet jointly we must find a balance between the two as the basis for our work together.

i. Clerking and agendas

A group needs a convener or clerk, either appointed or rotated within the group, who will conduct the business of each meeting and take a leadership role in helping the group work together. They may be responsible for planning the agenda as well.

Over a period of perhaps a year agendas should allow us to discuss the full range of our tasks. Drawing up a calendar of routine business helps ensure that we touch on everything at least once while leaving space for reflection and for issues as they arise. Some matters will naturally occur at certain times of the year; we can then slot other routine business around these dates, taking care not to overfill agendas at this stage. Listing and prioritising items as a new group of elders or overseers is a useful introduction to the work we will do together, and updating our calendar as the year progresses helps us with our planning in the following year.

We might also plan an outline 'regular' agenda, e.g. starting and ending with a period of worship, time for personal sharing, routine items, and good space for issues that need our attention now. But we will want to be flexible too. Sometimes pressing business means shelving routine matters on that occasion. We have to keep an eye on how often we do this so that important matters don't slide off the end of our agendas completely.

Joint meetings of eldership and oversight can benefit from varying the order of items on the agenda, or alternating the focus of each meeting, in order to give equal attention to both areas of responsibility. If our meetings are usually separate, it is helpful when we meet from time to time jointly (*Qf&p* 12.11) to assume no hierarchy between eldership and oversight. We can signal our reciprocal relationship by the separate conveners clerking these meetings jointly or alternately.

ii. 'Holding' our pastoral care meetings

Eldership and oversight meetings need to be held in the sense of *cared for* as well as *rightly* held. Meetings held in both senses of the word make it possible for our work together to be: Spirit-led, supportive, manageable and mutually accountable.

- **Spirit-led:** As with other meetings for business, eldership and oversight meetings are held in a spirit of worship that enables our discernment to be Spirit-led. We depend on a certain amount of structure, but this should allow our meetings to be creative and responsive.
- **Supportive:** The work of eldership and oversight engages our feelings and emotions as well as demanding action and hard work – and often quite a lot of bureaucracy as well. We meet together both to be sure of getting things done and to support each other in service that can involve significant personal cost. We need a regular space together that is honest and accepting so that it feels okay to talk about what we are willing and able to do. And this won't be the same for everyone. Some may feel overburdened while others feel guilty about not doing as much. If we cannot be clear about how our service affects us personally, our troubled feelings may hold us back from serving our meeting well.

> On occasion our meetings could include an activity that encourages relaxed discussion, or which helps us focus on our own needs through creative listening or worship sharing. An issue that arouses strong feelings in the group may reveal a need for a threshing meeting. We might even consider having fun together!

- **Manageable:** There is little point including ample time for sharing and mutual support if this makes meetings too long and too full, so that we end up tired and overstretched. Meetings work better when they are paced to engage our focused thinking and take account of the available energy and attention in the room.
- **Mutually accountable:** Whenever new people join the

group it helps to begin by agreeing ground rules on listening, confidentiality and plain speaking. And we must think about how the group will support its convener; a role that can bring singular pressures. We all share responsibility for how things are going. A useful way of keeping track is to include an item in our calendar towards the end of each year for reviewing the effectiveness of our meetings:

➤ What are our aims for these meetings?

➤ How far are we achieving them?

➤ Are we meeting often enough, or too frequently?

➤ If we meet separately, how well are our joint meetings serving the purposes of eldership and oversight?

➤ What is our practice regarding minutes, and how is this working?

iii. Minutes

The question of what to do about making and keeping minutes exercises eldership and oversight groups for good reasons, which are not always easy to resolve. We have to ask why it is important to keep a record. Who will it help if we do, and what will be lost if we don't?

Not all our business is of a confidential nature, so we shouldn't decide against making minutes on grounds of the sensitivity of matters before us. Minutes provide a useful record of decisions and action taken and help ensure that unresolved business is followed up. And we have to see our work as continuing beyond the service of any individual or of the group as a whole. Keeping sufficient records enables future groups to build on what we have learnt – and to avoid repeating our mistakes. Friends will also be glad of records in the event of an issue recurring or of it being relevant background in a new matter.

While the clerk or convener is usually the person who drafts a minute, all Friends present make the minute by agreeing its final form. Our group therefore needs to discuss what is appropriate to record within a shared understanding of confidentiality. Our guideline will be to minute the essential facts of a matter without revealing unnecessary personal details. For example, a decision to make a grant of money to or for someone should be recorded in a minute that gives the treasurer a clear instruction to make the payment, but it doesn't need to state why the person needs the money. Minutes of an especially sensitive nature can be kept confidential by storing them separately and noting the fact in the general minutes.

> Under data protection legislation a person has right of access to records about them held in any form, and this includes 'confidential' minutes. If we make our minutes with this in mind it doesn't stop us from being clear about a matter, but should help us to notice and remove any inessential facts, together with anything that is not factual, such as opinions or hearsay.

Do we make our minutes at the time in the usual way or by some other means? Guidance on this will always confirm that the usual way is how it must be done. But in practice many pastoral groups find they don't always achieve this. The matters we discuss are often very different from those brought for decision to a local meeting for business (LM), and we are trying to fit decision-making in with so many other necessary elements of our meetings. Friends report that they often run out of time and resort to taking notes rather than minutes. Others agree the substance of a minute but the actual minute is written up later and circulated – to those present at the time – for agreement on the sense of the meeting before minutes are signed and filed.

While both practices fall short of the ideal, the important thing is to keep a sufficient record and to be clear such records express the spirit of our discernment. But we may need to ask why lack of time is leading us to do things another way. Are meetings too infrequent? Are we overloading our agendas? Do we use the time we have in the best way?

A final point is to be aware of the usual arrangements for archiving minutes, which is likely to be an area meeting responsibility through an appointed custodian of records. Our group will need to decide when to deposit older records and to know the procedure for retrieving something we wish to refer to in relation to current business.

iv. Openness in how we work

We must remember that all the work we do in eldership and oversight meetings concerns the meeting community and individual Friends. And it may concern people in the sense of being a matter of concern to them as well. Do we pause to reflect on other Friends' perceptions of what *could* be going on behind closed doors?

> Not everyone is comfortable with the idea of meetings they are excluded from discussing their personal circumstances. They may understand the reasons and see the point, yet feel it distances them from Friends in pastoral care roles or from the system of care.
>
> Are we open to questioning how often it is essential that pastoral care meetings are held in private, which matters need to be discussed in that way, and which records held confidentially?

Friends do value openness in Quaker practice. Some meetings are considering this issue and finding fewer reasons and occasions to keep certain areas of their meeting's discernment hidden from view. For example, minutes of pastoral meetings may be made available to all Friends in the same way as LM (local) or AM (area) minutes, and notes of confidential matters, when needed, will be kept separately. In corporate systems pastoral meetings are open to everyone. Here too any sensitive matters will be kept confidential to the few Friends addressing them – perhaps within a care circle or as delegated by the meeting. Some elders' groups in traditional systems have adopted the same practice to encourage greater understanding of eldership.

❖ **Chapter 17:** *The Quaker way of right ordering* looks at the Quaker decision-making process in meetings for worship for business.

2. Connections with other groups

A formally convened local pastoral group will engage with other groups including the local meeting for business (LM), some other groups in our local meeting, our area meeting pastoral committee, and on certain matters with role holders in the area meeting.

i. Connecting with our other half

If eldership and oversight groups meet separately the first of these connections is with one another. It will be important for elders and overseers to meet jointly from time to time and to make good use of those occasions (see *Qf&p* 12.11 and 12.14). Practice varies, ranging from a joint meeting for learning or spiritual development every six months, to alternating joint and separate meetings for business each month. Other ways of sustaining good connections include exchanging minutes, or for both groups to send a representative to attend the other group's meetings. This latter practice enables every member of each group to have first-hand experience of the other over a relatively short period – depending on how often we meet.

ii. Connecting with local meeting for business (LM) and area meeting for business (AM)

As a local team we communicate formally from time to time with LM by minute on certain business, or by sending a report that we ask LM to discuss or to note: for example, a report on meetings for learning. Similarly, our group might communicate with other local meeting groups: we may receive a minute from the children and young people's committee, or send a minute to the finance committee. And we will routinely send minutes to the treasurer about money matters to act on. Some LMs agree to have a regular standing item on eldership and oversight, which helps the whole meeting remember the shared responsibility for pastoral care.

Communications with AM will be through the local meeting for business or our area meeting pastoral committee, though we may be in direct contact with the membership clerk and consulted directly by AM nominations committee. It all depends on practice agreed by the AM, which will be recorded in a memorandum of understanding held by our trustees. So we should check on that and also refer to *Qf&p* Chapter 4 for clarification on matters of right ordering.

iii. Connecting with eldership and oversight in the area meeting

Quaker faith & practice 12.06 tells us that we should meet at least once a year with others serving in eldership or oversight in the area meeting. If we cannot meet more frequently we are missing out on perhaps the greatest resource available to us. This is especially true of smaller meetings with possibly few Friends serving in pastoral care. We have so much to gain from the wider eldership and oversight body in terms of support, fellowship and mutually shared commitment to serving our local meetings, including the opportunity to learn from one another's different experience and ways of doing things.

When Friends from around the yearly meeting meet up on Woodbrooke courses or at eldership and oversight conferences, without fail they will report that a large part of their learning came from discussions and conversations with fellow participants.

Arranging to meet up regularly may not be practical in every area meeting, some of which are very far flung indeed; in others it might be a matter of imagining new ways of approaching the possibility:

"Elders and overseers have an annual residential weekend each spring. This is a major event in our calendar and not to be missed!"

"We hold a meeting for an hour before every AM. It isn't long, but our meetings are regular and long enough to do a couple of items of business. The main thing is we meet each other and form friendships."

"We cannot meet often but we build community by following up each AM elders meeting through online discussion in our Yahoo group. We get to know one another this way and exchange ideas."

"AM overseers' meetings take place quarterly on a Saturday. We do business in the morning, have a shared lunch and usually do a bit more business in the afternoon. Then we will do an activity, e.g. if an overseer has been on a course they might suggest discussing in small groups or we do worship sharing on a topic."

"Some people travel long distances to AMs, and some stay overnight with local Friends. AM lasts all day. Elders and overseers make the most of it by meeting in the lunch break, which is usually 75 to 90 minutes to allow most Friends time to socialise."

Establishing community among elders and overseers in our area meeting gives us access to greater resources than we can provide from within our local meeting, including:

- counsel, guidance and practical support in the event of difficulty
- a forum for sharing ideas and plans for change and development
- discernment to help a local group move forward.

And once we start making good use of these opportunities we will naturally find more reason to develop the wider corporate nature of our work.

The work of area meeting pastoral committees might include:

- reviewing the provision of pastoral care in each local meeting to ensure it is sufficient and working, and advising AM of additional needs
- discernment on matters of concern to the area meeting, and communicating this by minute to AM
- receiving and responding to minutes from AM requesting action
- receiving and responding to minutes from local meeting pastoral groups
- encouraging and supporting local meeting spiritual reviews

- undertaking AM spiritual reviews
- planning AM events for learning, community building or spiritual nurture
- arranging intervisitation between local meetings
- organising practical support for a local meeting in stretched circumstances
- reminding local elders and overseers of routine responsibilities and asking them to report any difficulties in their ability to attend to these.

3. Developing and reviewing our practice

A pastoral group is a community within a community and it requires similar attention to nurture and development as does our local meeting.

i. Induction

We may pay good attention to how we welcome newcomers to meetings, but do we also attend to the ways we welcome new appointees into our group? Each newly appointed Friend needs to have an induction that will give them confidence in understanding their role and how they can be helped to fulfil it. Certain things we can do as regular parts of our practice will contribute towards that induction:

- a welcome letter from the AM pastoral committee convener
- training opportunities, promoted and funded by the AM
- an induction pack with full information on the usual eldership and oversight practices and procedures in our local meeting and the area meeting, with signposts to further information
- a well-maintained and easily accessible collection of up-to-date resources
- a contact list of all Friends serving in eldership and oversight in the whole area meeting.

Our first meeting as a new group, or on the arrival of new appointees into an established group, should include activities for getting to know one another and opportunity to ask the most basic questions in an accepting and supportive atmosphere. Friends serving in eldership or oversight can feel daunted by the demanding nature of their responsibilities. Our group will want to ensure that the meeting gives appointed Friends all the support they require to serve well and develop their skills, including training, funding for resources and backing for their initiatives.

❖ The online resource **www.quaker.org.uk/tender-hand** includes examples of eldership and oversight welcome and induction material.

ii. Supporting 'apprenticeship'

Pastoral groups commonly include a proportion of Friends with more experience, e.g. where appointments are made on a rolling basis, or some Friends are serving a second triennium or have served in their current role previously.

> "We used to go by the triennium, but there were many exceptions, e.g. when people were released or they moved away. So we now appoint for three years from the start date, whenever that is. We gain from having continuity – our group changes quite often but usually only one person at a time."

> "Our elders and overseers are replaced on a rolling three-year cycle. About a third of the joint group are new each year."

> "Overseers appointed for a second term are responsible for supporting new overseers. We formalise this and we check that both the new and the experienced overseer are happy to be paired together."

New appointees learning the ropes should see currently serving Friends, and other 'old hands' in the meeting, as a resource, and not hold back from asking for information or advice. We all learn on the job, but we don't have to do that the hard way by approaching everything from our place of inexperience or limited information. Setting up 'mentoring' partnerships can be a helpful approach to supporting apprenticeship, particularly in a larger group. Mentoring partnerships might also be arranged between Friends in different local meetings.

iii. Building community in our group

How do we become a united pastoral community? A helpful induction is a good start but we have to build on that throughout our service together, especially in the ways we work as a team. Team working doesn't come naturally to everyone. We may need to share our feelings about working cooperatively before making assumptions we then find confounded, and to negotiate how much solo or teamwork we each feel comfortable taking on. There are plenty of tasks that can be delegated to individuals; we just have to be aware that decisions on principles and practice are agreed corporately and that we must keep others in the group informed. It matters too that we each commit to attending meetings of the group. This is not just about what we need personally; more importantly the group needs each of us.

> Building community also involves noticing and looking after our own needs. Friends can feel dispirited if their service isn't valued, or they feel unacknowledged or criticised.
>
> How will we support those of us who are under stress? What happens if conflict arises among us? Will we be able to address that with the same objectivity we seek to bring to difficulty between other Friends?

Knowing one another well helps us to find trust and to discover ways of dealing with difference and tensions between individuals, which will invariably occur. We can promote community building – with all our differences – by meeting together regularly. It's lovely if this includes social times too but our ordinary meetings will serve the purpose as long as we use them well, ensuring that our time together is more rewarding than burdensome. This will mean guarding against the kind of business meeting that ploughs through an interminable agenda of routine items, and agreeing that not every matter needs to be discussed or decided by our group. An important part of our role is to enable others in our community to contribute. When we get this right, pastoral care happens in many ways that don't demand our constant attention.

iv. Checking how well we are doing

Along with all else that has to be fitted into our work together we will want to include opportunities for reviewing our practice – to check it is serving the community's current and emerging needs.

> ➤ What are the meeting's needs at this time?
> ➤ How well does our practice meet these needs?
> ➤ Where are the gaps in our provision, and what can we do about them?
> ➤ What are we good at and less good at?
> ➤ How do we make sure Friends know who we are and what we are here for?
> ➤ How well do we maintain and publicise resources? What use are Friends making of them?
> ➤ Are we using these resources too, and keeping up to date in other ways?

Our own development and training needs are important elements in how our pastoral practice serves the meeting. We should note conferences and courses on specific aspects such as prayer, mental health, bereavement, conflict, etc. and consider who in our team would benefit from these opportunities.

People other than members of our group may also wish to take advantage of such training opportunities. Part of our responsibility for encouraging Friends to contribute includes helping them gain skills and experience of benefit to the meeting.

❖ **Chapter 17:** *The Quaker way of right ordering* includes guidance on seeking funding for training.

v. Spiritual reviews

From time to time the perceptions we gain by reviewing our practice should be part of a whole-meeting review of how pastoral care is serving the needs of the community.

> *Qf&p* **12.16** Whether elders and overseers are appointed or not, local meetings should regularly review their spiritual life and its expression in caring.

Undertaking a review every three years or so will help the meeting respond effectively to change. Change is inevitable in all communities; a meeting's circumstances change subtly with every Friend who leaves and each newcomer who arrives – and just with the passage of time as the world around us moves on. Change can also be disconcertingly swift. Attendance may increase or decrease markedly, or several 'seasoned' Friends either leave or arrive. Our children's meeting could dwindle inexplicably (it's not at all rare) or perhaps we will be blessed with an equally unexpected influx of families. And changes will almost certainly result in the wake of serious conflict.

Preparing for and meeting change that inevitably comes our way makes it possible for us to *plan* change as well. These are the two purposes of a spiritual review: the process takes Friends through stages of exploration and discernment, which enable them to see clearly how to respond to what is going on currently and to plan ahead in the light of emerging needs. A spiritual review can help our meeting whether it is experiencing change and Friends are wondering how to adapt, or the meeting simply wishes to be aware of areas that might need more or different attention, or it envisages significant development that the whole community seeks to pursue with confidence.

❖ *Spiritual reviews: Volume 3 of the Eldership and Oversight handbook series* provides a toolkit for designing a review process to fit our own meeting's circumstances.

Queries for reflection, discussion and learning

Chapter 3: Grounding our practice

Queries for individual reflection
1. Do I feel upheld by eldership, and are my needs noticed in my meeting? Where does my sense of being upheld or noticed come from?
2. How does our pastoral group work for me personally? How might I contribute to building a sense of community among us?
3. What do I value about being part of the area meeting pastoral community? How far am I aware of eldership and oversight in other local meetings? What difference do connections between local meetings make to me or to pastoral care in my meeting?

Queries for pastoral groups
1. How well are our pastoral meetings working to support our service and the meeting's needs?
2. 'Eldership and oversight need to work cooperatively and collaboratively at all times.' Is this true in our meeting? How can our group support this intention? What are the blocks to cooperative working?
3. How do our connections with the area meeting pastoral committee support our local meeting responsibilities? What might we do to strengthen those connections?

Queries for meetings

1. How far do we feel eldership and oversight in our meeting cover the responsibilities outlined in *Qf&p* 12.12 and 12.13?

2. Apart from those directly involved, how aware are we of what is discussed in pastoral meetings? Would it help the meeting if we knew more? Apart from confidential matters, which areas of eldership and oversight business might be more openly known about, and how?

3. What areas of meeting activity could we do with taking a closer look at, perhaps through a spiritual review process?

❖ These pages can be downloaded from the online resource: **www.quaker.org.uk/tender-hand**

THEME 2: Worship

Qf&p **20.11** Love silence, even in the mind... True silence is the rest of the mind; and is to the spirit, what sleep is to the body, nourishment and refreshment.

(William Penn, 1699)

Worship is at the heart of who we are as Friends and everything to do with pastoral care. It is of such importance that it is easy to overlook the fact that Friends are on individual journeys in their relationship with worship and may have other priorities that eclipse worship in their current experience.

Friends arrive in a Quaker meeting usually through one of three 'doorways':

Worship	**Community**	**Outward activity**
Some people are drawn to attend meeting through learning of our way of worship, which is also the first thing they encounter when they decide to give Quakers a try.	A good many are looking for a place where they will feel at home among people who share their spiritual and ethical outlook, and the wish to be part of a community is what first brings them along.	Others discover Friends through peace, environment, and other movements working for social and political change, or they learn that Quakers care about these things and recognise a 'fit' with their own concerns.

Whichever doorway into meeting we arrive by as a newcomer we find ourselves in the same place where these three elements co-exist, and it isn't long before we realise how worship for Friends is central to everything. If we discover this and it doesn't feel right after all we won't stay. People who attend for a while and then disappear are often those who have not found Quaker worship to be very answering of their spiritual needs.

The Friends who stay and become part of a meeting community are those who find the experience of worship meaningful, even if they continue to feel mostly connected by another aspect of being a Friend. This naturally includes Friends serving in eldership and oversight. Appointment as elder or overseer might reflect our leaning towards either the spiritual or community life of the meeting, or it might not. Many Friends serve effectively in each role at different times without feeling a need to adjust their outlook as Quakers, while others serve in both roles concurrently. And any of us may be primarily committed to wider Quaker concerns, drawing spiritual sustenance and insight from such engagement. The service of eldership springs from the diverse experience and leanings of ordinary Friends, and is relevant to all Friends in the same way.

Each chapter in this Theme addresses matters that are primarily the responsibility of eldership – whether that is the concern of elders alone, elders and overseers together, a pastoral group or the whole meeting. (The term 'elder' appears in these chapters occasionally as shorthand for any of those possibilities).

In *Quaker faith & practice* 12.12 the first four responsibilities (a–d) indicate how eldership supports meetings for worship. The following four chapters look at these sections in some detail to help us understand the responsibility all Friends share for ensuring the central practice of our faith is both rightly held and truly the lifeblood of our community.

Chapter 4: Meeting for worship
explores what 'right holding' of meeting for worship

means in practice, including taking care of the setting for worship, how we promote and share responsibility for right holding, and how we welcome children and young people in meeting.

Chapter 5: Vocal ministry

considers ways to foster helpful ministry, including encouragement and advice on speaking in meeting, raising awareness of the discipline of receiving ministry and addressing problematic ministry.

Chapter 6: Worship in the life of the meeting

looks at further ways in which Friends meet for worship, including meetings for worship for business, marriages, funerals and other special occasions, and raises possibilities for experimental or less usual forms of meeting for worship.

Chapter 7: Openings for the Spirit

discusses preparation for meeting for worship and the varied ways Friends support their spiritual lives, including spiritual practice, prayer, using the Bible and drawing on the whole of life as sacramental. It also invites us to think about diversity of belief and concepts of God in our meeting.

❖ The centrality of worship in Quakerism makes eldership a special case in pastoral care that merits more attention than is possible in these few chapters. There are a good number of books and resources on the subject, a list of which can be found online at: **www.quaker.org.uk/tender-hand**

❖ In particular, *Quality and depth of worship and ministry: Volume 5 of the Eldership and Oversight handbook series* offers elders and all Friends a resource for reflection on worship and ministry in the form of queries 'designed to be taken a few at a time'.

❖ *Living eldership* by Jenny Routledge is a discussion of eldership that seeks to cover previously unexplored ground. It will be of interest to any Friend wanting to reflect further on the spiritual basis and wider relevance of the role of elder.

Chapter 4: Meeting for worship

~

What's so amazing about Quaker worship? It is that for over 300 years groups of ordinary people have met together in silence, without the aid of a trained leader, or of liturgy, ritual or outward sacraments. Week by week they have shared in a corporate experiment of silent, yet open worship.

(Gorman, 2007: p. 1)

Meeting for worship is where it all begins. If we haven't been to a Quaker meeting before, we might make enquiries, read widely or even attend Quaker Quest sessions; but it is only when we settle into the stillness of meeting that we 'get it': *this* is Quaker worship.

How worship meets Friends' needs for spiritual nourishment, and how it expresses Quaker spirituality rather than something else, are responsibilities of eldership. The work of oversight supports those responsibilities in its focus on nurturing community. Our way of worship depends on us gathering in stillness and expectant waiting – together: Friends hold a *meeting* for worship in which fellowship matters as much as the silence.

This chapter looks closely at two of the responsibilities of eldership listed in *Qf&p* 12.12 to explore what 'right holding' of meetings for worship means in practice:

Qf&p **12.12 d.** to be responsible for the quiet gathering of the meeting for worship in order, reverence and harmony, for the arrangement of seating and for encouraging punctuality; elders will arrange for the closing of the meeting, normally by shaking hands;

Qf&p **12.12 b.** to promote the right holding of meetings for worship, remembering that responsibility for the meeting, including the fitness of the ministry, is shared among all the members of the worshipping group;

1. Taking care of the setting for worship

i. The meeting room

Qf&p 12.12 d. tells us that the arrangement of seating is significant to the quiet gathering of our worship. More broadly we must do what is necessary for our meeting room to serve its purpose, so that meeting for worship can happen 'in the manner of Friends'. Each meeting will have its own expectations about making the room ready, but they are likely to include the following:

- Seats facing inward, usually around a central table. Some meetings reserve a couple of adjacent seats for elders (though we shouldn't object if people sit in them) and often one near the door for a doorkeeper. We will check there is sufficient space around each chair or bench and leave an ample break near the entrance to the room so that it doesn't feel inhibiting on entering for the first time. Our aim is to signal that every arrival is welcome and readily included.
- At least one copy of *Quaker faith & practice* placed on the table (is it the latest edition?); often a Bible too and perhaps a vase of flowers. Copies of *Advices & queries* might be on the central table or placed around the room.
- Various other details, such as checking the hearing loop, lighting, heating and ventilation, providing cushions or

footstools, maybe a jug of water on one side with a glass or two, etc.

Anyone in the meeting might attend to these arrangements and others to do with people arriving for worship and being welcomed before and after meeting. The responsibility for arranging seating therefore soon merges with a wider responsibility of eldership and oversight for the practicalities involved in holding public meetings for worship. Some meetings organise these duties (e.g. on a rota); in others Friends help out as needed, perhaps according to whoever arrives first.

ii. Punctuality

Qf&p 2.47 Does punctuality matter? It is not merely a question of disturbing the peace and quiet of those already assembled... What is on my mind is more than that. If we were coming together to worship individually, each to enter into his or her own private meditation, then it wouldn't much matter whether all arrived by the appointed time. In private meditation the worshippers could each 'settle' separately, training themselves not to be disturbed by latecomers. But if our goal is to achieve a group mystical experience, deepening and enriching our individual experience, then, it seems to me, we need to start the process at the same time.

(Thomas R. Bodine, 1980)

Not everyone will agree on the need for the whole group to be present at the start of worship. Some meetings regard the first five to ten minutes as flexible time for people to arrive by public transport if this is limited on Sundays. Others ask latecomers to wait outside the meeting room (in silence to uphold the meeting for worship) so that they all enter together – which could be when children leave for their own activities.

But clearly it is good to promote punctuality as a habit that respects the needs of others and supports worship. If there are Friends who are repeatedly late we will want to do something about it, perhaps by speaking with the person privately to get to the bottom of the difficulty.

Should the problem be more widespread the meeting may benefit from having the matter raised for discussion on an occasion convened for that purpose, for example with the question: 'How does punctuality affect our worship?' This might be enough to improve punctuality, or possibly it will reveal underlying difficulties that require a whole-meeting approach. Could it help for an elder or overseer to remain outside the meeting room for the first 15 minutes to hold the silence with latecomers, including those for whom arriving on time is difficult or unpredictable? Might our meeting need to review the times for worship, or even the day?

✤ **Chapter 6:** *Worship in the life of the meeting* looks at variations on what Friends have come to regard as the standard model of an hour's Sunday morning worship.

iii. Quiet gathering

Coming to meeting with heart and mind prepared helps us have a sense of quietly gathering for worship as soon as we enter the building. Naturally Friends greet one another in a friendly way, but it is best to wait until after meeting to engage socially so that we each contribute to a calm atmosphere in preparation for worship. Elders and others encourage this best when it's done with a light touch, and in support of the responsibility of oversight for welcome and inclusion:

> *Qf&p* 12.13 **a.** to encourage attendance at meeting for worship and to make sure that newcomers to the meeting are welcomed and introduced to other members of the worshipping group;

So, for example, we don't abandon newcomers to a notice board or leaflet rack, but make sure they have someone to speak to who will help them feel at home. We welcome families with the information they need such as the arrangements for children's meeting that day and where a buggy can be safely stowed. We exchange a few warm words with the Friend we haven't seen for ages and agree to catch up with them over coffee.

Inviting Friends to go into the meeting room more or less as they arrive can support our intention for calm. In some meetings elders make a general invitation to move from the lobby five minutes before the time set for the start of meeting. In fact meeting begins as soon as the first person takes their seat in silence. Newcomers who are used to brief exchanges with other worshippers before a church service gets underway may not appreciate that this is our custom, but will soon pick it up if worship is clearly in progress when they enter the room.

Some things to discourage before meeting:

- conversations and catching up on meeting business
- a flurry of busyness in and around the kitchen
- noisy interactions generally
- popping in and out of the meeting room after the first worshipper is seated.

The aim is for everyone to be gathered in the meeting room at the due time 'in order, reverence and harmony'. From here on the role of elders is to participate in worship – little more and nothing less.

Qf&p **2.47** ...As a meeting 'gathers', as each individual 'centres down', there gradually develops a feeling of belonging to a group who are together seeking a sense of the Presence. The 'I' in us begins to feel like 'we'. At some point – it may be early in the meeting or it may be later, or it may never occur at all – we suddenly feel a sense of unity, a sense of togetherness with one another and with that something outside ourselves that we call God.

(Thomas R. Bodine, 1980)

Each Friend who finds their own still centre is part of the deepening experience of the worshipping group, and anyone finding it harder to settle will be encouraged by the presence of others who are fully engaged in the worship.

iv. Closing the meeting

Elders will usually arrange for two Friends to close the meeting at the agreed time by shaking hands – most commonly these are elders but practice can vary.

> "Our children are great timekeepers! On a few occasions meeting has overrun because the elders haven't noticed the time. But the children have. After a couple of minutes two of them shake hands and the meeting is duly closed. We discussed this in the elders meeting and decided it wasn't an issue. The children were exercising eldership, and that was okay by us."

There may be occasions when elders sense that the meeting needs more time. When this happens they usually discern their leading rightly. We allow ourselves to be guided by the Spirit during worship and for the closing of it too. Gentle stirrings around the room will no doubt tell us if the worshipping group is led differently.

2. 'Holding' the meeting

i. Promoting the right holding of meeting for worship

❖ It will help our understanding of the responsibility of eldership for 'right holding' to read *Qf&p* Chapter 2, which fully explores the spiritual purpose, history and practice of Quaker worship.

In essence our task is to ensure that meetings for worship are 'held':

in the Spirit
in the care of Friends, and
in the manner of Friends.

This amounts to much more than simply observing the *form* of Quaker worship. It involves everyone in the gathered group – including children, attenders and newcomers, as well as members and Friends undertaking eldership responsibilities – being aware of one another's presence and respecting the purpose we are all there for.

> *Qf&p* **2.77** The depth of Quaker worship, its richness, its power and its ability to meet the needs of each worshipper as well as the gathered group, depends on the commitment of every participant, and on the way we all come to our meetings with hearts and minds prepared.
>
> (Jack Dobbs, 1982)

Elders have a responsibility to promote Friends' commitment to worship, as Jack Dobbs describes. We commonly approach this in two ways:

1. by serving as an elder for a specific meeting for worship
2. through exercising eldership at all times, including any meetings for worship we attend.

1. Elders often take it in turn to serve at a meeting for worship, which may include being seated in the meeting room in good time, closing the meeting, inviting newcomers to

introduce themselves, handing over to the clerk to give the notices, and so on. As elders 'on duty' we may or may not be expected to have a more significant role in the right holding of that meeting than other elders present, or indeed the worshipping group as a whole.

2. Whenever we attend meeting for worship, and at all other times too, we will be mindful of our responsibility for the spiritual nurture of the meeting and of our example as experienced Friends who are able to lead the way. This will include:

- our own spiritual preparation beforehand
- our conduct before and after meeting and our quiet and grounded presence during worship
- action at other times, e.g. enabling learning and sharing
- positive eldering, e.g. supporting ministry
- being aware that others will be influenced by our example if we respond to a leading to minister.

The last of these is easy to misjudge. We model how ministry can support worship, not how to offer profound or skillful ministry. If we hope to discourage Friends from ministering too often, or at length, or in a teacherly way, or otherwise than as prompted by a true leading, then we will refrain from doing so as well. And we'll keep an eye on an impulse to break the silence with a self-consciously 'helpful' contribution made with good intentions, but not in the Spirit. Our authenticity and our habit of testing a leading is the best example we can give.

❖ **Chapter 5:** *Vocal ministry* explores this subject in greater depth and offers a simple process for testing a leading to minister.

ii. Sharing responsibility for right holding

The idea that all Friends share responsibility for meetings for worship may not occur to everyone. It is tempting for worshippers to look to elders alone as the Friends who will ensure the quality and conduct of meeting, and to underestimate the influence of their own presence and example. Friends may come to recognise this only gradually through experience and through the things the worshipping group does together to grow in community. We have to *feel* responsible for our worship in order to be properly aware of what it means to play an active part in right holding, which is largely a matter of recognising that we are each responsible for:

- our own experience
- the part we play in the experience of other individuals
- the contribution we make to the corporate experience.

For example, if we are distracted by raised voices outside, someone leaving the meeting room in a hurry, or vocal ministry that grates with us in some way, it is up to us how we deal with that, but not at the expense of other people's experience. Friends who hold the stillness throughout exert a positive influence, whereas any visible or audible disquiet can add to our distraction.

We share responsibility for this corporate act of worship by recognising our interdependence as a community – it matters to others too that we come to meeting regularly and on time, and that we each make good personal use of the worshipping hour.

iii. Children in meeting

When children attend meeting for worship it is always a gift, and one to be nurtured by good support from eldership and oversight. Meetings where children or young people are a regular part of the worshipping group may not appreciate how privileged they are. The majority of local meetings in Britain Yearly Meeting have no children, or just a few attending occasionally, and many wish they could change that fact.

> "We used to have four families coming regularly, mostly not all at once but we seldom had fewer than six children at meeting. We're now down to one family and I don't think they will stay. A children's meeting can disappear just like that. It's very sad. We miss them."

Other meetings might cherish their quiet and orderly worship, not at all sure that they would welcome having to adjust to a different way.

And it is a different way. Whenever children are present our meeting is an all age meeting for worship. We welcome children as equal members of our community and must place their needs to experience worship alongside the needs of adults. In most meetings with families attending, children join the main meeting for worship for a short period, perhaps ten or fifteen minutes at the beginning or the end of the usual hour. It would be a mistake to give the adult experience precedence during this period, but Friends can also make the opposite mistake of regarding the time everyone is in meeting together as *for* the children. Children appreciate experiencing worship exactly as it is held when they are not there; they want to know what the rest of us are up to and they don't want to be patronised.

Qf&p 2.74 Children have an uncanny knack of knowing the difference between living ministry, as opposed to words that are injected into the meeting for their good. This is why I feel Friends should at any time avoid deliberately speaking to children, for it usually means speaking down to them. In fact it is an excellent discipline for anyone who speaks in meeting to try to use words and ideas that can be understood by children, and yet speak to the condition of all present, because they arise from the profound depths which, in fact, produce things that are truly simple.

(Gorman, 2007)

Some Friends experience children in meeting as a challenge that they handle by making a real effort (which is much easier if children are well behaved and endearing). But naturally they won't always sit quietly. They might chatter or giggle or wander about – though it is astonishing how quickly even small children latch on to the atmosphere and copy the behaviour of those around them. Observing the difference between worship with children present and without, parents can easily feel anxious about how their children's presence affects other people's experience of worship.

There are two issues for eldership and oversight here – how to reassure parents and how to address attitudes in the meeting:

- Parents will appreciate the opportunity to talk about their concerns and to be reassured that the meeting doesn't expect their children to behave like the adults present, but values them being children. This is an especially important message for families new to meeting. When parents get to know others they will draw a lot of their confidence about being in meeting for worship from one another. So there is a lot to be gained from helping parents build community together. If there is a children's committee, or other Friends regularly participate in children's meeting, elders and overseers can work with them to support this aim.
- There is never a quick fix to changing attitudes! But our meeting can address them gradually by a consistent approach to welcoming families.

"Moving from a large meeting with an abundance of kids, to a small meeting with none, I asked LM to discuss what we would do if a family turned up. Our minute stated that we were a 'family friendly meeting'. In practice this meant being ready *every* Sunday to welcome children with some kind of provision, however improvised. Eventually, the families turned up!"

❖ **Chapter 10:** *All age community* looks further into the presence of children in meeting and at ways of building all age community.

Queries for reflection, discussion and learning

Chapter 4: Meeting for worship

Queries for individual reflection

1. What does meeting for worship mean to me? Where would I be without it?

2. Have I got a significant part to play in the quiet gathering and right holding of meeting for worship? If I have, what is it? What am I actually doing that makes a difference?

3. If I'm concerned about the quality or conduct of worship, what should I do about it? What effect will it have if I raise the issue – in my meeting or with other Friends?

Queries for pastoral groups

1. How do we seek to ensure the quiet gathering of meeting for worship and how can we encourage Friends to share responsibility for this? What hinders quiet gathering before meeting, and as it starts?

2. What does a rightly held meeting for worship look like and feel like? Are we conscious of doing anything towards this at the time or at other times? Are Friends in the meeting aware of our contribution, and does it matter if they aren't?

3. What part do children and families play in our meetings for worship? How can we foster the spiritual lives of our younger members through their

experience of being in meeting for worship with everyone else?

Queries for meetings

1. How well do our meetings for worship meet the spiritual needs of members of our worshipping community? How do people visiting our meeting experience worship here? Is there anything we would change if we could?

2. Are our meetings for worship rightly held? What part do we each play in ensuring this?

3. Does coming to meeting regularly matter? Does punctuality matter? How could we encourage Friends to recognise that their presence or absence affects the community as a whole?

❖ These pages can be downloaded from the online resource: **www.quaker.org.uk/tender-hand**

Chapter 5: Vocal ministry

~

This chapter looks at our responsibility for how vocal ministry contributes to meetings for worship:

> **Qf&p 12.12 c.** to foster helpful vocal ministry, seeking to discern the needs and gifts both of individual contributors to the vocal ministry and of the meeting as a whole: some Friends may hesitate to risk speaking in meeting because they lack confidence in their own call to speak – they will need encouragement; others may too easily rise to their feet without being clear as to the helpfulness of the message; sometimes it may be necessary to restrain unsuitable ministry.

The question of vocal ministry tends to arise as an issue in most meetings at some time or other. Spoken contributions might be entirely absent, too frequent, too predictable, or problematic in more or less concerning ways. It is such a significant issue for eldership that the term 'eldering' has come to mean only how we seek to influence the minister who is impeding worship in some way. We really need to redress that balance and reclaim the term to include actions that recognise and promote the positive life in ministry.

❖ Margery Mears Larrabee's Pendle Hill Pamphlet *Spirit-led eldering* clarifies why this is so important:

...what is spirit–led eldering? It is offering spiritual leadership, which is to support and encourage the life of the Spirit in an individual or group, or to raise questions and explore, with another person or group, ways in which they may be more faithful to the Spirit, or it is simply being prayerfully present. No particular act or behaviour in itself qualifies as Spirit-led eldering. It is the well-grounded intention and attitude of a compassionate heart and mind, led by the Spirit, that makes it so. When correction or support is offered that is not so guided, I see it as something other than eldering.

(Larrabee, M. M., 2007: p. 3)

1. Fostering helpful ministry

Qf&p 12.12 c. asks us first to foster helpful ministry. If we think about the way children learn, people no longer believe it is simply a matter of correcting their faults but recognise the importance of building on what they do well. Similarly, there may be times when we need to be clear with a Friend about unhelpful or unacceptable practice, but we should focus mainly on supporting what is good. In many meetings this will include encouraging Friends who never minister to heed Advice 13, which begins:

> **Advices & queries** 13 Do not assume that vocal ministry is never to be your part. Faithfulness and sincerity in speaking, even if very briefly, may open the way for fuller ministry from others.

One or more of the following suggestions might encourage less confident Friends to consider offering vocal ministry:

- opportunities for worship sharing. This is a relatively safe way for Friends to find their Quaker voice and yet be sufficiently challenging to prompt comparison with some aspects of speaking in meeting for worship. Worship sharing benefits from being facilitated by an experienced Friend

- encouragement to contribute in Afterword, which is another way to test out how it feels to speak in the gathered group. Afterword needs the support of eldership to work well – guidelines have to be clear and the space 'held'
- adapting the usual pattern of meeting for worship on some occasions, perhaps having half an hour's worship sharing followed by half an hour of worship or semi-programmed worship that encourages spoken contributions
- inviting Friends to participate in the regular reading of *Advices & queries* during meeting
- providing a simple guidance sheet – making it clear that it shouldn't get in the way of openness to being led, but offers an optional and personal means of testing a leading to minister.

Ministry in meeting for worship – listening for guidance

I return to the centre...

Worship begins ... we wait and centre...

I minister – clearly, trusting in that of God within me

I feel led to minister

I won't speak if my answer to any query is No – I'll return to the centre

Must I speak?

Am I led by the Spirit rather than the self?

Is it for now rather than another time or place?

Is this ministry to be shared?

Am I clear it isn't a political or personal annoucement?

Is it for anyone else besides the last speaker?

Supporting ministry includes remembering to let a minister know when we personally find their contribution helpful (and encouraging this practice). We should also ensure there are opportunities for sharing and reflection on the subject, such as discussion or creative listening in response to a prompt, for example:

'How we recognise and test a leading to minister'
'My experience of ministering in meeting'
'The place of spoken ministry in silent worship'.

The bigger picture is that everything we do to ground our spiritual practice, and to make connections with each other in matters of the Spirit, will help.

❖ The example guidance sheet above is adapted from one included in *Becoming Friends*; this version can be downloaded from the online resource: **www.quaker.org. uk/tender-hand**. The unit 'Silence and waiting' in *Becoming Friends: Living and learning with Quakers* includes further insights on speaking in meeting for worship. For information about the *Becoming Friends* course go to **www.woodbrooke.org.uk/becomingfriends**

❖ *Becoming Friends* offers guidance on various ways of sharing in groups, as does *Spiritual reviews: Volume 3 of the Eldership and Oversight handbook series,* which includes an appendix listing other publications on the subject. Explanations of worship sharing, creative listening and Afterword can also be found in the online resource: **www.quaker.org.uk/tender-hand**, together with guidance on how to facilitate them or support them with eldership.

❖ A brief description of Afterword is given in **Chapter 18:** *Keeping people informed.*

❖ For discussion of experimental and less usual forms of

meeting for worship see **Chapter 6**: *Worship in the life of the meeting.*

❖ There is more about practices for supporting our spiritual lives in **Chapter 7**: *Openings for the Spirit.*

2. Receiving ministry

Alongside a better understanding of the practice of *offering* ministry eldership hopes to support helpful ways of *receiving* ministry, which is also a discipline Friends get better at with experience. All the suggestions above for fostering ministry are how this complementary discipline can be encouraged too. As Friends we learn how to minister through becoming receptive listeners who open our hearts to the ministry others offer us, and we uphold ministry by letting what doesn't speak to us go with the thought that someone else present may have a different response entirely.

> **Qf&p 2.12** The right to speak is a call to the duty of listening. Speech has no meaning unless there are attentive minds and silent hearts. Silence is the welcoming acceptance of the other. The word born of silence must be received in silence.
>
> (Pierre Lacout, 1969)

When we discuss vocal ministry – in our eldership group or more widely in the meeting – it helps to start with sharing our experience of hearing ministry:

➢ Are there certain kinds of ministry we find more helpful than others, or less? (E.g. biblical, anecdotal, ministry that responds to or picks up on an earlier contribution, Christian, prayer, reading from Quaker faith & practice, etc.) Where do our preferences come from?

➤ If we find ourselves making judgments that prevent us from hearing the spirit of a spoken contribution, what are these based on?

➤ What do we do with ministry that speaks to us? And with ministry that doesn't speak to us?

➤ How do we respond to ministry we find annoying or that feels ill-judged and out of place? Are we able to receive it tenderly and let it go, or does it spoil meeting for us? What can we do about that?

Qf&p 2.69 …if anything should seem to be spoken amiss, the spiritually minded worshipper will have the wit to get at the heart of the message, overlooking crudity and lack of skill in its presentation, and so far from giving way to irritation at what seems unprofitable, he will be deeply concerned for his own share in creating the right spiritual atmosphere in which the harm fades out and the good grows. Many a meeting has known this power, transforming what might have been hurtful into a means of grace.

(A Neave Brayshaw, 1921)

3. Restraining unsuitable ministry

From time to time, supporting helpful ministry will mean taking action to let a Friend know that their ministry is actually hindering worship rather than contributing to it. Two common ways this becomes apparent require two different responses:

i. **Acting promptly** is called for when a Friend ministers inappropriately or in a way that disrupts worship *unexpectedly* on one occasion.

ii. **Considering a situation before acting** is always necessary in the case of a Friend who repeatedly ministers in an unhelpful manner.

i. Acting promptly

Prompt action isn't always a matter of acting in the moment during the Friend's ministry. We have to think very carefully before doing something that may well disrupt the meeting further. Sometimes we will choose to hold our breath, wait for it to stop and trust that Friends will allow the worship to do the work of healing. Prompt action then means being sure to speak with the Friend immediately after meeting. This conversation needs to start from the assumption that the Friend didn't intend to disrupt or hinder worship and wouldn't wish to again. So we will invite the Friend to explain why they ministered in that way, and only then will we explain why we felt it was unhelpful or unacceptable. Hopefully this conversation can lead to an undertaking that it won't be repeated, but we may have further work to do in helping the Friend towards a better understanding of the practice of vocal ministry.

If it is clear that something must be done to ensure the Friend stops and sits down, we have to model a Quaker way of going about this. So we will be calm and respectful and we will assume good intent in the Friend. Above all we won't order the Friend to sit down and we won't offer a critique of why the ministry is unacceptable. The most common approach follows a sequence such as this:

> ➤ First an elder stands and, as soon as there is a pause between words, thanks the Friend, inviting them to take their seat to allow the meeting to reflect on their ministry.
>> ➤ If that doesn't work the elder remains standing until the speaker notices and sits down.
>>> ➤ If that doesn't work, other Friends might also stand in silence. It is a very bold person indeed who carries on speaking in a room full of calm silent people on their feet!

After meeting we will naturally have a conversation with the Friend and give good attention to their feelings about being 'eldered' so publicly. They might be embarrassed, angry or hurt. Our first task is to listen and to be tender with those feelings. We can then look for the right moment to discuss why the action was taken, which might be for another occasion. When we do raise the matter we must be clear that we are asking for a commitment from the Friend that this will not happen again.

ii. Considering a situation before acting

What to do about repeatedly unhelpful ministry exercises elders in a different way. This may be a Friend we know well and respect, and it becomes increasingly difficult as time goes on to address our unease about their ministry for the first time. Or it might be a newcomer who hasn't yet noticed how Friends do things. Eventually we realise we will have to grasp the nettle. But it doesn't on that account become an urgent situation calling for an immediate response the next time it happens. If we have taken too long getting round to it we should take a bit longer and address it properly – that is, arrange to speak privately with the Friend, and do more listening than talking. Our aim is to help the Friend change their habit, and habits can be hard to break. So we must be patient and very supportive. However, if the Friend is unwilling or unable to cooperate we may need to consider other approaches.

4. Addressing more problematic ministry

It can happen that a meeting's worship is seriously affected by the repeated actions of Friends who are insufficiently aware of accepted practice, or who choose to ignore it, or who lack self-restraint. None of the foregoing advice about supporting ministry ignores the distress experienced in some meetings by spoken offerings that disregard boundaries. There will always be Friends who are unreceptive to the positive eldering of encouragement and guidance, and who appear not to be learning from others' example.

> "What do we actually do about the regular rambling minister with a deep need? How can we tackle that sensitively without offence, without the risk of hurt that will spill over into an escalating problem involving others too?"

This query expresses a familiar quandary. The elder who posed it was very exercised to act lovingly with the Friend, while aware that the meeting too needed her caring support. But her words hold an important clue: whatever we do may involve risk.

Elders may have to make a difficult judgment about the balance of risk involved in taking action. Perhaps we have tried various approaches with a Friend and got nowhere, and the meeting is hurting. Our main concern now has to be the meeting's need for rightly held worship. So we will put that need first, and try to do this with all the care for the Friend concerned that our action permits.

Any approach we agree to try needs to start with a private conversation in which elders invite the Friend to reflect on the problem from the meeting's perspective, and elders make it clear where their priorities have to lie. The conversation may not be easy for anyone so it is important that we give some thought to which person, preferably two, the Friend will be most likely to find acceptable. And we have to think through how we will respond if the process or the outcome is problematic.

The conversation will hope to discover how the Friend can be part of the solution, which might include some of the following:

- opportunities at times other than meeting for worship for the Friend to explore the matters that occupy their ministry, together with an agreement that they will test their urge to speak in meeting more faithfully
- appointing an elder or supporting Friend to sit alongside the Friend and, if necessary, to gently remind them of what has been agreed, or to ask them to resume their seat
- a 'contract' drawn up with the Friend in the form of an agreement that takes account of the needs of both parties. So it will state what the Friend agrees to do for the meeting, and what elders on behalf of the meeting agree to do for the Friend
- a separate meeting for worship held at another time for this Friend to attend – instead of the main meeting for worship – with others who are willing to support the Friend in this way.

A separate meeting for worship is very much a last-resort solution, but one which has worked surprisingly well in some meetings. Importantly, we will strive to ensure that any solution is a compassionate response that assumes goodwill on the part of the Friend. We must start there, even when there appears to be evidence to the contrary.

- ❖ The pamphlet *Dealing with difficult behavior in meeting for worship* (Friends General Conference) offers several strategies for addressing 'exceptionally difficult situations', along with guidance on all degrees and instances of difficult behaviour.
- ❖ **Chapter 14:** *Conflict and difficulty in the meeting* looks at addressing serious conflict in meetings.
- ❖ Sometimes a Friend presenting a difficulty for the meeting has a mental health condition, which we may need to address separately from our concern for the health of worship. **Chapter 15:** *Disability, vulnerability and times of stress* looks at our responsibility in this area.

5. Guidance on accepted practice

Mostly our concerns about vocal ministry are more routine, calling for regular attention but without the need for much intervention. Regular attention involves consistent eldership that encourages and supports good practice, as well as guidance or information that enables people to share responsibility.

Quaker Life produces several excellent leaflets on Quaker practice, which may give people the confidence of knowing what to expect and what might be expected of them, especially if a leaflet is offered with an open invitation for a conversation too. Much of what experienced Friends take for granted can seem mysterious and excluding if we don't take the trouble to explain it, so it is a courtesy as well as helpful to do so.

Elders in some meetings produce additional written guidance reflecting local circumstances with information that helps people recognise what they see going on at meeting. The following extract from a leaflet produced by Friargate elders concentrates on the place of ministry in worship. The leaflet invites Friends to see how accepted practice doesn't depend on having 'rules' but on an understanding that 'some of the customs and practice developed over time do help to deepen worship and draw the worshipping community together'.

Elders might find these ten points useful as an aid to 'holding' worship, which shouldn't be an arduous task but a natural service we can enjoy offering our meeting.

Tried and tested Quaker practice

- Beginning worship with an extended silence usually helps the meeting to 'centre down' and allows us to free ourselves of distractions. The spontaneous ministry of babies and young children is always welcome.
- While occasional silent reading, e.g. *Quaker faith & practice*, can help us settle into worship, habitually reading for a significant time may separate us from

fellow worshippers and thus lessen our contribution to the centring down.

- We are asked to listen to all vocal ministry in an open and accepting spirit and to allow it to settle deeply into the worship before contributing anything new.

- Spoken ministry is very welcome. *Advices & queries* reminds us: 'do not assume that vocal ministry is never to be your part'. Even a few hesitant words may be of great service and may also call out helpful ministry from others.

- Before rising, we may want to ask ourselves inwardly: is my message for the meeting or given for me personally? Does my leading come from the spirit or reflect a more secular concern, however important and passionately held?

- We are advised not to expect to offer vocal ministry every time we attend worship and not to speak twice in the same meeting.

- Books for spiritual reflection available in the meeting are often spontaneously and helpfully used in ministry. Experience suggests that it is not easy to integrate a ready prepared reading into the spirit of meeting for worship.

- Under the pressure of speaking, it is easy to forget to be audible. We all need to think of our listeners and consciously try to speak clearly, without haste, and loudly enough for everyone to hear us easily.

- We are asked to resist engaging contentiously with earlier ministry. When referring to earlier vocal ministry we are asked to try to avoid naming Friends as this can unintentionally exclude those who do not know the person named.

- It can be helpful for the last part of Meeting to settle into renewed silence. It can also be helpful to draw

the threads of the meeting together into a whole.
(*Finding our way into meeting for worship,* Friargate
Meeting (York) elders, 2011)

❖ A list of leaflets on Quaker practice is available from the
Quaker Centre at Friends House or by accessing the
online resource: **www.quaker.org.uk/tender-hand**

Queries for reflection, discussion and learning

Chapter 5: Vocal ministry

Queries for individual reflection
1. How do I feel about the practice of spoken ministry in my meeting, including my own contributions?
2. How far is 'unhelpful' ministry a problem for individual Friends to resolve – either in how they minister or receive ministry? Or do I see this more as a whole-meeting issue?
3. What part might I play in the way vocal ministry supports depth of worship, both during meeting and at other times?

Queries for pastoral groups
1. How is the Spirit faring in spoken contributions to our meetings for worship?
2. How do we encourage understanding of the practice and conventions of offering vocal ministry, and how far are we successful?
3. Are our strategies for addressing problematic ministry sufficient and workable? How can we support one another in our intent to affirm clear boundaries without compromising our care for a Friend? What support might we need from others in the meeting?

Queries for meetings

1. What contribution does vocal ministry make to quality and depth of worship in our meeting?

2. What is the role of Friends generally in fostering helpful vocal ministry?

3. What do we understand by the term 'eldering'? How can the meeting support positive eldering? Do we each have a part to play or is this the job of only some of us?

❖ These pages can be downloaded from the online resource: **www.quaker.org.uk/tender-hand**

Chapter 6: Worship in the life of the meeting

~

Qf&p 2.06 The treasure I had found [in meeting for worship] seemed startlingly simple, and I held this treasure quietly to myself, exploring its significance, feeling it almost too good to be true. Part of its simplicity was that I and others were to start just where we were at the moment and proceed at our own pace from there. How blessed that there were no restraints of belief. The promptings of love and truth were the starting places and we could move at our own pace to recognise them as the leadings of God – the beyond which drew me and others on from our limitations and despairs and smallnesses.

(Ruth Fawell, 1987)

Sunday morning meeting is only part of the picture of how worship is central to our faith and practice. The significance of worship in the lives of Friends means that it is a feature or the point of most other occasions – formal, informal and social – when Friends meet together. For example:

- worship at the start and end of meetings, whether for business or other purposes, such as pastoral meetings, meetings for learning or sharing, and social events
- worship we drop into or which a Friend requests when we are engaged in business or in discussion

- a few moments of worship at the start of a meal
- the practice of epilogue at residential events.

Elders will be concerned to encourage this Quaker habit, which serves a number of purposes. Most importantly it enables gatherings to be Spirit-led. It also brings spaciousness and silence into activities that otherwise may be so filled with words and busyness there is no time to reflect, and it acts as the glue in a community of Friends who share significant practices. We recognise one another, and ourselves, in the stillness.

But of course worship is much more than a Quaker habit; it is the way we conduct all our affairs as Friends and how we work together. This chapter looks at meetings for worship held for some of these other purposes or in different ways, including **meeting for worship for business, meetings for worship on special occasions and variations on our usual pattern for worship.**

1. Meeting for worship for business

Qf&p **12.12 e.** to ensure that the basis and method of conducting meetings for church affairs are understood; to accept responsibility for their right ordering;

Meetings for worship for business are the Quaker way of seeking unity on decisions through the same practice we are accustomed to in our regular meetings for worship: we gather in silent waiting for the guidance of the Spirit. The difference for many Friends is that the process of corporate discernment is much less familiar and can be hard to grasp. Eldership therefore seeks to help Friends understand the spiritual basis of the Quaker decision-making process and how it works in practice, and it helps if we can go about this in ways that will include Friends with different approaches to and understandings of the Divine. Arthur Larrabee offers a suggestion for how we might approach a common difficulty with the language often used to describe the Quaker business method:

> Historically, Friends have talked about seeking the will of God. My experience, however, is that today this concept is increasingly inaccessible to many Friends. How can we know the will of God? Perhaps there is another way to achieve a similar result. Instead of talking about seeking the will of God, would it not make more sense to talk about seeking a Godly outcome? In this way, we can seek an outcome consistent with what we know and understand of God without believing we can know God's will.
> (Arthur Larrabee, from a talk given in a special interest group at Britain Yearly Meeting 2013 – *Leadership and clerking: American style*)

Ideally everyone present in a meeting for worship for business should be aware of their part in the discipline of 'right ordering', described in *Quaker faith & practice* Chapter 3. As elders we encourage awareness and understanding of the discipline in three main ways:

- by our example
- through opportunities for learning
- in actions as needed during the meeting to affirm the discipline.

Each of these is part of how we uphold the meeting: the worship, the business, and each Friend participating, especially the clerks. As with much of eldership and oversight practice, the most significant contribution we make is our example.

❖ In *God and decision-making* (2012, pp. 47–48) Jane Mace describes the 'spiritual and mental exercises' that for her 'seemed to be what upholding might mean':

- keep my mind on the topic
- listen to other speakers
- appreciate the silence in the pauses
- question my own leadings and
- accept not being heard.

These five points could help us check that our own example is always a positive contribution to our meeting's corporate discernment.

An important part of supporting the work of the meeting for worship for business is to encourage Friends to attend. Some meetings find that it is the same Friends who regularly attend, and that its discernment is not truly corporate in the sense of the corporate body being the whole meeting – or a good proportion of it over a period of time. In the following extract Timothy Ashworth explains why our meetings for business need *different* people present for corporate decision-making to fulfil its spiritual purpose.

The Quaker way recognises that the diversity within the community is a gift without which the community cannot function; the diversity of the many members is *necessary* for the Spirit to operate.

…On the principle that worship reveals what a community believes, this business method practised in a spirit of worship reveals something that is foundational, not just to Quaker ways of doing things but also to the Quaker understanding that must necessarily flow from this: that inspiration operating through diversity is God's way of working.

(Ashworth and Wildwood, 2009: p. 98)

✤ *Rooted in Christianity: open to new light*, Chapter 7: Revealing worship, quoted from above, provides a helpful explanation of the spiritual basis of the Quaker business method.

❖ **Chapter 17:** *The Quaker way of right ordering* explores
more fully our responsibilities for upholding meetings
for worship for business.

❖ **Chapter 3:** *Grounding our practice* discusses the use of
the Quaker decision-making process in pastoral meetings.

2. Meetings for worship on special occasions

Qf&p **12.12 f.** to take responsibility for the right holding
of meetings for worship on special occasions such as
marriages and funerals, and, if memorial meetings are
asked for, to make sure that their purpose is clear to
those who attend – some meetings like to make special
arrangements for welcoming new babies or celebrating
other events.

Quaker faith & practice provides full guidance on holding
meetings for worship for weddings (*Qf&p* Chapter 16) and
for funeral and memorial meetings (*Qf&p* Chapter 17). Elders
will be particularly concerned with the spiritual needs of
Friends and others at these heightened moments of transition
in people's lives, and in each case the wider pastoral needs of
Friends and relatives will be met by eldership and oversight
working together.

❖ **Chapter 17:** *The Quaker way of right ordering* considers
the formal and legal aspects of weddings, funerals and
memorial meetings.

i. Marriage
Marriage after the manner of Friends: In the Quaker
understanding, the couple marry each other in the sight
of God and witnessed by the Meeting. No intermediary
performs the ceremony or pronounces the couple to be
married. This acknowledges that the process of becoming

'one flesh' cannot be created by any outside agency. Neither can it be prevented by anyone. The Lord brings the couple into unity. We onlookers can only recognise and celebrate that this has happened.

> (Quakers in Britain website: www.quaker.org.uk/ marriage-after-manner-friends, accessed 12.11.14)

Friends who were 'married in the meeting' often say how affecting and important this very simple ceremony was for them. Under the guidance of the area meeting's registering officer, elders and others involved in the preparation and holding of a Quaker wedding will want to ensure an experience of simplicity and spiritual depth consistent with the legal and formal requirements and the solemnity of the contract being entered into. This is quite a demanding responsibility, especially as there may be many people attending with no previous experience of a Quaker meeting for worship.

In a Quaker wedding the couple make their declarations not to each other but before God to the assembled gathering of witnesses, all of whom sign the Quaker wedding certificate. A marriage in the meeting is not only a commitment between two people; it involves everyone in the meeting. As elders and overseers we will encourage the meeting to recognise its role in upholding the couple in the journey of their marriage.

> *Qf&p* 16.07 Friends speak of marriage 'in the care of' the meeting. This is not merely a verbal reflection of the Quaker understanding of marriage as the Lord's work: it denotes two distinct, concrete responsibilities. First, the meetings (area and local) where the marriage is solemnised must care for the preparations for marriage...
>
> Secondly, every meeting has a pastoral responsibility for the care of all marriages within it, whether of members or attenders, whether both spouses are active in the meeting or only one, whether they were married at that

meeting or another, whether they were married according to the usage of Friends or in some other church or faith or by the civil authorities.

❖ We can help Friends become informed about the long-term commitment they are making to a couple embarking on a life together by encouraging reflection on the guidance in *Qf&p* Chapters 16 and 22.

❖ Further information and writing on the subject is available in the online resource: **www.quaker.org.uk/tender-hand**

❖ A good start might be the immensely readable 2006 Swarthmore Lecture, *Reflections from a long marriage* by Roger and Susan Sawtell.

❖ **Chapter 15:** *Disability, vulnerability and times of stress* is concerned with the many ways our personal relationships bear on our lives as Friends and the part pastoral care plays in supporting these.

❖ *Qf&p* Chapter 16 gives a detailed account of the legal, practical and pastoral aspects of Quaker marriage (same sex and opposite sex), including the circumstances when a meeting for clearness will be needed or might be offered.

❖ **Chapter 19:** *Making connections* looks further at meetings for clearness.

ii. Funerals and memorial meetings

Friends playing a part in the right holding of these meetings will usually have much less time to prepare than for a wedding, but should try at least to read the guidance in *Qf&p*, in this case Chapter 17. In a local meeting with little experience of conducting funerals or memorial meetings we should also seek guidance from more experienced Friends in our area meeting. The responsibility of area meetings to support local meetings with guidance and practical advice is outlined in *Qf&p* 17.14–15.

❖ *Funerals and memorial meetings: Volume 2 of the Eldership and Oversight handbook series* will be a helpful resource.

Chapter 10 in that handbook is a collection of first-hand experiences of such meetings for worship. It offers insights that can help us provide spiritual and practical support – both through the care we take in preparing for and holding a funeral or memorial meeting, and in attending to the needs of individuals. For example, it touches on some difficult subjects such as suicide and stillbirth, and strife in the family of the deceased. The handbook includes much practical advice and information that we will find immediately useful in helping a family to plan the meeting for worship and other details.

As in the case of Quaker weddings, funerals and memorial meetings will usually include non-Quaker friends and family who may not have attended a meeting for worship before. In line with any expressed wishes of the deceased and the family for planned contributions, such as music, readings, etc., Friends involved in organising the event will seek to ensure it embodies the spirit of a Quaker meeting and enables people present to engage in worship.

❖ A list of other relevant publications is available in the online resource: **www.quaker.org.uk/tender-hand**
❖ The Quakers in Britain website includes a leaflet for individuals to record their funeral wishes: see **www. quaker.org.uk/tender-hand**
❖ **Chapter 15:** *Disability, vulnerability and times of stress* explores questions to do with death, dying and bereavement from the wider pastoral care perspective.

iii. Other special occasions

Should we receive a request for a meeting to mark a special occasion, elders will probably suggest a simple meeting for worship – perhaps adapted to include planned contributions – which observes our usual Quaker discipline and stays within recognisable Quaker practice.

For instance, in the case of a meeting for worship to welcome a new baby we will need to be clear, to the parents and to family and friends who attend, that this will not be a Quaker version of a christening. Lewes Meeting's description of their practice offers an example of how a Quaker approach could be explained to Friends and others:

> Quakers do not christen children, but like other churches which do not recognise infant baptism, we have our own ways of welcoming new children into our meeting. Sometimes this is very informal; a couple just come to meeting, bringing their baby with them. After a while someone will stand and say a few words on behalf of the meeting. …
>
> Some people prefer to hold a special meeting to name or welcome a child, and they will plan with the Elders just what form this will take. Usually it is quite informal, with the children of the meeting sitting on a rug on the floor, quietly playing with toys, while the adults hold the meeting for worship around them.
>
> (Lewes Quakers, www.hitchin.plus.com, accessed 24.02.2014)

3. Variations on our usual pattern for worship

For some Friends, coming to meeting on Sunday plays little or no part in their present lives. Whatever the reason for their absence, a habit of worship may yet be an important part of how a Friend attends to their spiritual needs. But should the meeting just accept that its regular arrangements won't suit everyone living locally who would value attending meeting for worship?

Worship as it permeates the Quaker way observes few boundaries of when and where it can take place. It doesn't require a particular building to house it or certain qualified people to run it. Where there is a need we might hold a meeting in our own home, a hospital or hospice, a school or in the open air.

Qf&p **2.84** If we met more often for worship in each other's homes, it would remind us that God is with us in every place, at the kitchen sink and at the table; we should get to know one another more intimately, and could break bread together; the home atmosphere might make it easier to invite our acquaintances to join us; and any increase in numbers would lead to multiplication by cell-division; and an expanding coverage of the community.
(David W. Robson, 1971)

Friends may have needs or preferences for additional or alternative meetings for worship that are held otherwise than the usual pattern. The need in a community might be for a meeting to be held mid-week, in the evening or early on Sunday morning; for the times to vary – either shorter or longer than the usual hour; for a change of venue; for a different pattern to our worship on some occasions. None of these alternatives are unthinkable. Meetings are experimenting with different ways and finding that broadening the opportunities they provide for worship can be both enriching for their meeting community and no less authentically Quaker.

Because all meetings evolve over time, and sometimes encounter marked and sudden change, local meetings should regularly review their practice in the light of emerging or newly recognised needs among Friends (*Qf&p* 12.16). Emerging needs in our meeting might include:

- patterns of work or family life that prevent attendance on Sunday mornings, or at the usual time
- a new or growing presence of children or young people
- the absence of children and a wish to reach out to families
- the needs of Friends who find a full hour of silent worship too physically taxing
- the limitations of our usual venue for Friends with disabilities
- a need for Quaker learning to be incorporated when Friends are gathered in maximum numbers
- a wish among some Friends for worship more often than once a week
- low attendance at meetings for business and a wish to incorporate business more fully into the life of the meeting
- a desire to reach out to our local community.

Depending on Friends' needs for additional/alternative ways or times of worship, there are several options our meeting might consider. Each of the examples here is practised (and recommended) by a local meeting:

Meeting and eating
- Mid-week late morning meeting followed by bring and share lunch
- Early meeting on Sunday followed by breakfast
- Silent evening meal leading into half an hour's worship.

Two hour drop-in meeting for worship
People arrive at any time during the two hours and leave when they are ready. The success of these meetings depends on Friends slipping in and out quietly and being observant of the depth of worship in progress. If we invite others in our local community to join us, the conduct of Friends will often be enough to signal how this works.

All age meeting for worship
(discussed further in Chapter 10)
All age worship can take many forms, e.g.
- children simply stay for the full hour and occupy themselves quietly when they need to with books, soft toys or drawing materials
- programmed or semi-programmed worship on a theme
- worship on a theme that adults and children prepare for separately.

Half-and-half meeting for worship and worship sharing (either way round):
1. Start with worship sharing on a topic or text, and about half way through the hour a Friend invites the meeting to settle deeper into worship.
2. Following half an hour's worship, a Friend introduces a period of worship sharing to encourage spoken contributions on anything that has arisen for Friends during worship.

Half-hour weekday meetings
Held in a city centre meeting house for people to attend on their way home from work.

Extended Saturday meeting for worship
Two hours of silent worship, followed by a silent lunch, some gentle sharing of experiences in the form of worship sharing, and then more silent worship, for about 30–60 minutes. The whole session lasts about four hours, starting at 10.30 am.

Occasional programmed worship

Includes music, poetry or an art-based activity, such as the 'Appleseed' model.

Half an hour's meeting for worship leading straight into meeting for worship for business

Needs must! But this can work well in establishing that our meetings for business are meetings for worship, with a consequent improvement in how business is discerned and conducted.

A regular programmed meeting for worship

Hartshill Meeting holds two regular meetings each week. Meeting on Sunday morning is in the usual unprogrammed tradition. On Sunday evening there's a programmed meeting, which includes hymns, songs, readings, sometimes spoken prayers, and periods of silence as well as a 'message' from a speaker or someone within the group – usually written down beforehand.

❖ The Quaker Life learning resource *New expressions of Quaker community* offers tools for meetings to help them explore fresh approaches to expressing 'the core, the seed of Quaker community that would allow it to flourish in the local community and the wider world'. The outcome might include other styles or forms of worship such as the above, and possibly further ways of being more accessible and responsive to seekers and enquirers, including families with children, or those with busy working lives, while remaining authentically Quaker.

(Each local meeting received a copy of the resource; contact Quaker Life for further information.)

❖ **Chapter 13:** *Absent Friends* reminds us of members of our community who retain connections they find supportive, but who don't attend meeting for worship for various reasons.

❖ **Chapter 7:** *Openings for the Spirit* discusses how Friends support their spiritual lives at times other than meeting for worship.

Queries for reflection, discussion and learning

Chapter 6: Worship in the life of the meeting

Queries for individual reflection

1. How aware am I of worship being at the heart of meetings for worship for business, and of contributions offered as ministry? What do I do to support or encourage that understanding?

2. How well does our usual hour-long meeting for worship meet my spiritual needs, or fit with my other commitments or life style? What other ways of holding worship can I imagine working for me?

3. If I were to plan my own Quaker funeral, what would I ask for?

Queries for pastoral groups

1. What are the things we do to support worship as a Quaker practice that permeates all the meeting's activities? How might we instil a habit and appreciation of silence?

2. How well do we support the right ordering of meetings for worship for business? How can we encourage Friends' understanding of the spiritual purpose of business meetings?

3. Are we open to the possibility that experimenting with different ways and times might be a way forward for our meeting? Are there emerging needs in the meeting we should be considering? How could we find out

about needs for worship in our locality that are not met by our regular practice?

Queries for meetings

1. What must we do for our way of worship to be also our way of conducting meetings for business? Are there things that make it harder for this to be the reality in our meeting? What can we do to build on the strengths of our existing practice?

2. 'Instead of talking about seeking the will of God, would it not make more sense to talk about seeking a Godly outcome?' If we differ in our perspectives on this, how do we ensure we end up in the same place?

3. How do meetings for worship on special occasions contribute to the worship and community life of our meeting? Might there be special occasions in Friends' lives, other than marriages, funerals and memorial meetings, when worshipping together would be a right and spiritually helpful way of marking it?

❖ These pages can be downloaded from the online resource: **www.quaker.org.uk/tender-hand**

Chapter 7: Openings for the Spirit

~

Qf&p 12.11 Traditionally the first concern of elders is for the nurture of the spiritual life of the group as a whole and of its individual members so that all may be brought closer to God and therefore to one another, thus enabling them to be more sensitive and obedient to the will of God. So the right holding of our meetings for worship will be their particular care.

This chapter looks at the responsibility of eldership for spiritual nurture beyond our immediate care for meeting for worship. What else should we be doing to support Friends' spiritual lives? The first responsibility of eldership in *Quaker faith & practice* 12.12 spells out quite a condensed list of expectations which deserve to be looked at carefully. Everything that follows seeks to clarify our understanding of what might be involved and to broaden out the subject from these few words:

Qf&p 12.12 a. to meet regularly to uphold the meeting and its members in prayer; to guide those who share in our meetings towards a deeper experience of worship; to encourage preparation of mind and spirit, and study of the Bible and other writings that are spiritually helpful; to encourage individual and united prayer in the meeting.

Section 1 here looks at each of these expectations in turn, Section 2 broadens out the subject with more discussion and detail, and Section 3 reflects on Friends' understandings of God, which influence everything this chapter addresses.

❖ *Qf&p* Chapter 2 explores this subject in depth and is the place to turn for insights that will help elders fulfill this important responsibility.

1. Spiritual nurture and preparation for worship

Unpicking *Qf&p* 12.12 a. reveals four strands to elders' responsibility for spiritual nurture:

i. to meet regularly to uphold the meeting and its members in prayer
ii. to guide those who share in our meetings towards a deeper experience of worship; to encourage preparation of mind and spirit
iii. [to encourage] study of the Bible and other writings that are spiritually helpful
iv. to encourage individual and united prayer in the meeting.

i. To meet regularly to uphold the meeting and its members in prayer

The passage begins with a reminder that an important part of eldership practice is spiritual upholding of the meeting, and that we need to do this together. Some form of spiritual reflection will therefore feature in each elders' meeting. Holding Friends and the meeting in the light helps to deepen our understanding of the spiritual needs of the worshipping group, and it draws us together as a group of Friends serving the meeting too. We look further into prayer as part of this expectation in **iv.** below.

❖ **Chapter 3:** *Grounding our practice* discusses how we use pastoral meetings for this and many other purposes.

ii. To guide those who share in our meetings towards a deeper experience of worship; to encourage preparation of mind and spirit

Guiding Friends towards a deeper experience of worship means starting from where Friends are, with no assumptions about Quaker experience or spiritual inclinations. We can suggest ways of spiritual preparation Friends may not have considered, but the main task of eldership is to encourage people to discover an approach that feels right personally. We need to accept and seek to understand Friends' different beliefs or approaches to God in the meeting, the part spiritual practice plays in Friends' lives, and the importance individuals attach to different aspects of belonging to a Quaker meeting.

> "I first heard about Quakers through the Occupy movement. When I started attending, worship was secondary to having found a group of people who felt strongly about things that are important to me. That's still true, but meeting for worship is growing on me."

Below is a small sample of activities for learning and sharing on spiritual matters that Friends offered for this publication. Each idea provides an opportunity for drawing on whatever experiences and insights are real and alive for Friends, enabling each of us to discover with one another what is distinctively Quaker about our common ground.

- Sharing our spiritual journeys, e.g. 'How I came to Friends'
- Worship sharing on spiritual matters, e.g. 'What's happening in the silence?', 'The secular and the sacred', 'How do I pray?'
- A meeting for reflection following on from meeting for worship

- Spiritual friendship in groups or as partners (companions)
- 'Inner quest': A Friend shares something of their inner experience followed by worship sharing in small groups
- Worship sharing on a text, not necessarily biblical, prior to meeting for worship
- 'Friendly Bible study'
- Discussion topics, e.g. 'Somehow', 'Way will open', 'The beyond'

Some activities for encouraging spiritual reflection and sharing will be more recognisably in the nature of spiritual practice than others, and may attract different Friends for that reason. Once our meeting makes a start with some fresh ideas we will notice what works well and what elicits less response, and find that a natural snowballing of activity occurs as Friends take the initiative to set up a group or an event. Elders will want to support these, perhaps by offering an eldership presence where this would be welcomed or prudent.

❖ Further information on the above ideas and others can be found in the online resource: **www.quaker.org.uk/ tender-hand**
❖ The resource *Being Friends Together* provides access to a wide choice of relevant activities for Friends to use in their meetings: **http://together.woodbrooke.org.uk**. Further details are given in **Chapter 9:** *Belonging and commitment*, 4. Learning together.
❖ *Deepening the life of the Spirit: Resources for spiritual practice* by Ginny Wall provides elders with an excellent resource for use in the meeting and to recommend to Friends. It offers clear and accessible guidance on a number of spiritual practices that might interest Friends, either to practise on their own or with others, including guidance on how to set up spiritual friendship groups.

iii. [To encourage] study of the Bible and other writings that are spiritually helpful

Elders are often less comfortable addressing this aspect of the responsibility outlined in *Qf&p* 12.12 a. It is one thing to support a group of like-minded Friends wishing to study in this way, but another to promote 'spiritually helpful' writings as necessary to Friends' spiritual development.

The Christian roots of the Society are significant to an understanding of Quakerism today, and therefore to all Friends, not just those who come from Christian backgrounds. Elders may see a need to encourage greater familiarity with this history, including the early Christian experience that informed the insights of early Friends. Today's Friends can discover this from scripture too, but clearly elders cannot require Friends to read the New Testament. We can however offer the idea of using the Bible and other writings for spiritual reflection through the medium of some of the activities suggested in **ii.** above.

Perhaps we could also consult Friends on which versions of the Bible they would like to have available during meeting for worship. Some Friends are very attached to the language of the King James Bible; others may welcome a modern translation, of which there are several to choose from. It can be useful to provide both.

However we choose to promote the Bible as a resource we should bear in mind that from the witness of the earliest Friends to the leadings of the Spirit, Quakers have not given the Bible ultimate spiritual authority:

> *Qf&p* **27.28** ... because they are only a declaration of the fountain and not the fountain itself, therefore they are not to be esteemed the principal ground of all truth and knowledge, nor yet the adequate, primary rule of faith and manners
>
> (Robert Barclay, 1678)

iv. To encourage individual and united prayer in the meeting

As with promoting use of the Bible, elders may not agree on how they understand prayer, or how they might encourage others to pray.

❖ Anyone who is ambivalent about the concept of prayer will find *Qf&p* Chapter 2 (2.18–34) essential reading.

Whatever attitudes to prayer any of us might have, here we discover how Quakers understand and use prayer as an inward practice of deep reflection that we each make personally our own. There is nothing in *Qf&p* Chapter 2 to indicate right or wrong ways of praying, or that if we don't pray we are somehow less than Quaker. We simply find Quaker experience to warm our hands against and learn from, in so far as it speaks to our condition. In conversation with Friends about spiritual practice, conveying a sense of 'should' or 'ought' in relation to prayer – or any other practice – is unlikely to be useful. Our own perspective is little help to anyone else unless they *invite us* to tell them about it. But we can draw attention to this section in *Quaker faith & practice* for a window on a range of experience that may help Friends discover something encouraging, inspiring or just rather interesting. One of the ways this can work is in helping us see that whether we are comfortable using the word 'prayer' or we prefer to avoid it, we can each recognise elements of what Friends are describing as part of our own inward life. The following brief extracts from *Qf&p* Chapter 2 are quoted from the insights of a number of Friends:

"There is little point in praying that the sorrowing may be comforted and the lonely cheered, unless we ourselves set out to bring comfort and cheer to the sad and neglected in our own surroundings ... God does not do things for us – he enables us to do them for ourselves."
2.28 Elisabeth Holmgaard, 1984

"I began to realise that prayer was not a formality, or an obligation, it was a *place* which was there all the time and always available."
2.21 Elfrida Vipont Foulds, 1983

"There is no use trying to conceal how difficult it is to find time for private prayer in the congested schedules under which most modern people live. But at the bottom it is not a question of finding time ... [but] of the depth of the sense of need and of the desire... In this life we find the time for what we believe to be important."
2.32 Douglas Steere, 1938

"Prayer is not given us to make life easy for us, or to coddle us, but to make us strong ... to make us masters of circumstance and not its slaves. We pray, not to change God's will, but to bring our wills into correspondence with His."
2.24 William Littleboy, 1937

> "…let us not imagine … that a few sentimental good
> wishes from a distance are all that is needed.
> Whenever we intercede in prayer we must be prepared
> for an answer which places a practical obligation upon
> us. A prayer is always a commitment."
> 2.29 Thomas F. Green, 1952

> "Prayer is not words or acts, but reaching down to
> love: holding our fellows in love, offering ourselves in
> love; and being held by, being caught up in love. It is
> communion, an opening of the door, an entry from
> the beyond. This is the point where secular language
> fails, for this cannot be spoken about at all: it can
> only be known."
> 2.23 Harold Loukes, 1967

> "When I pray for others who are in need, it is a
> promise to make my own contribution, perhaps by
> writing, by visiting, by a gift, by telling someone
> whom I know could help."
> 2.27 'Anna', 1984

2. Spiritual exploration

As elders we would be missing something important if we
held back from promoting spiritual exploration out of a sense
that Friends may be unreceptive to the idea of spiritual
practice. The main thing asked of us in *Qf&p* 12.12 a. is to
'guide those who share in our meetings towards a deeper
experience of worship'.

> Guidance is not always a matter of offering suggestions; it is more to do with listening, with being responsive and alongside.

i. Spirit in the every day

❖ In his 1973 Swarthmore Lecture *The Amazing fact of Quaker worship* George Gorman examines structured approaches to preparation for worship – including reading the Bible, spiritual reflection, prayer and meditation – before describing his own way as one that 'seems to fit in with the Quaker sense that no strong line should be drawn between so called sacred things and those labeled secular' (p. 89).

...I personally do not find such an ordered, disciplined approach helpful, although I recognize its validity and obvious value to those who practise it. I have good reason to believe I am not alone in this, for there are a large number of Friends who have told me that their response is no longer along traditional lines. The approach we make we feel is in line with the widely held Quaker view, that the whole of life is a preparation for worship.

(Gorman, 2007: p. 89)

This was written at a time when most newcomers to Quaker meetings were previously churchgoers. Today a good many more have no previous church or religious background. The concept of prayer, or at least the word, may be unappealing or even alien to such Friends; they might find the Bible significant as literature or as a means of understanding our Quaker roots, but possibly not as spiritual inspiration. So it is not surprising that elders can feel unsure about how to fulfill the responsibility as outlined in *Qf&p* 12.12 a.

George Gorman focused on noticing what gave him joy

and insight, and also disclosed the dimension of transcendence. His preparation for worship included friendship and taking a vivid interest in people's lives, reading widely, letter writing and going for walks; an approach echoed here in the words of Friends responding to the query 'What brings you closer to God?'

"My work, which involves communicating with people on a deep level. I meet them in their distress and in their elation. Being able to share that is a privilege, it's spirit-to-spirit communication."

"On a clear night, the vastness of space, the big question – what's it all about?"

"Weeding. Shostakovich. Time spent with my cat on my lap."

"For me it's other people – people I meet in the flesh and also those I meet in history, and those I am aware of elsewhere in the world."

ii. Spiritual friendship

There is a long Quaker history of friendship between two people becoming a significant part of how they each find support and nurture on their spiritual journey. This might come about today by noticing that it is happening in a particular friendship and both of us agreeing to make this aspect of our friendship more intentional; or we might seek out a 'companion' who is willing to accompany us on our spiritual journey – and we on theirs. An intentional spiritual friendship makes regular time and space for sharing and exploring, and the Friends agree on how this works best for them – which might not be meeting up in person often, or at all if that is difficult to arrange. It could include telephone or Skype conversation; email contact; letter writing; sharing our journaling; reflecting on shared reading; doing an inspirational activity together (such as those George Gorman speaks about). Spiritual friendship is what we make of it.

Eldership can support spiritual friendship by making the meeting aware of the possibility and explaining what it is. Where helpful, elders may offer to meet with potential companions to discuss their understanding of the practice, what they hope to gain from spiritual friendship and the discipline involved in making a commitment.

Elders might also consider setting up spiritual friendship groups (as in the example of Sheffield Quakers, below). Again, these depend on commitment and agreed understandings for the duration of the life of the group – which might be decided in advance or discerned by the group over time.

Would you like to join a Spiritual Friendship Group?
Spiritual friendship groups are small groups which meet regularly at different times during the week, often in Friends' homes, to share our spiritual journeys, to worship together, or to discuss Quaker topics. The groups can take place in a variety of ways to suit the needs of group members.

There will be an opportunity to join an existing group, or to form a new one, after meeting on Sunday 23rd November (at 12 o'clock in Room 1). All Friends and attenders are welcome.

(www.sheffieldquakers.org.uk, accessed 16.11.2014)

❖ Elders may suggest the *Becoming Friends* course to newcomers. The course (online and available as a course book) provides a structured approach to helping newcomers develop an understanding of Quakerism, while exploring their own journey and connection with Friends. Becoming Friends 'companions' are Friends who have been trained to accompany and support individuals as they work on the course – in a role that has similarities with spiritual friendship. To find out more go to **www.woodbrooke.org.uk/becomingfriends**.

iii. Sharing our stories

Together with activities planned with spiritual exploration in mind, we can make opportunities (or encourage initiatives) for Friends to share and reflect on things that give meaning and purpose to their lives, but which have no obvious spiritual or Quaker connection. This could be anything from parenting to scuba diving, a pressured career to creative ways of making ends meet. It might help set the ball rolling to invite one or two Friends to speak to a group about something they are very engaged in, leading into whole or small group sharing from each person's experience of deep interest or engagement in their lives.

❖ The Quaker Life resource, *Being Quaker, doing Quaker* offers guidance on organising activities for sharing our stories. It is available to download at **www.quaker.org.uk/tender-hand**

> When we focus on the spiritual life of our meeting it's important that we don't think in compartments, but recognise how Spirit infuses the whole, how the whole of life is sacramental.

iv. Doing things together

Another approach is to encourage shared activities in the meeting that are engaging, fun and rewarding. Everything we do in the company of other Friends that uplifts us, or is just very enjoyable, feeds our inner lives and naturally becomes part of the worshipping life of the meeting.

> "We hold 'Creativity Days' with workshops to share our skills, e.g. bike maintenance, origami, recycling, bread making. And we do cooperative activities – sculpture, mural painting, juggling, patchwork "

❖ **Chapter 8:** *The meaning of community* and **Chapter 9:** *Belonging and commitment* look further into the relationship between building community and the spiritual life of the meeting. **Chapter 8** (3.ii) includes examples of community-building activities.

❖ A fuller collection of community-building ideas can be found in the online resource: **www.quaker.org.uk/ tender-hand**

v. Spiritual adventure

From everything discussed so far it might appear that the main work of spiritual nurture is to support and build on what Friends are inclined towards or already doing. But we shouldn't neglect the importance of challenge in spiritual development.

In the preface to Ginny Wall's book *Deepening the life of the Spirit*, Richard Summers invites us to see experiment as part of our exploring:

> We understand that who we are and what we do as Quakers flows from our spiritual lives, and is rooted in meeting for worship... We hope that Friends and meetings will be encouraged to experiment with these ways of deepening our worshipping lives so that we can share, today, the transformative experience of the Spirit of God

or inner light that has always been at the core of our tradition as Friends.

(Wall, 2012: Preface)

The idea of spiritual experiment, especially with others, can be daunting. It is really only possible where there is trust, respect for difference and a mutual willingness to be open with one another. Eldership and oversight can do much to deepen the spiritual life of our meetings by fostering among Friends these prerequisites for shared spiritual adventure, and by ensuring there are safe and inviting opportunities for Friends to give something new a try.

As elders we will need to keep a broad focus in the way we interpret our responsibility for spiritual nurture, building on the richness of experience and difference in approach among Friends, and offering challenge and opportunity to experiment too. This will include promoting and supporting spiritual practice of various kinds, providing the impetus or structure for setting up spiritual friendship partnerships or groups, enabling Friends to share their stories, and encouraging community building through shared enterprise, activity and joy. Our aim will be for people to learn from one another and to be mutually supportive in exploring the things that deepen their spiritual lives.

3. Belief and concepts of God

Thinking about God is naturally at the heart of religious and spiritual understanding among Friends. In Britain Yearly Meeting we are in a period when the question of how, and even whether, Friends speak of God is of particular consequence to many individual Friends and to whole meeting communities. It is also a moment when Friends need to take the longer view. In the last decades of the 20th century a tension between Christ-centred and Universalist perspectives was a major issue that exercised Friends, meetings and the pages of the Quaker press:

> *Qf&p 27.03* Can we settle the question, 'Is the Society of Friends Christian or not?' In the historical sense the answer is Yes: but that does not preclude the possibility that we may now be called to a new and wider perception of the Truth. We have the witness of the Society itself, as well as the example of Jesus, against turning yesterday's inspiration into today's dogma...
>
> (Lampen, 1985)

With the help of far-seeing Friends such as this the Society did eventually move on. British Friends are now tussling with questions around 'theism' and 'non-theism' and will no doubt leave the heat in this tension behind too. Reporting on a Quaker Committee for Christian & Interfaith Relations conference with the challenging title: *Faith – What's God got to do with it?* Michael Wright made this contribution to how Quakers might progress as a community of faith from here.

> I left Friends House that day with a very positive feeling that we have a challenge and an opportunity: to explore, in our unique spiritual discipline, new ways of discovering, describing and understanding our experiences of the divine. This might help us Quakers, and people in other Christian communities who are facing similar dilemmas.
>
> British Quakers are not alone in wondering what God has to do with faith: it is just that we are more open about doing so. That, for some, is threatening, for others liberating. It just might be transforming.
>
> (Wright, 2014: p. 11)

If it is true that British Friends are more open (than other Christian communities) with our wondering and questioning, we can aspire for this to be true in each of our meetings. It will not help our meeting communities if Friends ignore or discourage discourse arising from questions about God. We have to make it possible for difference – even the kind that brings with it the risk of contention – to be explored, and to continue towards understanding.

Tension of any kind among Friends is naturally a matter of concern to eldership and oversight. Friends' anxieties about diversity may be connected with how resilient or otherwise we feel as a community. We can easily feel strong when we appear to be united in essentials, less so when it becomes clear that our group encompasses significant or even fundamental differences. The way forward lies in having confidence in our ability to live creatively with difference and to learn from it, which is a much more resilient and enduring kind of strength.

The role of eldership in building confidence will be to encourage a spirit of respect for people's own experience and their genuine concern to find the language that embodies it. Friends from *anywhere* on the spectrum of belief or spiritual understanding can feel marginalised and not heard in a meeting where discussion feels too risky or it takes place in private corners only between people of like mind. If this is happening in our meeting, we will need to make opportunities for respectful and open sharing of religious experience and perspective, ensuring that Friends observe the discipline of listening with open hearts and minds.

❖ **Chapter 19:** *Making connections* suggests possibilities for structuring and facilitating this kind of sharing and notes the availability of learning resources that can help, details of which can be found in the online resource: **www.quaker.org.uk/tender-hand**

It has become clear to me that differences in our perceptions of God – the Light, the Seed, the Ground of our Being, call it what you will – don't matter a jot if we are able to meet and 'know one another in the things that are eternal'... and at the same time gain strength and impetus from the encounter. That is what happens in a Quaker meeting for worship.

(Durham, 2013: p. 40)

Queries for reflection, discussion and learning

Chapter 7: Openings for the Spirit

Queries for individual reflection

1. Where else apart from meeting for worship do I seek spiritual nourishment in my meeting community?
2. What spiritual practices or spiritual preparation for worship are meaningful for me? Do I have a part to play in supporting the spiritual preparation or prayer life of other Friends?
3. How do I feel about spiritual diversity in the meeting, and is this an issue for me? How might I contribute to exploration of belief and concepts of God, helping this to be enriching rather than divisive?

Queries for pastoral groups

1. How can we know about spiritual needs in our community? How will we ensure that eldership supports the spiritual life of the meeting in ways that are welcomed by and accessible to Friends?
2. How might we encourage and support Friends' personal spiritual practice? Where does prayer fit in? How do we feel about promoting use of the Bible and other writings, and how might we approach this expectation in the list of elders' responsibilities?
3. In what ways do we address spiritual diversity among Friends, including in our group? How could we go about making opportunities for exploration on matters

of belief and concepts of God in our meeting, or in the area meeting?

Queries for meetings

1. We each have different spiritual needs. How will we support one another on our individual journeys? Might we personally have needs and preferences in common with a few others? How will we find this out and respond?

2. In addition to meetings for worship, what are our shared needs for spiritual nurture? What could we do together at other times that will help deepen worship?

3. Are we aware of differences in spiritual or religious perspective in the meeting? How can we be more open to one another in a spirit of enquiry and learning?

❖ These pages can be downloaded from the online resource: **www.quaker.org.uk/tender-hand**

THEME 3: Community

One reason that we come to meeting for worship rather than worshipping at home is that we need community. It is a basic human need. Community roots us among others who are on similar spiritual journeys into the presence of God. When we come together only for meeting for worship yet have minimal contact with each other the rest of the time, we are not much of a community for each other. In that kind of distant community, it is easy for someone to become invisible first while present and then through not being there at all. The better we know each other, the less easy it is for that to happen.

(Bieber, 1998: p. 2)

A research project conducted jointly by Quaker Life and Woodbrooke in 2012 sought to discover what makes Quaker meetings 'vibrant'. Friends in their meetings were asked:

> What is it that you want to get from your meeting – as a place of worship, as a community and as a springboard for witness – and how well are your aspirations met?

One of the findings of the 'Vibrancy in meetings' project was that while almost all respondents said that meeting for worship was important to them, and the majority found it essential, the most-mentioned reason for attending meeting was fellowship. Does this mean that an awful lot of Friends are not really serious about their Quaker faith, but value attending meeting to be among like-minded people? Or is it that fellowship and community are essential to worship and our spiritual lives?

This Theme explores the idea that the kind of community we aspire to create together as Friends is all of a piece with our spiritual lives and how we hope to make a difference in the world. This is an ambitious aim that calls for our attention and our care; such a community doesn't come about by chance.

We often speak of 'building community' rather than finding or discovering it, which is an apt metaphor. There is a lot of hard work involved, and sometimes 'building' is exactly how it feels – as if with bricks and mortar, different 'trades' fitting in with each other and being at the mercy of the weather. It can be slow work too; we need to take the long view.

But we wouldn't be working at it if there were no rewards; Friends find plenty of reasons to build and nurture their communities. The challenges and the richness of opportunity that being a member of a community offers us are the subject of the following three chapters.

Chapter 8: The meaning of community
looks at the complex nature of a meeting community, the importance of taking part with a sense of purpose, and how we build community together.

Chapter 9: Belonging and commitment
considers welcome, ways of including everyone and how we grow in community through learning together and sharing our gifts. The subject of membership comes in here – why it matters and how eldership and oversight can support it.

Chapter 10: All age community
reflects on the significance to meeting communities of
the presence or absence of children and young people,
looking at the role of eldership and oversight in supporting
children's work and in welcoming and caring for families.

Chapter 8: The meaning of community

~

Both eldership and oversight continuously underpin the necessary – sometimes challenging – work Friends do to ensure their community thrives. During the writing of this chapter I heard the following spoken ministry (as I recollect it) offering a clear message that any Quaker meeting could learn from:

"When I was staying with a nursing order of nuns I once asked whether their vows entailed sacrifices that were hard to bear. Sister Anna hooted, 'Chastity, poverty and obedience aren't the problem! But living in a community together? Now that's the really tough one. We have to work at it every day. It isn't easy, believe me, and sometimes we fail spectacularly.'"

Here was a community of women who shared vocation, work, beliefs, practice and discipline, who spent a great deal of time together and knew each other very well; a community that had little of the variousness of a Quaker meeting and few distractions outside their work and community life to get in the way. These people found that being a community was difficult and needed to be worked at, and that this was by far the most demanding gift they had to offer God.

How much more will this be true of people loosely gathered together in a Quaker meeting? Even though Friends, unlike these nuns, have the release of separate lives away from meeting, we really shouldn't wonder that community might not come easily.

1. A web of connections

Qf&p 10.03 The Religious Society of Friends is organised into local meetings, each of which should be a community. It is our search for God's way that has drawn us together. In our meeting we can each hope to find love, support, challenge, practical help and a sense of belonging. We should bring ourselves as we are, whatever our age, our strength, our weakness; and be able to share friendship and warmth...

A local meeting community can appear at first encounter to be quite a simple organism. We join in worship, which is calm and orderly, no one especially appears to be in charge, and people are relaxed about what happens after meeting. We feel at home. After attending for a while we begin to settle in, but it could be rather longer before we discover the many parts and connections to this community:

- Its members are a mix of ages and circumstances and some people we hardly ever see. It includes Friends 'in membership' and others who are not, some who attend for a while and then move on, and it welcomes visitors and enquirers as equals.
- It has an internal structure of roles and offices, processes and procedures, which influences everything that happens in the community.
- It may contain a number of smaller communities such as committees and caring circles, and 'transient' communities such as task groups that convene more briefly.
- People meet and make community at other times for social activities, or for learning, discussion or spiritual practice.
- The local meeting is an integral part of the area meeting community in ways that affect many Friends actively and everyone less directly – even if they are unaware of it.

- It is not an isolated island but part of the archipelago of Britain Yearly Meeting. It supports Friends who belong to other Quaker communities, such as central committees, and encourages Friends to participate in the wider Quaker community.
- It has outward connections with other faith communities, charitable organisations, campaigning groups and institutions such as prisons, hospitals and schools.

Our community includes such a mix of groupings and connections that we would expect some of these to be more important to us personally than others. Along with other factors to do with our individual lives, our different perspectives and inclinations make for a diverse community of people who nevertheless have something significant in common. We are each making a choice to worship with *this* faith group rather than another, and we continue to do so for as long as the Quaker faith is meaningful and right for us. In all our variety, our shared faith is the lynch pin of our community.

But is that enough to hold us together? What if there are differences in our faith perspectives too?

2. Finding solid ground

The core of the Quaker tradition is a way of inward seeking which leads to outward acts of integrity and service. Friends are most in the Spirit when they stand at the crossing point of the inward and the outward life. And that is the intersection at which we find community. Community is a place where the connections felt in the heart make themselves known in bonds between people, and where the tuggings and pullings of those bonds keep opening up our hearts.

(Palmer, 1977: p. 27)

Parker J. Palmer speaks of three romantic myths that have replaced the reality of community in people's thinking. These myths – and the fallacies they contain – tell us much that can help us understand the challenge of finding solid ground on which to build community (Palmer, 1977, pp 19, 20):

• The myth of community as a commodity like any other we would like to acquire – as something we can aim for and go after directly:
    'We cannot have it just because we want it – precisely because the foundation of community itself goes beyond selfishness into life for others.'

• The myth of ideal community where being in easy contact with one another leads inevitably to supportive relationships:
    'Community always means the collision of egos. It is less like utopia than like the crucible or the refiner's fire.'

• The myth that springs from our wish to associate with people like ourselves, that real community will confirm the rightness of the way we see things:
    'In true community there will be enough diversity and conflict to shake loose our need to make the world in our own image.'

Palmer reminds us that our meeting does, and must, include people we would not have chosen to be with. Otherwise there is none of the challenge we need for finding fellowship. He also invites us to see that Friends will not succeed in creating true community by directing their attention on that end. It is more likely to grow around us as a by-product of joint endeavour focused beyond *our* needs as individuals or as a group.

There is a paradox here for eldership and oversight: how do we promote the growth of community among people who differ often in fundamental ways, while at the same time taking our eye off that ball? One thing we can do is to notice that this is exactly how it works:

In its review of oversight, a meeting undertook a 'care audit' to discover where and when caring happened. Various groups in the meeting reported that caring came about naturally as they got to know each other well. Groups that formed the strongest bonds were those doing taxing jobs for the meeting – elders and overseers, finance and property committee, etc. – and included short-term groups that disbanded when their task was complete.

There was something about having to get along as a mixed assortment of Friends doing demanding work they were tasked with and committed to, which strengthened their commitment to each other. They formed bonds that persisted after a committee was reformed or a group disbanded.

The example of this meeting's experience offers two linked principles to aid our thinking about building community:

- Purposeful activity with others is an excellent way of getting to know people.
- When individuals get to know each other better they form bonds that help build community in the meeting.

3. Taking part

i. There is plenty to do

We don't have to invent purposeful ways of contributing to the life of the meeting; there is invariably more to be done than there are people willing and available to do it. But lack of willingness or availability is two-edged: it denies some Friends the best way of feeling part of the community and it overburdens others.

> Many meetings find their community is actually two distinct groups: the committed regulars who attend business meetings and undertake roles in the meeting, and who know one another quite well; and others who see involvement as largely not for them, perhaps even feeling excluded from it. These people are not only distanced from the meeting but may not even know each other.

If we were only able to focus on one approach to building community it would probably be to encourage greater participation in service. As serving Friends we gain in so many respects, including the rewards we find in the service itself and the learning that comes through working with others. In a working relationship we very quickly notice our differences, but much that we like too, which in turn brings acceptance and willingness to recognise and value other perspectives. Undertaking a common task together is one of the most accessible ways of discovering and answering 'that of God' in others and growing in fellowship.

It is rather an ambitious idea that people might take on service before they dip their toes into other involvement in the meeting. Most meetings ensure there is plenty going on to bring people together – which may encourage some to consider service when they are ready. But we should be wary of seeing the meeting's job as providing tempting opportunities that will persuade people to forego other pleasures: if there is no more to it than that, their engagement won't last. Neither do we want Friends to feel obliged to participate solely out of a sense of duty. There has to be a third way.

ii. Purpose that brings its own rewards

As a community of Friends there are certain needs or wants we invariably have in common:

- to know one another
- to make connections
- to be useful
- to feel challenged
- to learn something new about ourselves.

If these essentially good things are not available to us in our meeting we will put our energies elsewhere. So we should see these as significant elements in any involvement asked of or offered to Friends. We find these needs and wants answered more readily when whatever we do together has a real purpose – above the purpose of fellowship. Friends considering an idea for bringing people together may find it useful to take into account whether it has a further purpose that could engage people's interest and commitment.

Each of the following activities achieves this through different means:

Activity that takes us out of our personal preoccupations through each of us being a necessary part of other people's experience
- walking group
- singing group
- 'eightsome' meals
- quilting group

Activity that deepens our spiritual lives
- prayer group
- Experiment with Light
- sharing our journeys
- worship sharing on a theme

Activity that expands our horizons
- learning more about Quakerism
- study that enriches our faith experience
- a book group
- cultural activities
- exploring 'green' issues

Activity focused on something that is needed and makes a difference
- supporting others in the meeting, e.g. newcomers, the children's meeting, absent Friends
- involvement in an external project, charity or cause
- linking with other faith groups in the local community
- practical work in the meeting house or garden
- outreach
- fundraising
- campaigning
- practical volunteering

❖ The online resource: **www.quaker.org.uk/tender-hand** includes explanations of these and other activities, and guidance on how they might be used in meetings.

As well as various opportunities for Friends to engage purposefully with a group of others, it is good to have occasions for *everyone* to come together regularly other than for worship or business, such as a regular shared meal or the occasional ceilidh. Whole-meeting activities are not necessarily easy to arrange – for example, if our premises are rented. But the gains for the community might nevertheless make it worth the effort of finding a way. Informal, purely social get-togethers are a necessary part of our community life, particularly as they seem to attract even those in our community who are resistant to most other ways of participating.

4. Building community in partnership

Qf&p 12.11 Traditionally the first concern of elders is for the nurture of the spiritual life of the group as a whole and of its individual members… The chief concern of overseers is with the more outward aspects of pastoral care, with building a community in which all members find acceptance, loving care and opportunities for service.

Though there is a difference of function, much of the work of elders and overseers is of the same nature. It is important that the two groups should at all times work in close collaboration and should, wherever possible, share their common commitment to the service of their meetings.

Eldership and oversight bring two essential perspectives to the common task of nurturing our worshipping communities. We are not solely a community that worships and prays together, and we are not just a group of people who care for one another and do things together. The above passage identifies overseers as having a chief concern for building community, but that doesn't happen in isolation from the spiritual life of the meeting. Elders and overseers therefore have to work in partnership and support each other's aims, which are complementary and indissoluble.

Qf&p 10.17 The spiritual welfare of a meeting is greatly helped if its social life is vigorous, and its members take a warm personal interest in one another's welfare.

Even when elders and overseers are working well together, building community is a considerable undertaking. It presents us with numerous needs and opportunities, and elders and overseers cannot personally act on them all. Partnership is necessary not just between elders and overseers, but with and between everyone in the meeting.

Often overseers do recognise the sense in sharing responsibility yet still end up doing most things themselves. It can be quicker and whole lot simpler just to get on with it. But if we see ourselves – or if others see us – as the people who do more or less everything, it can discourage people from participating in the care of their community and sharing responsibility for what kind of community it is or becomes. Sometimes those of us who are good at organising should sit on our hands. We will achieve more by enabling others to initiate activities – including coming up with their own ideas and their own way of going about it. A Friend might appreciate support or practical help, but we should resist taking over someone else's initiative.

We also risk giving the impression that only Friends who are especially caring are equipped to care, or that only people sufficiently connected or 'authorised' in the meeting can initiate activities or organise social occasions.

> "Friends value our overseers for being so dedicated, but see them as overburdened and wouldn't want to do the job. We have a perennial problem finding people willing to serve. Elders don't want to get involved either! But we've now decided to have joint roles. We have yet to see whether this will improve things."

Even the most efficient and hard-working small group of appointed Friends cannot achieve community on behalf of the rest. Whenever we initiate something we should encourage shared effort and input *at the outset,* and also watch that it is not always the same busy people who are asked to do things, or who offer. The benefits of making this a priority – even when our instinct says we will do a better job on our own – are more than just establishing a healthy principle; this is how Friends get to know one another and their meeting, and the way a sense of belonging grows.

❖ **Chapter 9:** *Belonging and commitment* looks further at ways our meeting can extend an inclusive and friendly welcome to get involved in the worshipping community.

❖ **Chapter 21:** *Leadership among equals* discusses the importance of sharing responsibility, encouraging initiative and enabling others to contribute to pastoral care.

Queries for reflection, discussion and learning

Chapter 8: The meaning of community

Queries for individual reflection
1. What are my needs for community, and how far do I find them met in my meeting?
2. What do I contribute to building community? How significant is my contribution towards achieving the community I hope for?
3. How do I respond to tensions and disagreements in the meeting? How might I be part of encouraging others to see diversity and difference as opportunity not threat?

Queries for pastoral groups
1. How do eldership and oversight complement each other in our community? What is our role in seeing that the spiritual, practical, social, business and outward strands of meeting life are interwoven and work as a whole?
2. How could we enable more people to get to know one another through purposeful activity together?
3. 'Sometimes those of us who are good at organising should sit on our hands.' What more might we do to encourage and support initiative and activity in the meeting? Are there limits or boundaries to this that we should be considering as well?

Queries for meetings

1. What are the many parts and connections that make up our meeting community? Can we map them, perhaps as a spider diagram?

2. 'In true community there will be enough diversity and conflict to shake loose our need to make the world in our own image' (Parker J. Palmer). How far do we recognise and work with this less than comfortable truth in our meeting?

3. How do we build community together? What opportunities exist that enable most individual Friends in the meeting to play a useful part? How might we expand or build on those opportunities?

✤ These pages can be downloaded from the online resource: **www.quaker.org.uk/tender-hand**

Chapter 9: Belonging and commitment

~

Building community goes hand in hand with encouraging a sense of belonging in the meeting. Friends gain this sense partly through knowing one another and participating in their community, and partly through knowing about their Quaker faith and feeling committed to the Quaker way. As elders and overseers we promote both ways of knowing more effectively when we have a good understanding of our own relationship with our worshipping community: what does our community ask of us and offer us, and what are we committing to when we come into membership of the Society?

1. One community among many

Quaker meetings, like most communities, are made up of people who are members of several other communities as well. These other communities – including family, place of work or study, societies and other organisations, etc. – may have no Quaker connections and no other Quakers among their members (or none the Friend knows about). This is a feature of our modern lives, but was not always so for Friends.

> Friends in earlier generations belonged to Quaker families, their workplace was often Quaker too, and their meeting was more than their spiritual home - it was the primary focus of all their relationships and connections throughout their lives.

- Some Friends today are similarly committed to their meeting as the primary community among several they may belong to. It's where they feel most at home, the group they are most willing to support with their time, involvement, service and money.
- Others cope with competing demands while sustaining a strong commitment to their meeting, and will do what they can to contribute.
- Some who attend a Quaker meeting regard it as just one group they find satisfaction in being part of. Their investment in the meeting's wellbeing may be lessened by a weaker connection.

Pastoral care is naturally focused on encouraging participation and commitment, but we recognise that people (and that includes all of us) have rich and varied lives beyond meeting, which for some may limit their connection with Friends. Our aim is not to achieve full engagement in the meeting, but to help Friends grow in commitment to a community that embraces them as they are. Without pressing people into more involvement than they find comfortable or possible, we can aim for everyone who attends meeting to find a place of welcome and possibility.

> Accepting people as they are includes seeing a Friend's choice to leave or to move to another faith community as within the natural order of things, not a failure on our part. We will wish them well on their journey wherever it takes them and be pleased to see them again if their journey brings them back into the community at any time.

2. An inclusive welcome

Every meeting will no doubt aim to be welcoming to whoever comes through the door, anyone who might want to and everyone who is already inside. Welcome is therefore what we do as a community all the time rather than a duty assigned to certain Friends on Sunday mornings.

> When meetings pay attention to the quality of their life together – creating opportunities for learning as well as service, nurturing a welcoming climate, eating as well as worshipping together, often doing fewer things, but doing them well – they have found it easier to attract (and hold on to) attenders and enquirers, and to think imaginatively and creatively about their shared life.
>
> (*Outreach handbook*, 2012: p. 5)

i. Newcomers and enquirers
People will pick up clues about our community from everything they observe – not just how we greet them, but what they see going on and how Friends relate to one another.

"One meeting I visited was so unwelcoming I'll never go back. I introduced myself at the end of meeting but afterwards no one spoke to me. They obviously thought their job was done by inviting visitors to stand up and say their name."

None of us should need to be on our best behaviour for newcomers; if we treat one another with kindness and respect it will be evident to anyone walking through our door. But we do have to be of aware of how things may seem to people unfamiliar with what Friends in the meeting take for granted. For example, when we respond to queries we might question how helpful it is to offer standard Quaker answers about our testimonies, witness, practices or beliefs. We are more likely to make a connection with someone new to Friends when speaking from our own experience, how it is for us personally – especially if we show we are interested in their experience too.

❖ The Quaker Life *Outreach handbook* is an essential guide for anyone involved in extending a welcome to their meeting – which is all of us. The section on 'Warmth and welcome' includes this summary of offering welcome:

- Welcome is a climate of hospitality rather than just a word; it is who we are rather than what we do.
- It is the responsibility of the whole meeting rather than just one person. If you see a new visitor, don't assume that someone else will say hello to them.
- If you are unsure whether someone is there for the first time, it's always worth taking the risk of saying hello, just in case.
- Catching up with Friends after meeting for worship is an important part of being a community; however, it can be off-putting and can leave people feeling left out. Try to include visitors in the conversation.
- Whilst we are sensitive to the danger of overwhelming newcomers and making them uncomfortable, on balance it is probably worth erring on the side of warmth. I have come across people who either struggled on through or who never went back because no one spoke to them. I have yet to meet anyone who stayed away because the meeting was too friendly.
- Listening is probably more important than talking. Rather than trying to explain everything about Quakerism, wait for the visitor to ask their own

questions and share some of what has brought them here.

- Someone reading the noticeboard for 10 minutes probably isn't that interested in the content of the notices. It is more likely that no one has spoken to them.
- For most meetings, the time after meeting for worship is when the real work of welcome begins. This can be a time of fresh encounter or of lost opportunity, and it is important to take the time to get it right.

(*Outreach handbook,* 2012: pp. 17–18)

❖ **Chapter 16:** *Communicating as Friends* looks at some of the things we can do to ensure that the messages received by people new to our meeting – including those who haven't yet crossed our threshold – are the messages we intend, and that they are viewed positively.

ii. A collection of minorities

Meeting communities are mostly not homogeneous. Friends may appear to have much in common but between us we also represent a number of minorities connected with such factors as:

- work, non-work, retirement, study
- family, partnership, living alone
- physical health, mental health, disability
- life experience, age, gender, sexuality.

"We include people by being aware of their circumstances, if that's possible, and by not making assumptions when we don't know."

We have to make sure that our usual meeting arrangements don't exclude certain minorities who have specific needs. There might not be issues of this kind among people currently attending – as far as we are aware – but hopefully we are all open to the possibility of welcoming new people.

Most meetings do take care to welcome newcomers, but can neglect to notice the people who have been coming for a while – perhaps for a good long while – and who for one reason or another remain on the periphery. If it is possible to know the reasons (we can always ask!) we can be sensitively aware of needs and accommodate them where that would be helpful. We may discover how we can keep a friendly and supportive connection with a Friend whose circumstances limit their involvement in the meeting, or explore with them ways in which they could contribute within those limits.

Knowing why some people stay on the edge of things might reveal a need for more positive ways of including people. From their perspective does it appear that there are 'us' who are well connected and responsible for what goes on, and that they are part of 'them' who are not really included? Are there sufficient opportunities for people to make a contribution that doesn't mean taking on a heavy responsibility? When people do get involved it tends to dispel assumptions about 'them and us' because it's clear how necessary everyone's contribution is.

> "When I became a functioning cog in the meeting was when I became a Quaker."

❖ **Chapter 8:** *The meaning of community* explores participation in the meeting.
❖ **Chapter 15:** *Disability, vulnerability and times of stress* addresses how our meeting includes people with needs associated with health, disability or advanced age.

iii. Transparency and openness

Creating a welcoming environment means making it easy for people to understand how the meeting works and what is going on. This tends to come naturally when Friends get involved, but it should be possible to find out in other ways too. Could it seem to some people that little or nothing is explained but that eventually things are supposed to become clear?

Explaining is part of how we achieve transparency, but even more important is a general climate of openness in the meeting. Achieving a climate of openness may be neither straightforward nor without its pitfalls.

> Where a sense of calm depends on not knowing what is going on in the silence, it can take very little emerging apparently out of nowhere to cause a real problem. Being more open will sometimes entail taking risks. But it may be better to take those risks often and in ways that are 'held' than allow assumptions and unease to grow through not being well enough in touch with one another.

Friends want to be more aware of the meeting community they belong to than just knowing how the processes work or what activities are planned. When there are more closed doors than open ones Friends may sense undercurrents or things going on behind the scenes that appear to exclude them.

Some meetings address this by including regular reports of meeting activities and the work of committees in a newsletter or website. In others, minutes of committees and various working groups are available for anyone to read in the same way as local meeting minutes. As elders and overseers, do we support openness by keeping our exclusive business to a minimum? There are practical solutions to maintaining essential confidentiality that could make it possible for eldership and oversight groups to report on their work, or even to produce open minutes.

❖ Issues of this kind are discussed further in **Chapter 3:** *Grounding our practice* and **Chapter 19:** *Making connections*

❖ **Chapter 18:** *Keeping people informed* explores matters to do with conveying information and how we receive information – what we do with it.

iv. Our meeting family

In time the connections we make as Friends strengthen our commitment and our feelings of mutual responsibility: we recognise each other as family. We get on with one another because we share significant understandings, and we find love and meaning in the family, which provides a home, company and care.

And before getting carried away with this comforting metaphor we shouldn't forget that families also endure all sorts of troubles and sometimes break down in discord. The tensions of 'family' life can be very occupying to a meeting; Friends can become wrapped up in matters that appear mysterious and off-putting to anyone less involved – especially newcomers.

Even when our meeting family is living in harmony we must notice who this cosy feeling may be excluding. Is our meeting the kind of family that pays good attention to its guests, takes particular care of its weaker members, and sustains connections with its neighbours and extended family? Does it accommodate difference and give voice to all ages? Has it got time and energy for the family member who isn't fitting in?

3. Sharing our gifts

Belonging to a community does mean contributing what we can of what we each bring from other experience. We all have skills and abilities that are valued in our working lives, in our friendships and in our families, but often Friends don't share these with their meeting. It isn't uncommon for Friends to know a good bit about one another's inner lives and yet be unaware of how someone earns their living, or used to.

- Do Friends feel their experience isn't worth sharing with the meeting? Is it that somehow their skills don't count, aren't good enough, or are irrelevant to the meeting's needs – or perhaps they are relevant but aren't in fact needed?
- Are some unable to offer service at this time? Do they fear that if they declare what they are good at or interested in they will be looked to for more than they feel able to offer?
- Do Friends prefer to keep that distance between their working lives and meeting?

Friends might need some encouragement to see that many of their qualities, talents and skills are spiritual gifts that have a place in their worshipping community too. Making this connection may lead some to find ways in which it feels okay to offer their gifts to the meeting.

> "We have a 'skills audit' over a shared lunch. We ask people to declare their unusual hobbies, skills or interests – whether or not they feel they are relevant to being or doing Quaker – and we build up a picture of this amazingly talented meeting! We also ask them to tell us about lapsed skills that they might still be interested in offering or reviving."

"A Friend facilitated a 'spiritual gifts' workshop – we worked in threes sharing what we were good at. The role of the two listeners was really important. It didn't feel like boasting – it was a lovely way to tell a couple of Friends something that made us feel good about ourselves."

Ideas such as these can be very useful for awakening reflection on service, but shouldn't be used as disguised attempts to glean information for nominations committees. If this is one of the purposes it must be stated, and that will affect what people feel able to 'declare'. Meetings may need to be more explicit about the various possibilities that exist for offering service, which might or might not include taking on an appointed role.

Whether or not Friends feel able to offer certain of their gifts in the service of their meeting community, an exercise in speaking about skills and experience with no strings attached might simply be a good way for people to be more aware of each other and to discover new connections. An activity along these lines could include discussion on the relationship between needs and gifts: how do we know our gift isn't useful or wanted if people are unaware of it; why should we assume that our need will be a burden on the meeting, rather than an opportunity for someone to offer their gift; what use is our gift if we don't share it with people who have a need for what we are able to offer?

Small connections all add up	A need is also a gift
When we share our talent for drawing or our love of dance with just one other Friend, that connection is part of building community.	When we make known our need for companionship, or for a lift to meeting, we make it possible for someone to offer their gift. So needs are also gifts: they release gifts in the meeting.

❖ **Chapter 19:** *Making connections* and **Chapter 21:** *Leadership among equals* each explore different aspects of how eldership and oversight can promote and support the sharing of gifts.

❖ Further ideas on sharing gifts can be found in the online resource: **www.quaker.org.uk/tender-hand**

❖ How Friends can participate purposefully in the meeting, including through service, is discussed in **Chapter 8:** *The meaning of community* (3. Taking part).

4. Learning together

Other than meeting for worship, and second only to service, learning together is key to how we grow as Friends and in community. What counts as a learning activity? Almost anything with a focus we can get our teeth into, and anyone might come up with an idea of interest to them that they would like to invite others to be interested in too. Learning and sharing activities often get off the ground best when they start out this way.

However, we will want to ensure that learning activities reflect the needs and wants of more than a few Friends with good ideas or particular interests. Our meeting as a whole has needs too. The resource *Being Friends Together* (referred to below) includes guidance on a simple step-by-step discernment process to help a meeting discover its priorities and decide on learning activities that will help the community grow. Being clear about our priorities and having a sense of direction as a meeting actually encourages Friends to come up with suggestions of their own, and provides a framework within which initiative can flourish.

"Everything is easier and more purposeful if the community is working, if it is pulling together. So we make sure there are plenty of opportunities for community to grow. We can't impose anything, there has to be a sense that we are part of this community voluntarily and that there is an assumption that we want to make it work."

As elders and overseers we may need to check an impulse to supervise every initiative, but we have a useful role to play in nurturing this important area of meeting life and seeing that it includes as many in the meeting as possible. For example, we will keep an eye on how well a programme of learning reflects the meetings 'vision': we may want to suggest a specific idea or approach from time to time where we see a gap in the meeting's agreed priorities or we spot emerging needs not previously discerned.

Some meetings appoint a committee or group to plan and coordinate learning activities, or a 'learning coordinator' who is in touch with everyone undertaking separate initiatives. If a committee includes an elder and/or an overseer, this link ensures that wider eldership and oversight perspectives, especially on inclusion, can be taken into account. One immediate suggestion we may need to make is that Friends offer 'learning' rather than 'study' groups, as some people find this a more inviting prospect. Study hasn't been a fruitful part of everyone's experience, and the word can be off-putting, but we all have things to learn and most of us enjoy learning.

With an eye on how learning together encourages a sense of belonging among Friends, we may want to make sure that a programme of activities includes opportunities to learn about who we are as a community, for example:

- the history/story of our meeting
- how our meeting's structures work
- who serves in which roles; who is active in Quaker service beyond our meeting and what they do
- how the life of our meeting is funded
- our previous Quaker experience before we attended this meeting
- the relationship of our local meeting with the area meeting.

❖ **Chapter 19:** *Making connections* offers further ideas and guidance on learning and sharing in meetings from the perspective of enabling good communications to flourish among Friends.

❖ Developed jointly by Quaker Life and Woodbrooke, the resource *Being Friends Together* was launched in October 2014. It provides easy online access to over 1,000 activities and resources for use by groups of Friends in their meetings, often as written material that can be downloaded for printing, and including video and audio resources. Friends can select materials or plan courses via structured 'pathways' or in any other way they choose, such as searching by keywords or 'catalogue' number. For further information, details of how a meeting can subscribe, and an opportunity to roam the site and try some things out for free, go to **http://together.woodbrooke.org.uk**

5. Membership

The usual way Friends express commitment to their Quaker community is by coming into membership of the Society of Friends.

❖ *Quaker faith & practice* Chapter 11 gives a full explanation of the history and spiritual purpose of this key aspect of belonging to a Quaker meeting and contains the most recent information we will need to guide Friends of any age through the process.

Area meetings have some latitude in agreeing procedures for admitting people into membership and might choose to develop their own processes. Friends advising those considering membership will need to be fully aware of the procedures in their area meeting and able to explain the options if more than one process has been agreed.

Procedures have to be simple and flexible enough to reflect individual and local circumstances. Experience shows that there is no 'one size' that comfortably fits all, and many area meetings have developed a variety of routes into membership in order to meet different needs.
(*Membership: Principles and processes*, 2013: p. 2)

i. Supporting people applying for membership

This is a listed responsibility of oversight (*Qf&p* 12.13 h.) but clearly involves concerns of eldership on the spiritual significance of belonging to a meeting community. Other members of the meeting might be involved as 'nurturing/ supporting Friends', and in the case of younger Friends a parent or guardian, or an advocate if the potential member is a person with limited capacity.

Overseers have further responsibilities for procedures concerning transfer of membership and enquiries relating to possible termination of membership. The formal and detailed nature of these procedures (all in *Qf&p* Chapter 11) is a good indication of the significance of membership in British Quakerism.

Friends offering guidance or encouragement to attenders wondering about membership often meet hesitancy connected with worries about being asked to take on roles. We may need to have a thoughtful conversation in order to disentangle questions about service to the meeting. It is true that certain roles are usually for members only (see *Qf&p* 3.24 i.), but it doesn't follow that all members will be expected to take on significant roles. Sometimes it's the other way round – a Friend would love to be considered for service they feel well equipped to offer, but has other reservations about applying for membership. Or it might be that nominations committee lets us know they would like to consider the name of an attender, with a query about any possible movement towards membership. In these cases there's good opportunity for equally thoughtful conversations about the meaning of membership.

We cannot always tell if or when a Friend might be ready to consider membership. Clearly we won't press recent attenders to think about the possibility, but we can stay alert to readiness in people who have been attending regularly for some years rather than assume that they haven't mentioned it because they aren't interested. There will always be an appropriate way to broach the subject; we just have to find it.

> "I was certain I was a Quaker after going to meeting for two years, but it was another two before I applied – because I thought you had to wait until you were asked. Then one day, an up-front Friend said, 'So when are you going to become a member then?' He wasn't one of the elders or overseers, just someone who thought I was probably ready."

❖ The Quaker Life leaflet *Membership: Principles and processes* summarises key points in *Qf&p* Chapter 11 on routes into membership and the significance of membership to the Friend and to the meeting. This will be especially helpful to overseers and others offering guidance; it could also be used as a starting point for discussion with a potential member. Copies of the leaflet are available from Quaker Life and can be downloaded: **www.quaker.org.uk/tender-hand**

❖ *Moving into membership: Volume 8 of the Eldership and Oversight handbook series* was revised in 2011 with a preface explaining that the revision process was necessarily limited and that some details will therefore be out of date. The handbook is useful background reading, but for current guidance on process we will need to refer to the latest edition of *Quaker faith & practice* (available online: **http://qfp.quaker.org.uk**) or to the above leaflet.

ii. Making a commitment

Becoming a member is part of our continuing spiritual journey. It doesn't signal that we have arrived at a destination, but that we are ready to commit to the next stage of being with Friends.

> As with marriage, we intend our commitment to membership to be lifelong, and as with marriage it can turn out differently, but it carries the same quality of significance and importance in our lives. Coming into membership is when an individual commits to a community and a community commits to an individual; and it changes both.

Not everyone sees it like this. Although the numbers attending Quaker meetings haven't changed significantly in recent years membership has fallen, which is concerning for both our Religious Society and our local meeting community.

Most meetings now include long-term attenders who either see no need to join the Society or who prefer to preserve that small distance. A further change from previous generations is the number of households with only one Quaker, which can significantly influence their relationship with their meeting.

It involves negotiation and understandings about how much time the Friend spends on their meeting or other Quaker activities, and it affects their financial contribution as well. Membership might just be a commitment too far for some partnerships in which only one is a Friend.

❖ **Chapter 15:** *Disability, vulnerability and times of stress* explores how we support Friends in their relationships of all kinds.

Qf&p **11.01** Like all discipleships, membership has its elements of commitment and responsibility but it is also about joy and celebration. Membership is for those who feel at home and in the right place within the Quaker community.

iii. Does membership matter?

- It matters to the individual Friend in expressing willingness, a desire, to be a dependable part of the Quaker community. Membership for most people today is not about readiness to commit to a community they grew up in, but to do with having arrived here from somewhere else. Friends describe it as a significant spiritual transition.
- It matters to local and area meetings that they include a healthy balance of Friends who understand our distinctive practices and where they have come from – Friends who will commit to playing their part in ensuring our meetings stay Quaker. The importance we attach to membership is clearly reflected in our structures and decision-making processes, not all of which are open to non-members.
- It matters to the wider Quaker community that Friends make this step in their spiritual journey for a number of reasons. It affects our charitable status and how the Society and constituent parts of it relate to other organisations, both religious and secular, and it gives us a public voice. A

committed membership influences how Quakers are seen in the world and the kind of underpinning the Society can provide to Friends who are actively engaged in Quaker witness. It is often noted that our influence and impact as a Society belie our numbers; that we 'punch above our weight'. Our weight is our membership.

> ➤ How do we continue to strengthen the Quaker community and uphold the Quaker way while being willing to be changed by those we welcome into our community?
> ➤ How can we encourage membership among Friends who insist they are not joiners, and who don't see how that affects the community they still want to be part of?
> ➤ How do we support active membership so that it doesn't become synonymous with being over-burdened and so deters others from joining?

There are no simple solutions, but everything we do to nurture our meeting communities will contribute to Friends in their meetings being part of the answer.

Qf&p 10.29 I feel very strongly ... that the spiritual life absolutely requires that we should not remain isolated. It is this deep need of getting out of a prolonged and dangerous relative isolation which urges me to ask now to be admitted among the Quakers. It is more and more clear to me that it is only in the bosom of a religious family, freely but very strongly constituted, that the individual can render to the world the services it sorely needs and which no politics, not based on a deep inspiration, can hope to organise.

(Pierre Ceresole, 1936)

Queries for reflection, discussion and learning

Chapter 9: Belonging and commitment

Queries for individual reflection

1. Which of the following best describes my relationship with the meeting?
    *   The Friend for whom meeting is their primary community
    *   The Friend strongly committed to meeting among competing demands
    *   The Friend who sees meeting as just one group among others they are part of.
    What tensions exist for me in this relationship?

2. Have I ever felt an outsider in an established group? What did it feel like? What can I personally do to ease someone's first or early experience of my meeting?
3. What does my membership mean to me? If I'm not a member, what is holding me back? In either case, how can I be involved in encouraging others in their commitment to the meeting and the Quaker faith?

Queries for pastoral groups

1. 'It's always worth taking the risk of saying hello, just in case.' (*Outreach handbook*). How do we each feel about putting that into practice? What advice might we offer others who find opening up conversations with strangers difficult?

2. Do we recognise the close relationship between needs and gifts? How will we encourage Friends to value the relationship, to acknowledge their needs as well as their gifts, and be willing to share both?

3. Do we need to explore other routes into membership than the process we are most used to? Might we consider providing training or a learning workshop for Friends who will be involved in these processes? How would we go about this?

Queries for meetings

1. How do we provide an inclusive welcome to 'whoever comes through the door, anyone who might want to and everyone who is already inside'?

2. How transparent are the inner workings of our meeting? What are the gains or risks connected with 'closed doors'?

3. Where are we as a meeting on the issue of membership? If we are affected by proportionately too few members, how will we approach the questions this raises? How does our meeting actively encourage, support and value membership?

❖ These pages can be downloaded from the online resource: **www.quaker.org.uk/tender-hand**

Chapter 10: All age community

~

The care of younger Friends and their families is a whole-meeting concern. This chapter concentrates on the role of eldership and oversight in promoting the growth and health of communities in which people of all ages share in the life of their meeting.

When children and young people come to meeting it is usually with a parent or other responsible family member, and while they are engaged in meeting activities there are clear boundaries of responsibility for their care. This is the essential context for work that aims to be inspirational, joyful, purposeful and inclusive. Our yearly meeting makes a substantial investment, through Quaker Life, in providing Friends and meetings with the best possible support for such important work.

❖ References throughout this chapter indicate some of the many resources available, all of which are very easy to access online: **www.quaker.org.uk/cyp**

1. Communities in the balance

The Religious Society of Friends in Britain is undeniably top heavy in terms of age. Friends in their sixties (the active retired) are the youngsters in some meetings and tend to predominate in Quaker service locally and nationally. Friends of working age are often busy doing exactly that – working to earn a living or to raise their families. Happily, the Society does include Friends of all ages, but proportionally fewer Friends are active in Quaker meetings the younger they are. This is a matter of concern to all who care about the health of our worshipping communities and especially if we are missing the vital presence of children and young people – as most meetings are.

The stark fact is that the majority of local meetings have no children attending at all. According to the tabular statement for the year 2012 only a third of local meetings held a regular children's meeting, and only one in four of these regular children's meetings were held every week. Encouraging families and making provision for children is sometimes argued for on the grounds that this is the future of the Society, that the children of today are the adult members of the future. Much more significantly, meetings gain from the presence of children, young people and their families *now*. They bring energy, challenge, inspiration and fresh perspectives that meetings need to become healthy vibrant communities.

i. Growing a children's meeting

Where Friends of working age are absent from meeting, so are their children. Sometimes we see the parents but not their children for a number of reasons; it can be difficult to break a pattern where one family's children don't come because there aren't any others to make it interesting and fun.

A few meetings are so settled as communities of older Friends that they would find it hard adapting to the presence of children; but on the whole meetings regret their lack of children and wish there were ways they could change it. If our meeting is in this situation there are things we can do and there is a great deal of support available to help us.

❖ The Quaker Life booklet *Resources and support for children and young people's work* provides an essential guide to accessing the right help and support for our particular circumstances.

❖ Among these resources is the leaflet *Being ready for children in your Quaker meeting*, which offers practical advice and clear steps for any meeting 'where, as yet, there is no regular children's meeting for worship, where children are not regular or even occasional visitors with their families'.

Elders, overseers and others who recognise how the absence of children affects their own community – and who also see the bigger picture in Britain of so many local Quaker meetings lacking a children's meeting – should do what they can towards bringing about change.

> As Quakers we have something special to offer children for their spiritual and faith journey. Our meetings, whatever size, can be welcoming, thriving, inclusive and positive places for all ages. If meetings are unprepared then children and families may feel unwelcome or uncomfortable and not come back. Love requires that we are ready.
>
> (*Being ready for children in your Quaker meeting*, 2012: p. 2)

This 'something special' is too good to keep to ourselves. Whether or not our meeting has a children's meeting, it is worthwhile reaching out to families in our area to discover how their needs and ours might coincide. The *Being ready* leaflet suggests some practical approaches we could try.

❖ **Chapter 6:** *Worship in the life of the meeting* invites us to consider how our meeting might offer opportunities for Quaker worship at times and in ways other than our usual Sunday morning meeting for worship.

ii. Supporting participation

In a Quaker community children need:
- To be valued, affirmed and cared for safely as individuals so that their different needs are met.
- Acceptance as a valid part of the Quaker community – this includes full participation in and contribution to the life of the meeting, only doing separately what cannot, properly, be done together.
- Freedom and nurture to develop spiritually. To be equipped and encouraged for their spiritual journey and quest.
- Encouragement and help in identifying and learning about what it means to be a Quaker in general and personally.

(What about the children in our meeting? Exploring the purposes of children's work, 2008: p. 1)

If our meeting is one of those blessed with children or young people attending we have an all age community. This is not just the period in meeting when children join the adults, or all age worship, or an event with provision for children. It is all of these and the rest of the time too. Our community will be richer for acknowledging this fact and making opportunities that bring all generations together for the same purposes.

"The children's meeting has been so involved in the life of the meeting; it's not just about having children around, it's about them really being part of shaping what we do."

It can be a challenge to get the balance right so that it feels natural as well as inclusive for worship, activities, learning and discernment to include all ages. Meetings will need to reflect together and plan their approach to communications and activities across generations. An inclusive approach asks adults to adapt the way they do things, including the way they are in charge. It means enabling younger members of the meeting to contribute and to take their share of responsibility for how things are done. Bringing about change in attitudes is invariably slow work, but Friends can help this along by degrees and in quite small ways:

- Encourage people of all ages to suggest things everyone could do together. We could be surprised by children's interest in 'real' Quaker business, witness or work, not only social and fun activities.
- Explain why Friends do something in a particular way each time children are involved in activities where adults usually know the ropes, for example, when there is a call for silence at the start of a committee meeting.
- Invite people of all ages to respond in their own way, which might not be to say things out loud. Don't base everything on talk.
- Note differences in attention span.
- Avoid asking adults to do childish things and expecting young people to behave like adults. No one should need to act like a person from another generation in order to fit in.

A special issue of *Journeys in the Spirit – Connecting as a community* explores possibilities for greater participation by young people in the life of their meeting. This is a need articulated by young people but experienced by all Friends who are working to build all age community in their meeting. The pack of resources accompanying the special issue offers us really practical things we can do to link our provision for young people aged between 12 and 18 with the wider meeting.

This special issue looks at young people's participation. Participation means that *"young people should be fully integrated within the Yearly Meeting and have a real impact on all aspects of our life and work so that the whole meeting can grow from this involvement"*. (Meeting for Sufferings Minute 4, 7 May 2005)

(*Connecting as a community*, p. 1)

❖ *Connecting as a community* is available at **www.quaker. org.uk/tender-hand**

❖ Some of the ideas and suggestions in this section came from reading an inspiring article by Christie Duncan-Tessmer, 'Weaving children and adults into full meeting life', in Philadelphia Yearly Meeting's *Pastoral Care Newsletter* of January 2008.

iii. All age worship

Worship that includes people of all ages is perhaps the most important element in all age community life. Often the times when we have our strongest sense of community – of how we all gain from one another's presence – are the 15 minutes or so when children commonly join the adults in meeting. Being alongside children as they learn to enjoy the quiet company of adults and each other is one of the more extraordinary experiences of being a Friend, and something we should cherish with our good attention and care.

Children in earlier times may have accompanied their parents for the whole of meeting for worship, which was often longer than is usual today, but we are in a different age with different expectations. Could it be that both adults and children are missing out to some degree?

"We found that our children can 'cope' with much longer periods of silence than we would have imagined and that they can experience a deeper silence in which the Spirit can be powerfully felt."

Increasingly meetings recognise that they want rather more of their worship to be all age and inclusive, and are experimenting with various ways of enabling that to happen. All age meetings for worship are one response to that need. If we want to find out how we could go about this there are a number of resources we can access.

- Quaker Life has produced a practical guide: *Spring into all age worship*, which includes sample plans to use as they are or to adapt.
- The monthly Quaker Life publication *Journeys in the Spirit: Children's* edition offers further ideas for all age worship. It is available by subscription from **www.quaker.org.uk/cyp**
- More suggestions can be found at **www.quaker.org.uk/ideas-store**

Many of the ideas in these resources are based on a theme and include planned elements, often with a creative activity for all ages to engage in. While most Friends are prepared to enter into the spirit of programmed or semi-programmed all age meetings, not everyone is so willing to put their own need for silent worship on one side, even occasionally. Meetings address this in different ways, including providing an alternative separate silent meeting, or having the children join the main meeting for only part of the time, or holding 'all age' worship in the children's room with just some of the adults joining them.

"There was a somewhat tense situation, with some Friends feeling so strongly against the decision to hold an all age worship in the meeting room that they have not worshipped with us since."

"We have established the practice of starting meeting for worship earlier than usual on these occasions so that Friends who wish can have a full hour of silent worship before the children join us for all age worship."

"I can't pretend all age worship is my cup of tea, but then again it isn't about me. It helps to integrate children and families and we all learn through it. That must be a good thing."

This Friend's accepting attitude is common, which is helpful to the extent that it allows all age worship to happen. But it won't flourish as a meeting practice if Friends regard it as principally for the benefit of the children and only incidentally for the adults. How can we make all age worship more of everyone's cup of tea?

An approach that is nearer to the usual silent unprogrammed meeting for worship might work better for some meetings. Here is Warwick Meeting's experience of another way (from an account of the event by Anna Edelston):

"The meeting was designed to be as similar as possible to normal Sunday worship, with the addition of the children in the meeting for the hour. We set out a number of response materials in the middle of the room: natural bark blocks, wool and drawing materials. The children were free to play with the materials, or sit on the floor or a chair quietly. The parents generally sat around the children, intermixed with other adults.

The worship proceeded as in a regular meeting. The children (aged 4–7) responded very well to the silence. They spent most of the time interacting with the materials, with some sitting quietly at different periods. The children were, on the whole, peaceful for the entire hour. One worshipper spoke of how it brought back to her memories of stillness in her own childhood and how spiritually nourishing that experience still is today. Some of the younger children needed parental attention from time to time, but this did not disrupt the worship. Nobody worshipped separately in the alternative meeting room, which had been set up for those not feeling able to join the main meeting.

When asked what she recalled of that meeting (now some months in the past), my 7-year-old daughter responded, 'I enjoyed it... I felt elated.'"

With worship at the heart of everything we do as Friends, elders and overseers will be concerned to find acceptable ways for it to be more inclusive more often. Elders will want to support the spiritual intentions of the occasion by working with the Friends planning all age worship. And both elders and overseers might be involved in addressing any difficult feelings in the meeting alongside their support for those taking the initiative on the meeting's behalf.

Hopefully the decision to have all age worship will have evolved from as many people as possible in the meeting talking about it – including elders, overseers, children's committee, the children and young people.

... Take a proposal to local meeting. Encourage people to ask questions, voice their doubts and anxieties, and share their hopes. Free the way for people to come to all age worship with open minds and hearts. Challenge people to live adventurously.

(*Spring into all age worship*, 2013: p. 3)

2. Care of children and young people

❖ In addition to the constantly updated guidance and support provided by Quaker Life, *Pastoral care of children and young people: Volume 7 in the Eldership and Oversight handbook series* is a very useful resource. It provides a practical guide to many of the issues we encounter through the responsibilities outlined in *Qf&p* 12.12 i. and 12.13 f., and makes an excellent first read for Friends who might be unsure of the role they can play.

There is no need to reiterate here guidance provided in that handbook, or by Quaker Life, but we will look further at two aspects of our meeting's care for children and young people that especially concern eldership and oversight:

i.   working together with others responsible for the care of children and young people
ii. caring for the individual child or young person.

i. Working together
Eldership and oversight share their responsibility for the care of children and young people with a number of other people in the local and area meeting:

1) Children and young people themselves

Children and young people's right to participate in decision making concerning matters which affect them

is enshrined in Article 12 of the United Nations
Convention on the Rights of the Child, to which the UK
is a signatory. The benefits of enabling and empowering
children and young people to have a voice and take on
responsible roles are being increasingly recognised.

*(Report of the Quaker Life consultation group on
children and young people's inclusion, 2008: p. 2)*

It isn't easy to involve younger people in the usual processes
of decision making in the meeting. Practical obstacles include
the timing, length and manner of business or committee
meetings, and finding young people willing to take on roles.
Could adults consider meeting with young people on their
terms instead? For example, members of a committee might
join the children's meeting on occasion to engage with them
in discernment processes they have been involved in planning.

❖ The *Journeys in the Spirit* special issue *Connecting as a
community* suggests various things we can do as a meeting
to give young people opportunities for their voices to be
heard and to participate in discernment of decisions that
affect them.

2) Children and young people's committee (CYP)

Usually some Friends are appointed to coordinate children's
meeting activities and events and to ensure good practice in
all aspects of the needs of younger Friends. Elders and
overseers should liaise with such a committee, offering their
support and involvement. This will be important to encourage
understanding in the meeting of how children and young
people's work is integral to the life of the meeting community,
not an add-on that doesn't really concern other Friends.
Quaker Life underpins the work of CYP committees with
workshops for meetings, resources, guidance and training,
which elders and overseers too should access to help them

contribute usefully and appropriately. They might work with the committee to draft a children's work policy that expresses the aims of children's meeting within a framework of good practice and matters to do with meeting safety.

3) Parents and other responsible adults

The involvement of family members is essential and usually easy to ensure, but we should see that the meeting doesn't become over-dependent on their service in this area of the meeting's life. Parents have needs for varied involvement as much as any other Friend – and they need to attend meeting for worship as well.

> One way for a meeting community to attend to the care and nurture of children is to create opportunities for their parents to attend meeting for worship. This is often an overlooked way of supporting children. If parents can be nurtured by worship, their children will benefit.
>
> (Sayers, 2014)

Elders and overseers can support parents' needs by working with the CYP committee on ways to bring further volunteers into the programme.

4) Volunteers working on the children's programme

Volunteers may be glad of offers from elders to work with them in supporting worship in children's meeting, and for overseers to advise on individual or group care needs. Children aren't always angels! Volunteers need to know that support is available should they be faced with challenging behaviour or if they are struggling to manage a boisterous group.

5) The whole meeting

Regular space for children and young people's work on the

agenda of local meetings for business can help Friends to feel involved, consulted and informed. Even if there are occasions when there is nothing to discuss or report it keeps this work continually alive in the minds of Friends. From time to time we might engage the meeting in thinking about care of children and young people, perhaps with discussion based on one or two of the queries offered at the end of this chapter.

> Moving beyond tolerating our children in meeting is not something that, once achieved, can be forgotten. It is something that needs to be regularly affirmed if it is to become part of the culture of the meeting community.
>
> (Sayers, 2014)

6) Area meeting children and young people's work advocate

We need to be aware of our meeting's links with the area meeting and establish contact with this Friend to learn of the support available. For example: our children and young people's advocate might be able to facilitate connections with other children's meetings in our area; small meetings might combine resources with one or more others, perhaps rotating a children's meeting between them; they could help us set up a Link Group for young people across the area meeting.

7) Area meeting safeguarding coordinator

This Friend will advise on the steps to take for safeguarding and child protection. Our area meeting can plan its own procedures with the help of the latest edition of *Meeting safety,* and sample policy documentation is also available from Quaker Life. If it all appears a bit daunting (it is simpler than it looks), the human face and practical guidance of our safeguarding coordinator will be important as we think these issues through.

❖ *Meeting safety* is a short document giving a brief introduction to safeguarding. Always use the latest edition, which is available at **www.quaker.org.uk/tenderhand**

ii. Caring for the individual

Eldership and oversight seek to care for the spiritual, emotional, community and welfare needs of children and young people in the meeting. Between this focus of pastoral care and the children's meeting programme – which naturally includes the same concerns together with an emphasis on learning, and looking outwards too – our meeting seeks to care for the whole child.

Whole children and young people are individuals with individual needs; elders and overseers should attend to these separately from the needs of their peers and of their parents and other family members. We will always observe guidelines on safe and appropriate contact with minors, and within those guidelines look for opportunities to support children in their individual relationships with adults in the meeting.

"One of the reasons I started coming to meeting was because our two children were missing out on close relationships with people older than us. At meeting, they get lots of conversation and attention from various 'grannies', and they thrive on it."

Meetings provide for eldership and oversight of individual children and young people in various ways. 'Linked Friends' (explained in *Pastoral care of children and young people*) is a way of involving at least as many adults in the meetings as there are younger people and has the advantage of continuity over longer periods than is usual with elder or overseer appointments. Both 'Linked Friends' schemes and arrangements for children to have named overseers or elders usually include consulting children about which Friend they would like to be paired with. What matters in any arrangement is that children and young people have someone in particular who is there for them and who will value and invest in the relationship.

> In our meeting we want to create a structure which allows the easy flow of ideas, enthusiasms, requests, questions, and cries for help or of anger between children and young people and the whole body of the membership of the meeting.
>
> (*Pastoral care of children and young people*, 2001: p. 4)

Queries for reflection, discussion and learning

Chapter 10: All age community

Queries for individual reflection

1. How do I feel about the presence of children in meeting, or their absence? Do I enjoy being involved, or do I prefer to leave this to others? Where do my attitudes to children and young people come from, and how have they changed over time?

2. What can I personally do to connect with and support a child or young person in my meeting?

3. How can I support Friends in the meeting who are very involved in children's work? Am I aware of the demands of this service? How can I express my understanding and appreciation?

Queries for pastoral groups

1. How do we exercise care and spiritual nurture of children and young people as individuals? Are we sufficiently aware of the spiritual and other care needs of children and young people? How can we find out?

2. Are we aware of families who don't attend or who don't bring their children to meeting for various reasons? How could we 'reach out to families in our area to discover how their needs and ours might coincide'?

3. How well do we liaise and cooperate with the Friends responsible for children's work in the meeting? How might we support that work more actively?

Queries for meetings

1. What do we understand by 'all age community'? How can we integrate children and young people more fully into the life of the meeting?

2. How will we make sure that everyone involved in the care and inclusion of children and young people in the meeting is aware of our written policy on this? If we lack a written policy, how will we go about drafting one? If no children attend our meeting currently, are we aware of the area meeting policy, and should we write a statement on our intentions regarding welcoming families?

3. Whether we have a thriving children's meeting, or we are getting by, or we have no children at all, do we support and engage in connections across the area meeting on children and young people's work? How might we contribute to keeping this work high on the agenda of our area meeting?

❖ These pages can be downloaded from the online resource: **www.quaker.org.uk/tender-hand**

THEME 4: Caring

The focus in these chapters is on the experience of caring and receiving care, on what Friends actually do to care for one another. How we go about this is inevitably influenced by circumstances specific to our local meeting, including how it organises and sustains its pastoral care provision.

Chapters in **Theme 1: Pastoral care** are useful background to the broad subject of caring covered here. They describe how eldership and oversight are structured and conducted to ensure that every aspect of our worshipping and community life supports our meeting's spiritual purpose. The practical approaches we take to caring for one another reflect and depend upon all those underpinnings, while keeping a clear focus on attending to the diverse needs of individual Friends.

Diversity as a feature of Quaker meetings has significance for the care we provide. Our community is built on the fellowship and contributions of individuals, each of whom has needs and gifts for spiritual nurture, belonging and outward connections in varying degrees. We can be certain too that many will have care needs of one kind or another, and that caring will be among the gifts Friends have to offer their community.

When we are thinking about care in the meeting we must look beyond the part we play as elders and overseers towards the giving and receiving of care as it involves everyone. This Theme discusses the idea that care is much more than something that *we* do for others who we (also) identify as needing it. A caring meeting enables everyone to contribute and to be part of how needs are met. Just as importantly, it encourages the kind of community where needs are noticed, made known, uncovered, anticipated and planned for in the normal course of being among Friends.

Some needs we have as members of a community can appear to be quite slight and maybe nothing to get exercised about, such as our needs for company, for being valued, acknowledged and taken seriously. When it comes to caring for children we don't doubt the importance of these 'small' things, but we can overlook their significance too in the lives of adults. We may need to check that our busyness with tackling the really challenging issues doesn't lead to neglect of simply being a good kind Friend, or that it makes us blind to someone's need for a little tenderness. These are the small things that bind us in community; the strength of which makes addressing the bigger things possible.

Because care depends so much on the good functioning of the community, the needs of the whole worshipping group may have to take priority over the needs of an individual in cases where attending to one seriously compromises our ability to attend to the other. This is just one complicating factor among many angles on the subject of care discussed in the following five chapters.

Chapter 11: Addressing need
explores three basic approaches to addressing need: providing for needs we know about or can anticipate, being a community of Friends who take responsibility for our own needs and being prepared to meet less common or unexpected needs.

Chapter 12: Receiving care
reflects on the experience of being cared for, looking at mutual care, invisible care, self care and how we would each respond to being on the receiving end of guidance.

Chapter 13: Absent Friends

considers the many causes for absence, the pitfalls of making assumptions, and how pastoral care might respond to a range of needs implicated in absence.

Chapter 14: Conflict and difficulty in the meeting

discusses how the health of our community influences difficulty in the meeting, the needs of individuals on all 'sides' of a conflict, and the response of eldership and oversight to significant challenges.

Chapter 15: Disability, vulnerability and times of stress

touches on a wide range of care needs including illness and infirmity, dying and bereavement, living with physical disability or mental ill health, and dealing with stress in relationships. It also reflects on supporting Friends who provide care in stressful circumstances.

Chapter 11: Addressing need

~

How can eldership and oversight prioritise the needs of the worshipping community, while being responsive to the legitimate needs of each person – of whatever age, temperament, life circumstance or religious disposition?

On the face of it that's quite a tall order. But it is important to see the two as linked: a meeting cannot care for individuals by neglecting the community, nor can it sustain community at the expense of caring for Friends.

The different – and changing – needs of the community and each individual within it are met from a number of sources: sometimes by the ways a meeting nurtures the spiritual life and builds community; sometimes by Friends, not only elders and overseers, guiding others or caring for one another; sometimes from networks of family and friendship, or from sources and organisations other than the Quaker meeting. We can gain a good sense of the most appropriate source for addressing a need by recognising and working with the three main ways a community cares for its members:

- providing for known or anticipated needs
- taking responsibility for our own needs
- being prepared to respond when needs arise.

The aim for our contribution as elders and overseers – which will only ever be part of the whole – will usually be to find a balance between these approaches, and through service that is not intrusive and doesn't dominate how the meeting functions as a community. We also have to be aware of the boundaries of our role and of our own limitations. Not everything about a Friend's situation or circumstances is for eldership or oversight to resolve, nor are we expected to be social workers or professional carers.

> It is worth bearing in mind that our responsibility is simply to ensure that Friends are supported in the things that enable them to be members of this worshipping community. These things might well be many-layered and far reaching – we are whole people living whole and complex lives – but we should be aware, and sometimes remind ourselves, of appropriate limits to our influence in Friends' lives.

1. Providing for known or anticipated needs

Some things elders and overseers can anticipate providing for are noted in *Quaker faith & practice* 12.12 and 12.13. The lists of responsibilities draw our attention to matters that may affect Friends personally but which they often have in common with others, and sometimes with everyone.

> *Oversight* has responsibilities for: welcome; encouraging attendance, involvement and the possibility of membership; attending to practical matters affecting individuals in their relationship with the meeting; supporting Friends living elsewhere. (*Qf&p* 12.13)

Eldership is responsible for: right holding of meetings for worship; seeing that there are opportunities for spiritual nurture and for learning; ensuring meetings for business are conducted in right ordering.
(*Qf&p* 12.12)

Eldership and oversight are jointly responsible for care of individuals, including attending to the needs of children and young people.
(*Qf&p* 12.12 and 12.13)

Taking time to discern needs and opportunities in the meeting, and planning how best to employ our resources, are essential in eldership and oversight practice. But we have to be prepared to adapt and change as well – our processes and procedures are only tools not rules. Tools become out-dated (they might require new parts or even replacing) so it matters that we observe how our practice is serving Friends, as individuals and as a community. If our community feels lacking, our worship is dry or Friends are discontented, we should look again at the arrangements for addressing needs – including the contribution of Friends other than elders and overseers – to see if these are sufficient or still working. For example:

> ➤ When there are opportunities for Friends to learn together but people don't turn up or a group soon fizzles out, is it clear why?
> ➤ Are attenders generally not expressing interest in membership? Why is this, and what could make a difference?
> ➤ Are our families disappearing? Should we give better attention to the needs of children and young people in the meeting, or is there another reason?

A significant influence on how well eldership and oversight can anticipate and plan to meet needs is whether all Friends or just a few are involved in identifying them and how they are addressed. Each meeting has its own distinctive 'profile' of needs: there might be a predominance of elderly Friends, poor transport links, a lot of families, or many attenders and only a handful of members. Needs associated with circumstances such as these might be relatively easy for elders and overseers to identify, but is the meeting generally aware of how a prevalent need or coincidence of needs might be straining its resources? And do people know that they all share responsibility for the welfare of their community?

If not, part of planning for anticipated need could include raising an issue in a setting where everyone is invited to think about it and discuss how it might be addressed. Or it might help to have a more open-ended enquiry, perhaps starting with the question, 'What are the prevailing needs in our meeting?'

❖ Either a meeting for learning or a threshing meeting – as described in **Chapter 19:** *Making connections* – could be useful for engaging everyone in understanding an issue, perhaps for the first time, and as a forum for planning what to do about it.

In fact *any* gathering of Friends in the meeting where concerns and ideas are exchanged might play a part in helping Friends to identify and plan to meet common, and less common, needs in their meeting.

2. Taking responsibility for our own needs

This is 'our' in the sense of each person in the meeting: *Qf&p* 12.12 and 12.13 indicate how eldership and oversight can approach this:

Eldership includes reminding Friends that we share responsibility for how meeting for worship is held and upheld, that we can learn how to participate in meetings for business, and that the extent to which the meeting is part of the life of the local community is a choice we can influence or act on.
(*Qf&p* 12.12)

Oversight includes encouraging Friends to take part in the life of the meeting and to be involved in the ways our meeting seeks to nurture caring friendships.
(*Qf&p* 12.13)

The joint responsibility of eldership and oversight here is to encourage an understanding among Friends that depth of worship, a friendly, welcoming and supportive community, and the meeting's connections with the wider community, are in their own hands. In other words, we should be active in helping Friends see that they can to a large extent meet their own needs as members of the meeting. This will include being explicit that Friends' involvement and initiative is welcome and not out of order. When we are not clear about that, or the way we work implies the opposite, we may well inhibit Friends' ability to take care of what matters to them about their meeting.

As individuals in a meeting we each have a responsibility to consider whether any of our further needs are matters for eldership or oversight and how a Friend or Friends might help. And then we have to make this known; we shouldn't expect people to work out what's wrong from how we are being rather than from what we are saying.

But expressing need isn't always an easy thing to do. For Friends to feel okay about playing a part in how care is provided, and comfortable about conveying what their needs for care are, there has to be a climate of shared responsibility and mutual support. The ways eldership and oversight care for the whole community should encourage each of us to feel that we can ask for or access support and contribute to the care of others. How Friends build a climate of mutual responsibility and caring together inevitably hinges on getting to know one another and being willing to play a part; pastoral care is most effective when it succeeds in unlocking the potential in us all for active participation in our community.

❖ **Chapter 8:** *The meaning of community* explores issues raised here in more detail.

3. Being prepared to respond when needs arise

i. Occasional needs
Quaker faith & practice 12.12 and 12.13 note several examples that most meetings will address at some time or other:

> Advising on and making arrangements for meetings for worship on special occasions, such as funerals, memorials and weddings; providing guidance to couples intending to marry.
> (*Qf&p* 12.12 and 12.13)

> Comforting the dying and the bereaved; caring for and visiting Friends who are sick or infirm; arranging meeting for worship in the homes of Friends unable to attend.
> (*Qf&p* 12.12 and 12.13)

> Advising Friends in financial difficulty and ensuring financial help is available where appropriate. (*Qf&p* 12.13)

Occasional needs are more or less usual depending on a meeting's size and other factors. The less frequently they occur the more occupying and demanding our response will feel, so thinking things through beforehand helps us to be ready for these occasions. In some instances, a meeting may benefit from having access to experience more widely available in their area meeting. This is just one of the ways Friends can use the resources of area meeting pastoral committees.

Other occasional needs include difficulties that are not so uncommon that we should be surprised – and unprepared – when they become apparent. Addressing a difficulty with a Friend is also part of our care for the Friend. For example, oversight includes helping to resolve misunderstandings and eldership includes the possibility of having to restrain unsuitable vocal ministry. Both possibilities can prove to be very difficult to address and we risk addressing them badly if we are unprepared; a misjudged response may just create further problems. In difficult situations we should make sure we consult with others if at all possible. If there is no choice but to respond in the moment, the best advice is to try to calm the situation and gain some time for a more considered response.

❖ **Chapter 14:** *Conflict and difficulty in the meeting* includes guidance on addressing difficulty of various kinds, which a meeting might use to help Friends be more aware and better prepared.

ii. Unexpected needs

I once burst a tyre by colliding with the kerb at a petrol pump. I know how to change a wheel but my knees are no longer up to it. The forecourt was full of people walking to and from their cars and they could see my predicament, so I approached several people who looked stronger than me for help, without success. Then I spotted someone crossing the forecourt right from the other end. "Could you do with a hand? I saw what happened – and the look on your face." Andrew changed my wheel, accepted my thanks and a tissue to clean up, and waved goodbye.

I felt cared for. And I could tell that Andrew felt good doing something for me that it would have been a struggle for me to manage on my own. I wasn't expecting to need help and he hadn't expected to offer it. But the need arose and someone I'd never met before simply responded.

In the light of this example of in-the-moment care, preparing for the unexpected sounds like a contradiction. How do we prepare? And if we have to act in the moment, how can we test our leading? Most people will be able to recall similar acts of uncomplicated caring and how that felt, which might serve to encourage us when an opportunity arises. We shouldn't feel over-anxious or deterred from just being a good Friend responding to a need, but clearly not every situation will be so straightforward.

In more challenging circumstances our response will be influenced by how far we feel we are acting alone or supported by others. We are better equipped to respond to the unexpected, and to have a good sense of the rightness of our action, if our habit as an eldership or oversight group is to agree practice and share experience together. There will be occasions when we will be glad to be aware of strategies that are new to us but which other Friends have found helpful. We will also be more able to judge when an immediate response is not the answer in a situation, but that it should be discerned with others who may help us decide what to do.

iii. Needs we fail to spot

Sometimes a need comes to our attention like a bolt from the blue because we have made easy assumptions about a person that prevented us from really knowing them. For example, it is a common experience to learn with complete surprise of the break-up of a relationship and then, looking back, we recall signs of something wrong that we dismissed at the time. Perhaps we will get better at reading the signs with experience, but more realistically we have to consider the possibility that an unexpected occurrence could give rise to unexpected feelings in us, which may affect the usefulness of our response.

It may be that we have failed to notice a problem because we are personally invested in everything being okay, for example:

- We don't notice bad feeling brewing between two Friends who are both dear to us until it erupts in open hostility.
- We are unaware that a Friend is unhappy in a role we encouraged them to take on until they suddenly resign.
- We don't recognise a Friend's deteriorating mental health condition until it becomes critical.

Belatedly discovering a situation in which we feel implicated places additional demands on our personal resources, especially if our first reaction is to feel guilty about not responding sooner. Being prepared for this possibility means recognising that we may have to attend to both needs (theirs and ours), but that the Friend's need comes first. We should try not to allow our own feelings of either shock or guilt to get in the way.

How we anticipate dealing with difficult situations will be different for each of us and complicated by the fact that we can feel daunted just thinking about possibilities. It is a bit unreal too. In practice most needs that become apparent will be of a kind inviting a response which comes naturally to us, and sometimes it will take two or more heads rather than one to be sure of the right natural response. Opportunity to consult other serving and/or experienced Friends will invariably be the way we get things right for and with someone who could do with our care, and will play an important part in how we look after our own needs as well.

❖ **Chapter 12:** *Receiving care* looks further into how we take care of ourselves.

❖ **Chapter 15:** *Disability, vulnerability and times of stress* addresses some of the more personally demanding care needs we could be called to respond to.

Queries for reflection, discussion and learning

Chapter 11: Addressing need

Queries for individual reflection

1. How do I care for people? How involved am I in noticing, or enquiring, or responding to need, and how are my responses received? Do I feel my care is valued?
2. Is caring a burden at times? Do I find it difficult to limit my involvement or the time a Friend takes up? How well do I cope when my care is rejected or criticised?
3. In what ways do I take responsibility for meeting my own needs as a member of my worshipping community? How can I do this without feeling disconnected or left to my own devices?

Queries for pastoral groups

1. How can we ensure we 'prioritise the needs of the community as a whole, while being responsive to the legitimate needs of each person'? If we have had to make a difficult choice at some time, how do we feel about that now (or how would we make that choice)?
2. How do we prepare for needs or circumstances we don't often meet? Is there a point in giving scarce time to this? In what ways would it help when the unexpected happens?
3. Are we prepared to learn from getting things wrong? How will we do this in our group without blaming or scapegoating?

Queries for meetings

1. 'A caring meeting enables everyone to contribute and to be part of how needs are met; just as importantly, it encourages the kind of community where needs are noticed, made known, uncovered, anticipated and planned for in the normal course of being among Friends.' To what extent are we this kind of caring meeting?

2. Are arrangements in the meeting for caring for people sufficient and working? Where are there lacks or difficulties in providing for Friends' needs?

3. Do we invariably look to certain Friends to provide most of the care? As a caring community, how can we all support and care for one another? What does or will this mean in practice?

❖ These pages can be downloaded from the online resource: **www.quaker.org.uk/tender-hand**

Chapter 12: Receiving care

~

In every meeting there are certain Friends who are especially caring and kind, who are just very good at noticing and responding to need, and who go out of their way to be there for others. While not aspiring to be such exceptional carers most of us feel able to attend to people's needs as part of our responsibilities for care in the meeting. Caring for one another is an essential part of the life of our community, and clearly we must nurture and support the gifts of caring among Friends – the exceptional and the ordinary.

But alongside the attention we give to providing care we should be aware that care is a transaction between at least two parties. At its simplest it involves a person who cares and another who is cared for, and the experience of this other person should naturally influence how Friends provide care.

It might feel selfless and benign to provide or offer care, but it nevertheless amounts to a 'good deed' someone does for someone else, and the person on the receiving end may have a more complicated response. To understand this other side of care we need to ask ourselves how comfortable we are with receiving help and support. All Friends, including elders and overseers, are subject to the caring attention of eldership and oversight. But do we find this as straightforward as offering care? Does anyone?

This chapter looks at our 'role' as Friends who receive care from five angles:

- how we feel about being cared for
- mutual care
- invisible care
- self-care
- receiving guidance.

1. How we feel about being cared for

It might be that we feel very supported and grateful to receive the care of Friends. Anyone offering care will certainly hope that's how it turns out and will be at least disappointed, if not dismayed, if the response is very different.

Receiving help and support is not necessarily easy and is sometimes even unwelcome. Some people experience oversight as patronising and want nothing to do with it – most meetings where Friends are grouped in circles or lists for the purpose of oversight maintain an additional list of people who choose to opt out. We can experience discomfort being on the receiving rather than the giving end of care for various reasons, including that it can make us feel dependent or powerless. And to make matters worse, we can then find ourselves feeling guilty about appearing ungrateful.

The fact that most of us will have no difficulty recognising this experience indicates that we should take it into account when we offer our care. We have to be aware of the possible consequences and be mindful not to react negatively when our help is rejected. Someone who has a clear need, yet experiences this kind of discomfort, might respond by keeping a distance from Friends, by not getting involved in the meeting, or by asserting that everything is fine, even in their distress. Friends who are prickly or abrasive when we offer care may only be protecting themselves. Their response might be less to do with our offer than with their own discomfort in expressing a need or accepting help.

Another possibility is that we have misjudged the kind of

care that would be useful or welcome. An urge to do something (and perhaps be seen doing something – because we feel accountable in our role) can impede our ability to be sensitively receptive and responsive. Not every need demands that we take action; we have to distinguish between our wish to be helpful and the needs of the person we are hoping to help.

> "Over the years with a chronic illness I got used to fending off kindly but too frequent and sometimes intrusive attention. The most acceptable approaches were those I could respond to with, 'No, but thanks for asking'. Much harder was unsolicited advice or repeatedly being asked how I was when there was nothing more to tell that was different from last time. I began to feel that somehow I was being found guilty of not getting better! It was exhausting having to take such care not to offend by declining help. I frequently felt not properly heard."

2. Mutual care

Care in Quaker meetings is not only a transaction between a giver and a receiver of care, but encompasses the possibility that the roles might be reversed. The Friend who provides care may be a Friend who needs care too and it should be possible for anyone to offer this.

Caring for one another can also be simultaneous. For example, when we respond to someone's need for practical support they reciprocate by lending us a listening ear in our family worries or they make sure to call on a different Friend for help on another occasion.

Where care is invariably provided by certain Friends in the meeting, for instance by overseers or a few dependable caregivers, it is easy for a sense of *them and us* to arise, which inhibits the natural to and fro of caring for one another. We can affirm that we are all *us* through fostering a climate of mutual care in the meeting. Mutual care asks more than that we care for others. It involves:

- putting ourselves in the shoes of anyone we are caring for
- allowing anyone we care for to care for us
- the meeting (usually through eldership and oversight) being explicit about the need for everyone to care for each other.

Finding a balance between encouraging mutual care and providing care will help our meeting build a community of equals who share responsibility for how safe, accepting and inclusive the community feels. As appointed elders or overseers we have to remember that our term of service will come to an end and that someone else will serve in our place. If we have avoided being on the receiving end of Friends' care thus far we could find the transition not at all comfortable. Nurturing a climate of mutual care makes for easier transitions between appointments as well as more positive attitudes to receiving care.

❖ **Chapter 11:** *Addressing need* discusses how our meeting can encourage a climate of mutual care in the meeting.

3. Invisible care

This is perhaps the best kind of care to receive: we are aware of a climate of support and feel confident that should we have a need, it will be safe to make that known without the 'danger' of either being swamped or feeling a burden. This is the kind of care that visitors to our meeting will pick up on. And for anyone not attending meeting for any reason, it makes a difference to how connected with their community they are in their absence. Invisible care is all the small and not so small things a meeting sees to so that Friends feel included, welcomed, respected and accepted. It includes potential care – you might never have occasion to call on it but you know that you could.

But we shouldn't confuse invisible care with deciding what care to provide for a Friend without being in touch with them about that. Friends who are uneasy about oversight are often especially bothered by the idea that their needs or circumstances could be discussed behind closed doors, and that 'people who know best' will make a decision that affects them. Our care can be both invisible and open: eldership and oversight might work in ways that encourage an invisible climate of inclusion and care, but it should always be possible to know what is going on. Friends will be able to know this either because they are included in discernment and decisions that affect them as individuals, or because everyone is kept informed about plans that affect the meeting as a whole.

4. Self-care

I have become clear about at least one thing: self-care is never a selfish act – it is simply good stewardship of the only gift I have, the gift I was put on earth to offer others. Anytime we can listen to true self and give it the care it requires, we do so not only for ourselves but for the many others whose lives we touch.

(Palmer, 2000: p. 30)

Receiving our own care may not come easily. It is not unusual for Friends to defer tending to their own needs repeatedly because someone else's need jumps into the space and *has* to come first. That someone else might be a family member, a personal friend or someone in the meeting; the need could be urgent; there might be no other likely person around who could help (or who is being asked); it may be perfectly possible for us to lay aside other things; and we may do this again and again.

On the other hand we could take Parker J. Palmer's advice and see self-care – and the time and space we give to this – as essential to our care for others. For example, we might regard it is an investment in eldership to spend time in worship together, to explore our own spirituality through worship sharing, or to give time for discussing our different perspectives on concepts of God and belief. We could choose to give the area meeting for business a miss this month to have a break from Quaker responsibilities and go on a family outing instead. We could put that unwritten report further to one side and do a bit of gardening, listen to some music or watch a TV drama.

In some meetings the responsibilities of oversight can feel especially burdensome and time-consuming, allowing no room for us to consider whether the situation and how we are addressing it is inevitable, including the toll it takes on us. One Friend responded to research for this publication by explaining:

> "Our ministry is taking care of the half or more in the meeting who are disabled and elderly. I just don't have the energy to take care of all these people."

Maybe we have to question our own and our meeting's understanding of what is expected of oversight and ask: how can Friends be *adequately* cared for, including ourselves? This kind of questioning can feel quite hard, especially in the face of Friends' real needs.

Even in less pressing circumstances we could encourage one another to put our own needs first from time to time. But we do have to be cautious about offering advice that can appear to be a reproach. 'You should take better care of yourself' might well be received as more critical than helpful. Similarly, a Friend working hard to serve in their role can feel criticised when another reminds them of the advice: 'Attend to what love requires of you, which may not be great busyness.' (*Advices & queries* 28). We should remember that the advices are intended for us to judge when to administer them to ourselves, not prescribe them to others. We find urging to activity in *Advices & queries* too; what we are really being advised towards is a balance. Almost nobody can diagnose a balance for somebody else; we should always be alert to the possibility that our well-meaning counsel to other people might in fact be addressing a need in ourselves.

The most helpful support and encouragement to look after ourselves will come from Friends who are willing to listen to us relating our experience, perhaps at length, and who will refrain from telling us about theirs – just yet; and from the Friend who can listen without giving us the benefit of their advice – until we ask for it.

> "As a new clerk I was so grateful for the support of the previous clerk, who was always available on the end of the phone whenever I needed a bit of advice. And thinking back, he never actually advised me what to do, but just listened as I ran my thoughts about a dilemma past him until I was clear in my own mind."

We can encourage these essential listening skills in ourselves and each other by sharing and listening in structured setting, for example, worship sharing or creative listening as a group, or by using techniques such as paired listening, spiritual interview conversation or a meeting for clearness. Our self-care might include asking Friends for opportunities of this kind, and we can encourage self-care generally in the meeting by raising awareness of the possibility of listening support for anyone who would value it.

❖ **Chapter 19:** *Making connections* looks at a number of such possibilities for encouraging sharing and listening in the meeting.

5. Receiving guidance

There is a further aspect to the experience of being on the receiving end of care to bear in mind. As members of a Quaker meeting we implicitly agree to be open to the guidance of eldership, and also to be overseen in matters more to do with our involvement in the life of the meeting. Are we as comfortable with this as we are with being providers of eldership and oversight? Friends who are practised in offering others advice and guidance, who embrace this as part of their role, can still find it hard to receive the same.

Most Friends accept the discipline of the Quaker business method; our clerks depend on a common understanding of what that means and they look to experienced Friends – elders especially – to uphold the discipline. If we want to encourage in the meeting a similar understanding about the disciplines that eldership and oversight ask of Friends we should first reflect on our *own* possible response to being 'eldered', or to overseers discussing a concern about our actions.

Elders and overseers might perhaps find this idea more unsettling than Friends who share corporate responsibility with everyone in the meeting. Surely our appointment signifies that we can be depended on to act in all things as Friends should? Hopefully that is true. But keeping to a common discipline is both a shared responsibility and a shared obligation: how we respond to Quaker discipline is as important as how we uphold it.

Queries for reflection, discussion and learning

Chapter 12: Receiving care

Queries for individual reflection

1. How do I feel about the possibility that some Friends will make it their business to be aware of my circumstances? How might I respond to an approach by someone concerned for my welfare? Would it matter who offered me this attention?

2. Do I, or would I, feel able to let another Friend know about support or care I needed in connection with belonging to my meeting? Does it make a difference to me if caring is a two-way process?

3. If I am involved in a lot of caring, do I also attend sufficiently to my own care needs? How do I go about this?

Queries for pastoral groups

1. How good are we at prioritising calls on our attention, and at asking Friends in the meeting for practical support by sharing the load?

2. Eldership and oversight can be very demanding and sometimes difficult and upsetting. How do we support and care for one another through thick and thin?

3. How would we feel about being 'eldered' or knowing that Friends were concerned or critical of something we had done? Would we be able to respond well to being offered advice or guidance as a result?

Queries for meetings

1. How visible or invisible is care in our meeting? What are all the small and not so small things our meeting attends to in quiet ways that affect how Friends feel included, welcomed, respected and accepted?

2. Do Friends feel there is a sense of 'them and us' in the meeting, which is affecting the way care is provided for? How might we address that impression?

3. To what extent are we a community of equals who share responsibility for how safe, accepting and inclusive the community feels?

❖ These pages can be downloaded from the online resource: **www.quaker.org.uk/tender-hand**

Chapter 13: Absent Friends

~

Running a workshop with a local meeting I was a bit taken aback by the response to my suggestion that we begin by thinking for a moment about anyone prevented from attending the event. I did my best not to keep glancing at my watch as Friends spent a good deal of time – way over what I had allowed for in the programme – collectively recalling and writing on sticky notes more and more names of people connected to the meeting, however distantly, and posting them on a wall. At the end of the day, these Friends gathered for a photograph in front of the wall of names so that the whole meeting was included.

I learnt a lot from that meeting where everyone mattered and everyone was held in the Light.

Absence from meeting is commonly just part of the way some Friends have to organise their lives. Not everyone is available to attend every week: Friends might be working, on holiday or visiting family, or have competing weekend commitments that frequently keep them away from meeting. The Friend who is the only Quaker in their family may limit how often they attend in order to find a balance of priorities in family life. Some Friends worship with more than one faith group and will divide their time and other involvement accordingly. If these Friends nevertheless regard themselves as committed members of the meeting, then so should we.

The Friends who come to meeting more regularly may just have fewer current complications in their lives than some others – who are no less welcome and no less essential to the community.

Being responsive to the presence or absence of people who regularly worship with us is a responsibility everyone in a meeting shares. Many Friends say that at the start of meeting for worship they look around and bring to mind the name of each Friend present. Those of us who do this as a way of settling into worship will notice who is not there too and we can remind ourselves of the reason, if we know it. Some reasons for absence are readily known and being aware allows us to uphold absent Friends in their other commitments, or in the circumstances preventing their attendance.

Knowing about absence also makes it possible for Friends to respond to need. If the reason is not known and we are at all concerned, we should naturally enquire, taking care to go about this with sensitivity. Often Friends hold back from making contact for fear of getting that wrong. We have to bear in mind that when we take our unease about an absence seriously, and act on it, we will sometimes discover a need that calls for our timely attention.

1. Needs connected with absence

i.   Absence due to illness, injury or incapacity, bereavement, pressing family or home circumstances, or work stress, etc. will involve us in some form of response depending on the circumstances – including the Friend's wishes, their support outside the meeting, and the resources we have to help in practical ways. At the very least we will express our loving concern and willingness to help and we will stay in touch throughout a period of need.

ii.   There might be Friends who have difficulty attending meeting because of a practical problem to do with transport or the facilities at our venue. Perhaps the chairs are not very comfortable or we lack an accessible toilet or hearing loop. Where changes to existing arrangements are not possible we could perhaps offer an alternative such as worship in a Friend's home.

iii. The absence of families with babies, children or teenagers may suggest we should look into the reasons. We might learn about the parents worried that their baby will disturb the quiet, the child who doesn't want to come or who does other activities on Sunday, the young person who prefers the company of people their own age, the parent who is unhappy with arrangements for children's meeting, the attitudes of adults in the meeting towards children's work, etc. The reasons and how to address them will be a matter for elders and overseers and Friends who work with children's or young people's meetings to consider. Answers could possibly lie in provision for children and young people at times and places other than meeting for worship on Sunday morning.

iv. Some Friends are absent because they no longer live locally – or not currently – including young people living away from home or members living abroad or elsewhere. Others might be away regularly for family, work or other reasons for weeks or months each year. We shouldn't neglect to stay in touch with these Friends, who continue to be part of our meeting in their absence. If we have lost contact with members they are still a responsibility of oversight unless and until their membership is terminated.

v. Where absence involves a member or attender moving permanently to an address covered by a different area meeting, overseers are responsible for informing the new area meeting about this (Qf&p 11.22). And in some cases it could be helpful to contact them occasionally during the period of settling into a new home, job or community.

vi.   Some Friends may still have connections with, or recollections of, people who were once well established in the meeting but who moved away some while ago and perhaps transferred their membership. Our community is always more than the Friends who currently worship together; it includes its history too. There might be pastoral needs linked to the permanent absence of significant Friends who have a continuing influence on our community, including Friends who have died – recently or some time in the past.

vii.   Perhaps the most taxing cause of absence we could learn about is conflict or difficulty between Friends. The Friend who stays away may be angry, offended by a recent occurrence at meeting, or worried about something they said or did. We must certainly address conflict when we become aware of it, but not by rushing in. We have to consider an appropriate response with others before taking any action.

viii.   If we are lucky we may also get to hear of the Friend who attends sporadically because they feel burdened by their role in the meeting, or who is disaffected, concerned about the way things are in the meeting, or waning in their commitment to the meeting or their Quaker faith. A Friend might find they are not so much journeying with Quakers as pulled off on the hard shoulder. Tact and sensitivity will be called for in how we approach the Friend and the kind of support or guidance we offer. There are likely to be lessons we can learn from Friends in these circumstances – we should listen with open minds to their experience, without assuming that the problem is either all to do with the meeting or all a matter of personal perspective.

ix.   Are we aware of people who would not be attracted to the idea of attending our meeting for one reason or another? Is our community seen as too elderly, too middle class, too narrowly of one mind (theologically or in our outlook) or not family-friendly? Some things about who and how we are as a meeting will be out of our hands, but not all. Every meeting should consider how it appears to non-Quakers and not-yet-Quakers for clues to what would make a difference.

❖ **Chapter 4:** *Meeting for worship* and **Chapter 9:** *Belonging and commitment* each look at further aspects of including people in their different circumstances and ensuring everyone is made equally welcome.

❖ **Chapter 14:** *Conflict and difficulty in the meeting* includes guidance on appropriate first steps to addressing difficult situations that could possibly lead to a Friend withdrawing from meeting.

2. Checking our assumptions

When we note people who are often not present and have no information that tells us why, we should at least wonder what is preventing them, even if there is no reason to suspect a problem. We cannot safely assume that a Friend's repeated or prolonged absence isn't a concern without knowing the cause.

Only by checking our assumptions can we be sure that we aren't neglecting a need we could helpfully respond to. But this doesn't mean we have to quiz Friends or ring them up whenever they fail to appear. If our meeting values Friends knowing and caring for one another we will find natural ways of being in touch that don't feel intrusive. Perhaps we will speak with others who know the Friend – lightly and with sensitivity, observing confidentiality where necessary. There is usually someone who knows more than we do, someone who is closer who can reassure us or alert us, if we enquire.

"After we moved we had loads to do on the house, and Sam wasn't keen on driving 18 miles there and back, so we didn't go to meeting for months. I started missing it but Sam didn't and eventually I went on my own. People were very surprised when I turned up because they'd got the idea from somewhere that Sam and I now attended another meeting. In all that time no one had thought to give us a ring and find out!"

We should also notice our own feelings concerning a Friend's absence and recognise how these might affect our response. For example, our assumptions about a reason for absence might make us feel a bit impatient. Do we suspect that a Friend likes to come to meeting occasionally for a peaceful hour, but has no interest in anything else going on and no sense of being part of a community? Do we see another Friend's irregular attendance as being critical of the meeting in some way? If we think we are quite certain why someone rarely attends, and the reason disappoints or irks us, we must check those assumptions – there is always the possibility that in reading the signs as they appear to us we are seeing something to do with ourselves, not the Friend. We have to keep an open mind and try to understand the absent Friend's perspective. In turn, they might need to recognise how their absence affects others in the meeting.

Another response we might spot in ourselves is relief that a certain Friend has stopped attending. If this is someone who is disruptive or who has caused upset to others we could be justified in seeing their absence as some kind of solution. But it is important to see a solution for the meeting separately from a solution for the Friend; our care for members of the meeting doesn't cease if they withdraw because of conflict. The difficulty as experienced by the Friend still has to be addressed and it may be even more pressing that we attend to this if a deteriorating situation has led to that point.

3. Quaker-related absence

In most meetings some Friends will be away from time to time because of Quaker commitments. We are possibly aware of the absent Friend serving abroad as an Ecumenical Accompanier or in conflict resolution, but do we always know who is attending a conference on our behalf, meeting with a central committee or a trustee body, or on a course at Woodbrooke? There may be other Friends whose absence is connected with their employment by Quaker organisations, such as Woodbrooke or Britain Yearly Meeting, and others who have to be away through volunteering their work as facilitators, associate tutors or external elders.

We don't have to know everything about where Friends are on Sunday mornings, but we should at least make it our business to be aware of Friends who are fulfilling Quaker responsibilities, engaged in Quaker witness or pursuing Quaker interests. These Friends want to know that their home meeting values and supports their ministry or their learning and growth as Friends.

A not uncommon response to 'Quaker' absence can have a very unfortunate effect. Friends who are relatively unfamiliar with the wider Quaker community can see those who are often away through Quaker commitments as both neglecting their meeting and asserting some kind of superiority over others. It is not unusual for 'national' Friends to feel unsupported by their local meeting, even experiencing an element of hostility.

"I'm sad to say I've stopped attending my local meeting. I couldn't go regularly anyway because of committee weekends plus time with my family on other weekends. I felt more and more disconnected and picked up that some people in meeting were criticising me for getting my priorities wrong. It made me very uncomfortable and actually a bit angry that they have no interest in the work I do for Friends."

If perspectives of this kind are present in our meeting we should make sure that we are not colluding with them in any way – by our inaction, for example. Every Friend serving the Society more widely or engaged in ministry elsewhere is a member of a local Quaker community; their service springs from the spiritual nurture and fellowship they find there, and they need this in order to serve well. Each local meeting should see itself as essential to the work of Britain Yearly Meeting in the support it provides to anyone serving nationally or beyond. It is also the responsibility of these Friends to bring their experience back to the local meeting, and meetings should encourage them to do this.

4. Contacting absent Friends

When we know or suspect a cause for someone's absence, or if we are hoping to find out, how do we make that first contact – to ask how they are, let them know we are thinking of them, offer our help or just to have a chat? This might be easier if we know the reason (but not always); less straightforward if we are unsure, so it will be important to choose one or more ways most likely to be acceptable *and* successful.

i.   **Post:** Sending a friendly card or a brief letter to someone we haven't seen for several months makes no assumptions and extends a welcome while offering an opportunity to be in contact if they wish to.

ii. **Telephone:** Sometimes a quick and friendly phone call is the best way to be lightly in touch, but think first who is the right person to do this, because it might not be you. When we contact someone not seen in meeting for a while and we are hoping to find out why, the most helpful advice is to say a little, listen a lot, and never rise to provocation. A phone call by the wrong person at the wrong time or in the wrong spirit risks making a tricky situation more difficult. We can guard against that risk by consulting a few other elders or overseers for their perspective and together deciding what to do. We may still not get it right but we have to trust that if we test our intentions to ensure they are thoughtfully discerned, we are doing our best to help and everything we can to avoid causing upset.

"In difficult situations, we find the most appropriate person to intervene – we have different strengths and weaknesses and are also aware of natural connections between people. I am organised and friendly, but not tactful. I am not a good choice if somebody has personal difficulties."

iii.   **Visiting:** The same advice applies to visiting a Friend in their home. This is often a welcome act of kindness and care that makes all the difference to someone who is feeling cut off from meeting. But if we don't know the Friend well it's a good idea to speak first with someone who has better knowledge of the person or their circumstances. It might in any case be a welcome courtesy to phone first and arrange our visit.

iv.   **Email:** A good use of email might be to ensure that absent Friends – with their permission – receive all the usual information such as newsletters, minutes and diary notices. But we should be wary of attempting to reach out personally by email. It is famously easy to misread words whose positive or benign intention we would understand perfectly well if we heard them spoken in person. We might wonder what would be so different if we wrote the same words on a postcard, but, strangely, experience tells us that it is.

v.   **Electronic media:** Friends who use Facebook or Twitter are probably in touch with one another even if they don't attend meeting. But perhaps our meeting has a Facebook page that could be used for extending a welcome, sending good wishes to absent Friends generally and posting information about what's going on so they feel part of the community. If our meeting website is kept constantly up to date Friends will get into the habit of checking there too.

vi.   **Extending an invitation:** By whatever means feels right in the circumstances we could invite a Friend personally rather than generally to attend an event, such as sharing lunch or all age worship, or to meet up socially if we know the Friend well enough. We would have to make a careful judgment about whether to reach out in this way, but it offers the opportunity of the most tangible connection and might be exactly what's needed.

Once we are in touch with a Friend concerning their absence – or anything else – we will take our lead from them, offering appropriate attention and action. Taking our lead from Friends is where all our care should start; there is almost nothing we can do *for* Friends that is not better done *with* Friends.

❖ Questions raised here, and others to do with communications among people in the meeting, are explored in more detail in **Chapter 16:** *Communicating as Friends* and **Chapter 20:** *Being in touch in a modern world.*

Queries for reflection, discussion and learning

Chapter 13: Absent Friends

Queries for individual reflection

1. What keeps me away from meeting – occasionally or often? Do I feel that others notice and care? How is that observation or care expressed, and is it welcome? If no one enquires about my absence, how would, or does, that affect me?

2. When I notice others are absent how do I respond? If there is someone whose absence I am ignoring for any reason, why is that?

3. Are there some people in meeting I scarcely notice at all? How might that affect them, and how does it affect me?

Queries for pastoral groups

1. How do we respond to repeated or prolonged absence that has no apparent cause? How far do we accept variations in attendance, or prolonged absence, as the normal run of things?

2. Are some reasons for absence easier to accept than others? What might be the implications of making assumptions without checking?

3. How effective are our routine ways of keeping in touch with absent Friends? Are there things we can do that might encourage absent Friends to stay in touch, even while they are unable or choose not to come to meeting?

Queries for meetings

1. Do variations in attendance affect our meeting community? What difference does it make whether people come regularly, infrequently or sporadically?

2. Do we hold back from enquiring about absence out of feeling it is none of our business? What might be the possible consequences of no one taking the trouble to contact an absent Friend?

3. How well do we support and uphold Friends who are often absent on Quaker business of one kind and another? Do we know what these Friends do or where they are when they are not worshipping here? How can the meeting encourage and enable any of us to tell the meeting about our wider service and involvement?

❖ These pages can be downloaded from the online resource: **www.quaker.org.uk/tender-hand**

Chapter 14: Conflict and difficulty in the meeting
~

Conflict is inevitable in any system that is vital and growing. Therefore, a meeting that is vital *will* have conflict. The only Friends communities that are free of it are cemeteries and a very few meetings that are dying. Friends need to examine our attitude to conflict. We need to acknowledge that violence and conflict are not the same. We need to view it as an opportunity for growth rather than a problem to be avoided if possible. Handled well, it can be used for deepening the life of the meeting and strengthening relationships within the meeting.

(Greene and Walton, 1999: p. 80)

This chapter aims to help elders, overseers and others have confidence in their ability to respond in taxing circumstances and to address difficult situations. A great deal of helpful literature and expertise is available in our yearly meeting on conflict resolution; so our exploration here will not duplicate those resources.

❖ In particular, *Conflict in meetings: Volume 4 in the Eldership and Oversight handbooks series* offers a very readable and authoritative account of approaches to conflict resolution, which includes a sequence of appendices mapping the field and guiding the reader to further publications and resources. An updated list of these and other relevant resources can be found online at **www.quaker.org.uk/tender-hand**

Perhaps that publication has stood the test of time so well because conflicts in meetings actually haven't changed much over the years. Meetings have always experienced apparently incompatible expectations, opinions, hopes or interests, and incidents of misunderstanding or a clash of personalities.

The presence in our meetings of people whose behaviour on occasion causes upset is nothing new either. We are all capable of doing or saying things we regret from time to time, and most of us have some way in which we can be stuck or unhelpful, or at least that other people find difficult. Not infrequently those ways are related to our strengths. Quakers historically have had an ability to confront wrongs and be 'difficult' in the face of other people's certainties. This fact makes it easy for us to explain, or even self-applaud, our behaviour as 'plain speaking' or taking a stand against what is clearly wrong (in our view) when possibly we are just being inconsiderate and needlessly provocative. Friends' historic experience of shared discernment, of testing leadings and supporting community, came about for good reason. Today we still depend on those tried and tested practices, while bringing new insights and improved skills to the task of addressing age-old troubles.

"Some Friends see 'plain speaking' as an opportunity, not a discipline..."

1. Supporting helpful processes, strategies and behaviour

So people will be difficult and conflict will happen. Caring for Friends and our meeting in ways that enable the good energy in these tensions to lead to growth is both a challenge and entirely consistent with our care in other times and circumstances. Our primary task is to nurture the development of a healthy and vital worshipping community – a resilient community. So we have to focus on supporting everything that makes our meeting worth belonging to and worth contributing to. Chapters throughout this book identify behaviours, actions and processes that contribute to this aim.

The health of our community is influenced largely in two ways:

i. The nature of our corporate life
This centres on how our meeting is grounded in worship and includes the ways our systems, processes and practices work. These areas of meeting activity are where addressing conflict should start, *including when we are in the thick of it*:

> ➢ Is our worship rightly held and at the heart of our community?
> Depth of worship will nourish our meeting and support our relationships.
> ➢ Are our meetings for business in right ordering and well attended?
> Right ordering will be the bedrock of how we are able to respond in testing times.
> ➢ Are nominations and appointments working well for the meeting?
> Spirit-led nominations practice fuels a vibrant and effective community.

> ➤ Are there good opportunities for fellowship and learning?
>
> Meeting one another in things temporal as well as eternal helps us empathise and respond with humanity.
>
> ➤ Does our pastoral care system meet our community's needs?
>
> A caring community is able both to attend to hurt and to confront those engaging in hurtful actions.

ii. Individual behaviour and actions

The attitudes and behaviour that support community are the same as those that allow conflict to be addressed constructively. Briefly, our behaviour is helpful when we seek to meet that of God in others and allow our actions to be prompted by love first.

> Love is patient, love is kind. It does not envy, it does not boast, it is not proud. It does not dishonor others, it is not self-seeking, it is not easily angered, it keeps no record of wrongs. Love does not delight in evil but rejoices with the truth. It always protects, always trusts, always hopes, always perseveres. Love never fails.
>
> (1 Corinthians 13, 4–8, New International Version)

Below is a reminder of some of the positive behaviours that are especially relevant when we are thinking about conflict: how Friends build a peaceable community and the resources they can draw on when conflict happens. These behaviours and actions are what each Friend can do personally; they are not things elders and overseers can 'organise' or demand of Friends (even should we wish to!). Our task is to nurture a climate that encourages everyone to know where their Quaker heart is and to act on it. A big part of that will be how we model the behaviours we want to promote: if our own conduct consistently reflects Quaker principles, the Quaker way *will* catch on.

Behaviours and actions that support community

Including

- noticing who is on the edge of things and bringing them in
- relating to children as equals
- making welcome our personal priority after meeting for worship
- actively discouraging cliques
- thinking about our use of language: assume there is always a stranger present
- being 'disability aware': ask what people need rather than make assumptions.

Supporting worship

- coming to meeting regularly and on time
- welcoming the presence of children
- holding the meeting in the light; prayer
- finding ways of laying aside ministry that doesn't speak to us
- accepting that imperfect ministry is the more common sort: avoid 'judging' other people's ministry
- offering ministry: distinguish between different kinds of promptings, be self-observant
- thanking a Friend for ministry we found helpful.

Playing a part

- identifying as part of the meeting (not outside looking in)
- getting involved in the life of the meeting, attending social and other activities
- being willing to undertake service
- supporting and upholding those appointed to roles in the meeting
- offering personal support to someone who has taken on a responsibility
- volunteering one small thing we can do personally that could make a difference.

Communicating

- listening with an open mind and putting our agenda aside, at least until another has finished speaking
- allowing others space to think, respond and find the right words
- listening for the meaning beneath
- checking a message for clarity with someone else before posting or announcing
- making our announcement a request or invitation (not an instruction)
- taking extra care with electronic communications.

Caring

- listening
- making time
- kind words
- looking out for one another; noticing and responding personally to need
- staying in touch with absent Friends
- supporting those who are caring for others.

Peace making

- assuming good intent first
- considering that when someone acts in a way we find unacceptable they might be under stress or in distress, and that a bit of support might be what is needed
- checking with the Friend(s) concerned what we believe we have heard or witnessed; consider we might be mistaken
- holding back from responding *immediately* if we are annoyed or angry
- being firm and clear (not aggressive) when we feel another person's behaviour oversteps acceptable boundaries
- looking after our own needs when we feel threatened
- asking 'What does love require of me?'

You might find it useful to add your own examples to these not-exhaustive lists and use them as an aid for reflecting on the health of your meeting community.

> ➤ Are behaviours of these kinds common in our meeting?
> ➤ Do we model behaviour that supports community?
> ➤ How might we encourage helpful behaviour in those who practise it?
> ➤ How might we encourage it in those who often don't practise it?

Helpful behaviours call for our *active* encouragement, acknowledgment and support. Sometimes Friends are uncertain that what they have done or said is okay, let alone positively helpful. We can thank people personally for their ministry, their service, their support, their involvement or their kindness; we can send a brief appreciative email or a card, or give them a ring. It is easy to underestimate the good we do by simply expressing our appreciation.

❖ **Chapter 21:** *Leadership among equals* clarifies why Friends need to model Quaker practice and behaviour, with suggestions for putting this approach into practice.

❖ Chapters in **Theme 3: Community** explore ways of building community through positive actions and attitudes.

2. Responding to conflict

i. Being alert to the early signs of trouble

If among Friends there is a marked absence of actions and behaviours that support community, it should be enough to give us concern that the meeting will be less able to hold together when things go wrong. We can be watchful and prepared for when difficulty does arise, but our main concern will be to focus on strengthening community.

> ➤ We build community through the ways we get to know one another.
>> ➤ When we know one another we are much more likely to empathise with someone else's experience and to care about their feelings.
>>> ➤ Empathising with and caring about someone else goes a long way towards our ability to resolve differences.

More often, positive relationships among Friends will be the norm, and every now and then a difficulty erupts that unsettles a number of Friends or sometimes the whole meeting. Continued active encouragement of what is going well underpins any approach we take to address behaviour that causes difficulty or concern, as will continuing with our normal community building activities.

Unhelpful behaviour is not uncommon. Anyone might respond to provocation or stress uncharacteristically or fail to see how their actions might have consequences for others. And just as we can identify behaviour and actions that build community, we can readily spot the opposite. Behaviour is unhelpful if it upsets or hurts someone, causes difficulty or undermines or hinders community. It might range from being careless about the effects of actions on individuals or the community, through to asserting dominance over others.

Unhelpful behaviour

Relating to others

- judging and criticising, especially when not done openly
- hurtful criticism disguised as plain speaking or concern
- tale-bearing, gossiping; talking about people while neglecting to speak to or with them
- dismissing or denigrating the views, beliefs or actions of other Friends

- scolding and accusing
- sarcasm; intimidating manner or body language.

Relating to the meeting

- distancing oneself from the meeting, engaging in 'us and them' perspectives
- expecting others to do things and complaining about the way they do them
- grumbling and complaining, and encouraging or fanning grumbles
- creating factions or taking sides
- taking pre-emptive action without consulting others
- dominating discussion groups
- obstructing business meetings.

> Many of these examples of unhelpful behaviours spring from a climate of distrust in which depersonalising others is an available option. They can also occur in otherwise healthy communities between individuals or several people caught up in disagreements or disputes.

If we spot people behaving in any of these ways in relation to individuals, groups or the meeting as a whole, we should take it as a warning that trouble is likely to ensue. Tactfully drawing attention to problem behaviours, with an offer to listen and an opportunity for conversation, will often be sufficient to encourage more helpful behaviour or discourage harmful actions.

So our first response is to presume that Friends do not want to cause trouble; that they do hope to be prompted by love. The consistently 'difficult' Friend may be accommodated too, and their manner tolerated, as long as they are receptive to this approach.

Behaviour by anyone in the meeting that has gone beyond being unhelpful to becoming repeatedly unacceptable will probably need to be addressed differently. We look at problems of this kind below in **3. Serious difficulty in the meeting.**

ii. Doing something about it now

We shouldn't assume that a healthy climate in our meeting will be enough to prevent the damaging effects of unhelpful behaviour when it does arise. It is certainly easier to address difficulty in a healthy meeting, but not less risky to ignore. When we meet unhelpful, hurtful or excluding behaviour in Friends we must act in good time, giving us a better chance that intervention will be appropriate and useful. The longer we leave it the more danger there is that difficulty will escalate or become entrenched. Some difficulties can be slow growing and long lasting. Do we just tolerate the Friend who is constantly critical of how things are done and who undermines Friends serving the meeting? If we fail to act it can be taken as accepting or agreeing with what is going on. We also fail to support anyone who is adversely affected by another's actions.

It is less easy to ignore a difficulty involving specific incidents that trigger accusations and counter accusations, and which spill over into the life of the meeting. But even then we may hope it will all blow over; or maybe we delay because we are simply at a loss to know what will help. We have to appreciate the risk we are taking – on behalf of the meeting and on behalf of people who are hurt – and we have to recognise that everyone involved in a situation of difficulty is in need of timely care, no matter who is 'at fault'.

> "Recently when there was a conflict in our meeting, it would have been great if several of us could have spent a week or so talking to lots of different people, sorting through what had happened and supporting Friends in moving forward. But most of us don't have the time, so things don't happen in a timely way. And two months later, when something is said, or followed up, it's too late. The damage is done."

"A group of relative newcomers became assertive and critical of the way things are done out of misunderstandings about Quaker practices and discipline. By the time we realised we had to do something about this the criticisms had damaged relationships in the meeting."

iii. Listening with individuals first

Having embarked on attempts to address a difficulty we will find ourselves doing a great deal of necessary listening. The skills of active listening may not come naturally, but can be learnt. Part of our preparedness for conflict will be thinking and talking about the subject when there appears to be no need for it! That is also the time to practise skills in our pastoral group. It is serious stuff, but we can have fun while we learn and gain confidence in a safe, supportive and experimental setting.

> ...role play, resisted as it is by many people, provides an excellent vehicle for practising in a safe environment with opportunities for feedback. ...fictional case outlines can be used as scenarios for trying out clearness, threshing or other meetings, for practising individual skills...
>
> (*Conflict in meetings*, 2005: p. 53)

People involved in a conflict situation will naturally explain what happened from their own perspective. The first account we hear is unlikely to be the whole story, but differing accounts should not be taken as indicating that some Friends are being untruthful – anyone may have only partial knowledge, or perhaps some of what they know is what they have heard, and so on. We may need to meet with Friends individually, asking what each person:

knows
has witnessed
has heard about
thinks is going on.

We will want at least to discourage further problematic interactions and we can ask this of each Friend we speak with. A request will probably need to be specific, for example, no emails or telephone conversations on the subject, or to certain Friends.

What we hear in these conversations may vary markedly between people who see themselves on opposite sides of an argument. It is very difficult to separate feelings from facts when recalling an upsetting incident. If we felt wounded by something the other person said we may remember that person raising their voice, using aggressive words or intimidating body language, and we can sincerely believe it happened. It is not uncommon to hear this from both parties, each describing their own manner as moderate and restrained under extreme provocation.

So quite early in our conversations with each person involved we must ask: How has this affected you, how do you feel about it?

> Feelings count as much as facts, but it is important not to get caught up in seeing degrees of hurt as indicators of right and wrong. Feelings are only proof of feelings, they are not proof that things have been said or done. All 'sides' in a conflict may feel pain as well as anger, and for some people anger is simply how they deal with their pain. When people fall out with each other it often has as much to do with how a person responds to a trigger as with the trigger itself.

Strong feelings, whether experienced as hurt or as anger, require attention first. Our conversations with people involved in a difficulty are not only for the purpose of establishing facts and achieving cooperation. People also just need to be heard. Being heard can be a large part of how people feel able to move forward; it might in itself be enough to resolve a problem. Ways other than one-to-one conversations that give individuals good time and opportunity to be heard include:

- worship sharing in pairs or small groups – for people who are having difficulty in talking through a challenging issue in discussion or conversation
- a meeting for clearness. This is not a tool for conflict resolution, but an opportunity for an individual to explore a dilemma or a difficult decision in a setting with others who help them focus and find clearness for themselves. Guidance on this process is available in a leaflet published by Quaker Life (see below).

iv. Options for action

Only after we have listened to individuals' accounts of what they claim has happened, and to the feelings around that, should we go on to consider what to do next. Available options will be influenced by the kind of problem being addressed, who is involved, and what we feel is possible in our meeting. And our focus will not be entirely on making something stop; we will probably be aiming for *something else* to happen in its place. 'Something else' might include two people agreeing to work with each other in a new way, the formation of a group to take an initiative forward, or the meeting engaging in discernment together on a matter that had not come out into the open before.

Openness is something to aim for in addressing difficulty, and if this can be achieved early on it has the potential to defuse ill feeling going on in corners or among cliques. The following are a few suggestions for how openness may help a situation:

- Where there are conflicting views, might a skilfully led threshing meeting or a discussion group enable people to hear each other without rancour?
- Where processes have not been followed or leadership has been ineffective, can we own the problem as a whole meeting and discuss a way forward using our business method?
- Can we channel the energy of disgruntlement into a creative and practical plan for doing something in our meeting differently?
- Where there are unhelpful assumptions about roles, might we hold a 'roles fair' where people explain what they do and invite questions?

v. Listening in a group

Arranging an occasion for everyone who is involved or concerned to listen to one another as a group may help a situation that has progressed beyond a few people. Depending on the nature of the difficulty, the occasion might be conducted as worship sharing or in the form of a threshing meeting – either of which could be useful after Friends have had the opportunity to be heard one-to-one. The guidance in the Quaker Life leaflet *Threshing meetings* provides a helpful structure we should follow if we opt for that method of airing contentious matters.

Opportunities to meet all together can be effective where there is reason to believe that Friends have the will to move forward from a place of conflict to work for the good. But engaging the whole meeting won't be an appropriate response in every case. Facilitating a group addressing a matter of conflict or contention is not easy. We should only undertake this if we can call on the service of Friends in the local or area meeting – or beyond if necessary – with the skills and experience to handle it well. Even skilled Friends can be challenged when feelings are running high or when one or more people behave in a manner that they, or others, regret. In any event, no one should undertake this alone; we may agree that one person will take a lead in facilitating the group, but we should plan it together, be prepared to offer support to whichever Friend is facilitating, and meet afterwards to debrief.

> Perhaps the most important attribute of the peacemaker is a manner that affirms the personal worth of each and every person, which as Friends we term 'that of God in everyone'. Translating this belief into action is not always as straightforward as it seems. Some people 'bring out the best in us', and we respond openly and easily. With others, we are uncomfortable or defensive. Active conflict resolution demands an ability to relate, not to the outward, presenting behaviour of other people, but to that which is buried beneath it: to see a 'problem person' as a person with a problem.
>
> (*Conflict in meetings*, 2005 p. 43)

vi. Ground rules
Whether we are working with individuals or with groups we should begin with agreeing some simple ground rules:

- respect for each other
- listening especially when disagreeing
- sharing the time
- confidentiality.

As facilitator we will need to be active in ensuring ground rules are observed. We may find we also need to remind people specifically about not attributing motive or intent to another person. When we notice assumptions about motives we can prompt people to ask about these. It makes a big difference to how a conversation or discussion progresses if we stay clearly within a spirit of enquiry and check all attempts at accusing others – present or absent.

> It's completely obvious that you did it deliberately to humiliate me...

> I don't understand why you did that. I felt so humiliated. Can you tell me what was going on for you?

> Everyone knows he went ahead just to suit himself...

> I thought he went ahead just to suit himself. But he never explained – so maybe we should ask him?

vii. Frameworks

Working within a clear framework can help a problem-solving or conflict resolution process to progress effectively. The following are two approaches that elders and overseers might feel equipped to try:

  a) A framework of four simple questions can be useful where a problem between individuals, or wider in the meeting, has aroused strong or painful feelings and there is a prospect of mounting damage.

    1. What is the problem?
    2. How do you feel about it?
      Or: What is its effect on the community?
    3. What would you really like to happen?
    4. What could you *actually* do?

It is tempting to shorten this by deciding what the problem is and then moving on to discuss what can be done about it. But this leaves out exploration that allows Friends to be properly heard, and which could open other possibilities. Our feelings and our hopes are not incidental but essential to our discernment. Working with a framework such as this may require close direction and/or careful facilitation to discourage Friends from re-entering previous circular arguments.

b) A framework more applicable when there is less urgency takes the positive in a situation as the starting point for a process of discernment – as a group or between individuals:

1. What do I value about this meeting / group / process / other person, etc.?
2. What is our shared vision for the future?
3. What might threaten the development of our vision?
4. What could we do to preserve or enhance what we value and to achieve our vision?

The focus is positive throughout, including in stage 3 when Friends are asked to hold their vision clearly in mind in order to consider what could threaten it. The point is not to get sucked into giving up on a shared vision because there are too many obstacles. So it will be important to give good time to *finding* a shared vision in stage 2 and not move on until it's clear people have achieved this.

viii. When resolution stalls
It can help at some point in a process to step back from our first impressions for a more considered view of what is going on. We naturally hope to avoid actions that people will perceive as punitive or ascribing blame, but may yet find that the process of addressing conflict actually makes things worse and

that we have to reconsider our approach. Resolution could take some time; we must be aware of that and might have to accept the possibility that it will not be complete.

Whatever we do there could still be people unwilling or unable to move on, people whose bad feeling is less to do with a presenting problem than with other factors that are personal to them. A Friend might not be amenable to anything that could address a difficulty, yet continues to demand attention to their hurt or complaint. They may also persist in causing or inflaming trouble.

In the first case, when we notice a pattern of repeated calls for attention the most appropriate response could be to withdraw our efforts to help, even if we believe that to do so will give the Friend more reason to complain. This may be what it takes for the cycle to be broken. In the case of someone persistently causing trouble, there is nothing for it but to confront them and ask plainly for the actions to stop – which may achieve something, or it might have exactly the same negative effect as withdrawing our attention. We can hope that negative effects will be short lived, but they could worsen or become entrenched – and our meeting may then be in serious difficulty. We consider this unpalatable prospect in 3. below.

❖ Further examples of frameworks for problem solving or conflict resolution are included in literature on the subject listed in the online resource: **www.quaker.org.uk/tender-hand**

❖ On the same website (**www.quaker.org.uk/tender-hand**) are resources for practising listening and other conflict resolution skills, including fictional case study scenarios for role play or discussion.

❖ *Conflict in meetings* (pp. 42–54) provides explanations and guidance on listening and responding in conflict resolution settings, questions that get to the heart of the problem, ground rules and creating the right environment, and the importance of practice.

❖ **Chapter 16:** *Communicating as Friends,* 3.ii discusses difficulties associated with remembering and recalling inaccurately.

❖ The two Quaker Life leaflets noted above, *Threshing Meetings* and *Clearness,* can be downloaded from the Quaker website, **www.quaker.org.uk.** Printed copies are available from the Quaker Centre at Friends House: 020 7663 1030.

3. Serious difficulty in the meeting

i. Drawing boundaries

Occasionally meetings experience difficulty that is so serious it threatens the very survival of a community. Difficulty of this kind with one person or more may persist over many years unchecked because Friends just don't know what to do. We can hold back from being clear and firm out of a belief that our response must at all times be inclusive, and we try one thing after another to accommodate the Friend(s) without success.

> As communities we agree to live within boundaries of what is acceptable and what is not. Just as a child needs these boundaries asserted, modelled and sometimes explained, so do some adults who push at boundaries in ways that upset individuals or which threaten the community.

If meetings tolerate actions or behaviour that damage relationships, Friends may well lose heart and disengage, or even leave the meeting. Why should they stay when nobody cares enough about their experience to address the person causing them pain? Failure to challenge someone who intimidates or bullies others risks handing them power and exposing their victims further. And we fail to care not only for the victim but also for the offending person as a member of the community, a member who actually needs the community to be clear about boundaries, as we all do.

ii. Seeking outside support

In such cases, and others where an alternative angle on an issue could help, we may need to consult or request the involvement of Friends from outside our local meeting. This could be especially useful when Friends are drawn into taking sides in a conflict; it may be essential when we feel out of our depth, or we need to signal that we are taking the matter seriously and will not be giving up on addressing unacceptable actions or the hurt experienced by Friends. Support should be available from the area meeting pastoral committee, or from a group set up for the purpose of advising on disputes, as recommended in *Quaker faith & practice*:

> **Qf&p 4.23** Area meetings are recommended to appoint a group of experienced and knowledgeable Friends who would be available to give general assistance in the amicable settlement of disputes. If help from outside the area meeting is needed, enquiry should be made of the clerk of Meeting for Sufferings, who may suggest Friends qualified to give it.

Another option is to ask for support from Quaker Life staff who may offer advice and possibly arrange for visitors from the Quaker Life Network to contact us.

❖ Up-to-date information on the support available from Quaker Life, and how to access this, is included in the online resource: **www.quaker.org.uk/tender-hand**.

4. Mutual support

Possible causes of difficulty in meetings emerge in every aspect of eldership and oversight addressed in this book. The causes are numerous – almost anything that matters to Friends invites different perspectives and approaches, and any of them can give rise to conflict. Nevertheless, discovering conflict is invariably a dismaying experience. We can find ourselves asking wryly: 'Why can't Friends just behave themselves, accept differences and get on with being a community?' 'Why can't we all remember our testimony to peaceful living?' 'Why must we have so much of our time taken up like this?'

Our ability to handle the dismaying effects of conflict – as with other stresses inherent in our service – comes importantly through the support we find in our pastoral group. Here we build community through prayerful reflection, discernment and learning how to uphold our meeting in all its ups and downs. Here too we may have to address our own needs for understanding and to be heard. Our efforts to help may not succeed, and we shouldn't expect they always will, but that can feel hard. It is not unusual for peace makers to find they are held responsible not just for failing to resolve conflict but also for making it worse or even being the cause of it. Whatever the outcome, we will be glad to be in community with other committed Friends who are able to weather a storm or two together.

Queries for reflection, discussion and learning

Chapter 14: Conflict and difficulty in the meeting

Queries for individual reflection

1. What part can I play in supporting helpful behaviour in the meeting? How aware am I that my own actions and ways of being a Friend have an influence on others?
2. What do people find difficult about me? Am I able to empathise with someone who causes difficulty by behaving badly or unwisely?
3. How do I respond to conflict? Do I avoid it; am I anxious to find a compromise; do I want to win? How might my response affect my ability to support others in resolving their differences?

Queries for pastoral groups

1. This chapter lists many behaviours and actions that support community. What can we do to build on the positive ways Friends interact and contribute in the meeting, and encourage more of these?
2. How can we be more alert to signs of difficulty? What are we looking for or what are we turning a blind eye to?
3. What conflict resolution strategies do we feel competent to employ? What nature of difficulty would lead us to look for help outside our meeting?

Queries for meetings

1. 'Our primary task is to nurture the development of a healthy and vital worshipping community.' What can we do as a meeting to actively support the helpful behaviours that contribute to our resilience as our community?

2. When disagreements or difficulties arise between Friends, how will our community support all the people affected? How will we each avoid getting involved in conflict by taking sides?

3. What does it mean to behave as a Friend should? What are the boundaries of acceptable behaviour we agree on as a meeting?

❖ These pages can be downloaded from the online resource: **www.quaker.org.uk/tender-hand**

Chapter 15: Disability, vulnerability and times of stress

~

Some care needs require us to be especially sensitive and understanding in how we address them. These may include matters that are part of the everyday nurture of the meeting community, such as elderly Friends who need a fair bit of support, or mental illness, which is often a hidden but very present care need in many meetings. Other needs arise from time to time, and occasionally come as a shock – no one can anticipate disabling injury or a diagnosis of cancer. And our experience varies a lot. In meetings where family stress or break-up is not uncommon Friends will know how to respond helpfully; in others a split relationship can shake a community to its core.

The demands of providing appropriate care for particular circumstances can feel quite challenging, and might require Friends to become aware of relevant good practice and resources, but essentially all the approaches discussed in previous chapters in this Theme still apply. We are not expected to be specialists in anything, just good caring Friends who are willing to do our best in a loving spirit.

As described in those previous chapters our care for *any* Friend starts with making it possible and easy for people to make their needs known, should they wish to, and then we can consider with them how the meeting might respond. In some circumstances we may learn of a need the meeting could respond to other than by a Friend sharing this directly; for example, another Friend may alert someone in the meeting, or we may notice or hear of a possible need. If this does happen we should check our concern with the Friend personally wherever we can. In some instances it may be helpful to consult family members or friends, but we mustn't bypass the Friend concerned. If we do speak with others we should always let the Friend know about this and preferably ask their permission first.

When we become aware of a need we haven't met before we are better able to address it if we have at least thought about the possibility beforehand. A newly formed group, or one welcoming new members, will benefit from taking time to share current or past experience of care needs with each other. It can help us talk about less likely situations and how prepared we feel to respond appropriately.

This rather lengthy chapter comprises eight often quite short sections, each providing an introduction to a care need we could encounter in our meeting.

1. Living with disability
2. Safeguarding of vulnerable adults
3. Illness or infirmity
4. Mental health
5. Ageing
6. Dying, death and bereavement
7. Supporting relationships
8. Inclusion of offenders; prison ministry.

As introductions only, these sections anticipate that the next step for any reader engaging with questions raised here will be to seek further information.

❖ The online resource: **www.quaker.org.uk/tender-hand** has information on accessing specific guidance on all these care needs, including signposts to resources, publications and organisations that can help.

❖ References in each section draw attention to a few immediately relevant resources and to other chapters in this book where a subject is addressed.

❖ Everything included here needs to be read with the guidance and discussion in other chapters in this Theme in mind, especially **Chapter 11:** *Addressing need* and **Chapter 12:** *Receiving care.*

1. Living with disability

Each person living with disability has unique needs and we will ask individual Friends to let us know what these are. But any public gathering should anticipate some common needs. Whether the gathering is in a meeting house or rented premises, a meeting will want to ensure the best provision for inclusion and accessibility that is possible in its circumstances. In matters to do with premises, the role of Friends with pastoral responsibilities will be to notice or learn about lacks that could be addressed and to raise these with the meeting.

There may be several other issues concerning equal inclusion that Friends should be alert to and may need to address. For example, we could come across carelessly excluding attitudes among Friends, unhelpful nominations practice, or an unchecked assumption that the meeting's usual processes, arrangements and resources are accessible to all.

❖ The Quaker Disability Equality Group (QDEG) offers advice and information on basic good practice and sometimes quite small things a meeting can do to make a difference. Guidance on their website **http://quakerdisabilitygroup.org.uk** can help us undertake a disability 'audit' of our meeting as a first step towards raising awareness and ensuring good practice in each area of meeting activity.

BYM has a legal obligation to ensure that disability equality issues are addressed…

In particular, QDEG seeks:

- to promote the full inclusion of all disabled people within the Society
- to raise awareness of the diversity of needs among disabled Friends
- to enable the skills and experience of disabled Friends to be valued and fully utilised
- to provide advocacy for disabled Friends at all levels within BYM
- to provide advice and share expertise.

(Extract from QDEG's Aims – http://quakerdisabilitygroup.org.uk accessed 22.5.2014)

2. Safeguarding of vulnerable adults

Meetings may have a duty of care for people who are not fully able to care for themselves. In law this includes children and young people under the age of 18 and people in some other circumstances that are less easy to define.

Most safeguarding matters concern children and young people, so the document *Meeting safety* (see below) is written largely with those groups in mind. If the issue of safeguarding vulnerable adults affects our meeting we should check the requirements with our area meeting safeguarding coordinator. Trustees are the area meeting body responsible for safeguarding and for drafting a safeguarding policy, which will be agreed by the AM (area meeting for business). The following extracts from one area meeting's safeguarding policy may help Friends decide whether they need to explore the matter further.

Adults are regarded in law as having the capacity to make decisions, unless the contrary can be proved. ... Adults can become vulnerable, temporarily or permanently, because of illness, frailty or disability.

Sometimes adults who appear vulnerable in various ways attend Quaker Meetings... Friends actively involved in caring for a vulnerable person may take on a position of trust. In this role, they deserve oversight, as the tasks could be (a) onerous, (b) misinterpreted by third parties, (c) need sharing, to ease the load.

...

The issue of protection or safeguarding becomes relevant when the *context* around the individual is examined. Is the person able to look after him/herself? Defend him/herself from common dangers? Does the person need care (beyond the usual reciprocal care of a friendship or partnership)? Does he/she receive care (whether formal or informal)? What it is the quality of the care? Good, abusive or indeed a bit of both? The answers to these questions ... give clues to the need to report the situation of an adult to an agency with a statutory responsibility to investigate.

(South Wales Area Meeting
safeguarding policy, 2012: p. 4)

Importantly, Friends should never *investigate* a possible safeguarding matter themselves; this applies to all Friends, including elders and overseers. We must work with the safeguarding coordinator to decide whether a matter should be reported to the authorities, and then do as guided by this Friend. A further caution we must observe is not to talk about our actions with other people in the meeting who are not directly involved in a process advised by the safeguarding coordinator.

❖ *Meeting safety*, updated regularly by Quaker Life, gives a brief overview of safeguarding within Quaker meetings and includes an introduction to other organisations Friends work with in this area.

3. Illness or infirmity

We all get ill from time to time, sometimes seriously; others live with chronic illness or physical infirmity. Caring for Friends in these circumstances will therefore be a concern of every meeting.

Where a Friend is unable to attend meeting for worship – at all or regularly – we should offer to arrange occasional meetings in their home, if they would welcome that. Attending to the spiritual needs of Friends who are unwell or infirm could be our clearest priority. A listening presence, and sometimes just sitting alongside a Friend in a spirit of worship, is often the most welcome support we can provide.

The needs of a housebound Friend will probably include regular and friendly contact including social visits, though we should not assume this. For example, fatiguing illness and some other conditions can make conversation or even the presence of someone in the room painful and exhausting.

An offer of practical help with a task a Friend cannot see to in their present circumstances might be gratefully received, but we should be wary of encouraging an expectation that Friends will provide ongoing practical and other caring support. Long-term support may well be available from other sources, such as family members, the caring and medical professions, social services and some charitable organisations. Our Friend may prefer us to provide for their needs, but we have to weigh their wishes against other calls on our time and availability in the meeting. The contribution of eldership and oversight might be better directed towards helping our Friend access support and providing advocacy in the process.

"When I was diagnosed with MS the Friend who helped me most was the one who let me swear and rage down the phone. She didn't just listen passively but encouraged me with some choice profanities of her own. We would both end up laughing like drains."

Physical illness often brings emotional upset and frustration at being 'out of action'. There may be financial or career consequences and effects on other family members that add to a Friend's anger or fear. Anyone offering support must be able to allow the Friend to express their distress and worst fears and be sufficiently robust emotionally not to get entangled. The Friend with a strong need to fix things and make everything better will not be the right choice.

❖ There are many organisations, websites and online communities that provide support to individuals and families dealing with specific conditions. The people affected are usually aware of these, but Friends offering their support might also find it useful to access information that may help them respond appropriately.

4. Mental health

All of us experience mental distress at times, personally or in those close to us, perhaps when a relationship ends, or we are bereaved, or are under particular stress at work or in the family. Many of us, about one in four, will also at some time suffer a mental health problem severe enough to meet the criteria for a psychiatric diagnosis. Quaker meetings probably attract a disproportionate number of people in this situation, who find support in the quiet reflective atmosphere and acceptance.

(Guidelines for overseers dealing with mental health issues, Manchester & Warrington Area Meeting, 2013: p. 1)

Mental health is a broad and very significant subject for eldership and oversight that merits treatment in much greater depth than is possible in this publication. The figure of one in four noted in the above extract speaks for itself, as does the observation that Quaker meetings attract a disproportionate number of people with mental illness. So we are almost certain to be addressing mental health needs in either subtle or more overt ways. The meeting is also likely to include people with mental health conditions who we are unaware of, and who nevertheless find nurture and support through worship and being part of the community.

"We have two main mental health needs in our meeting. One Friend has a long-term condition, which makes him difficult and sometimes disruptive and he can be quite hurtful to other individuals. We also have at least three people with depression – they are often withdrawn or very negative and hard to get to know properly. Both kinds of mental health issue concern us and deserve our loving care."

Our immediate concern when we become aware of need will be to offer our support or to find unobtrusive ways of making a difference to the Friend's experience of meeting. Being sufficiently well informed about the effects of mental illness can be a great help to everyone involved.

As this could be the whole meeting it might call for an opportunity to learn about and explore mental health issues together. There are various approaches to this we could consider, including calling on expertise in our area meeting or contacting Quaker Life to request a facilitator experienced in mental health matters. And a well-maintained collection of resources enables us to find advice and information, both for when we feel ready to explore further and for when a need becomes apparent. A few key points that may help us get our bearings in a complex field include:

- Where a Friend is aware of their condition and has some insight into how it affects others there is much that Friends can do to provide appropriate support and understanding. And we should ask the Friend for guidance on this.
- Depression is common and often hidden. It can be very hard for a depressed person to initiate or even accept social contacts. When we extend a hand of friendship it needs to be clearly free from any expectation or agenda of our own. Offered lightly our connections may encourage someone for whom each day is a real struggle.

"One of the Friends who offered me the best support would ask 'How are you?' and he accepted my reply of 'Terrible, thank you, and how are you?' without probing further. It was lovely to be asked, and even better that my reply was putting him in the picture, but that I didn't want to dwell on it. I knew that if I wanted to say more, I could."

- If a Friend with mental illness exhibits disruptive or hurtful behaviour we may well have to insist on boundaries to safeguard both the Friend and the community. There could be a point when we have to weigh the needs of an individual and the needs of the meeting and take difficult decisions about where to put our limited resources.

- There are also limits to how involved we should be. With concern for the Friend and for our own good we must preserve our stable grounding; we do not jump in with someone in the whirlpool of their suffering.
- Even when it is clear we are helping in some way we shouldn't expect to be thanked. This otherwise usual response to thoughtful actions may just be beyond someone who is consumed with their own concerns.
- A common response when we are negatively affected by a person's behaviour is to believe it is intentionally directed at us. It helps to recognise that anyone's actions may have causes and triggers unconnected with us personally.
- We need to feel okay about asking tough questions of ourselves: Do we feel up to this? How well are we coping? How will we cope if a presenting difficulty escalates?
- There is help and support available for meetings struggling with mental health issues, and we mustn't hold back from seeking this. The health of our meeting may also be at stake.

A couple of publications, both published by Friends General Conference (FGC) in America, would provide a good practical introduction for a pastoral group to discuss. They are likely to be in your meeting library, or can be obtained from the Quaker Bookshop or online:

- ❖ 'Pastoral care for persons with mental illness' in *Grounded in God: Care and nurture in Friends meetings,* ed. Patricia McBee, FGC (Philadelphia), 2002

- ❖ *Dealing with difficult behavior in meeting for worship,* by a task group of FGC, 2007

- ❖ The online resource: **www.quaker.org.uk/tender-hand** lists further publications on the subject and includes information on how to access support from Quaker Life and from other organisations that can help.

5. Ageing

Old age is not in itself a problem – either for the ageing person or the people close to them. An older person could need some support in practical things, but not in everything, and may still have more to offer than they need to receive. We are all affected by myths and stereotypes about ageing, which can result in discrimination and small acts of exclusion. Our group or our meeting might benefit from an opportunity to explore assumptions together.

If some older Friends are becoming quietly invisible we should make opportunities for reviving real connections. A Friend might be experiencing a sense of loss at being less actively involved and would welcome the opportunity to do something for the meeting that really matters. By recognising that old age brings different gifts we can use our imagination to discover ways the meeting and individual Friends could benefit from these.

We can also support attendance at meeting by older Friends and encourage their greater participation in the life of the meeting with some quite simple practical measures, for example:

- attending to comfort/disability needs in the meeting venue
- arranging transport
- including older Friends on committees and ensuring they can attend business meetings, social events, etc.
- providing written material in large type
- keeping in touch
- offering practical help at home where appropriate, and guidance on sources of help.

Friends who no longer or rarely attend meeting will be in our minds too. We must maintain contact and find ways of extending our community outwards to include them, such as visiting, holding meeting in their homes and being in contact with family members supporting an older Friend.

✤ *This is who I am – Listening with older Friends: Volume 9 of the Eldership and Oversight handbook series* offers guidance on supporting Friends in old age through encouraging conversation and reminiscing, referred to in the handbook as 'Meeting for Listening'.

> Meetings should recognise and support those whose ministry is to the needs of older Friends. Not everyone feels called to this service, possibly even within our pastoral group. Rather than just be pleased that at least some people are, we should recognise the stresses involved in caring for older Friends and give our valued carers opportunity to 'debrief'. This might include offering our encouragement and support for them to reduce the amount they do personally, and equally encouraging others in the meeting to get involved.

Our support could be especially important for Friends giving their time to caring for people and family members affected by dementia. Dementia and milder forms of decline in mental and intellectual capacity affect many in later years. Our care may be needed either for a Friend with dementia or a family caring for a relative with the disease, or both. A diagnosis of dementia can come as a great shock and the time ahead is likely to be both stressful and very sad.

✤ The Alzheimer's Society: **www.alzheimers.org.uk** can help us support a person with dementia and those caring for them. The website includes the following tips for carers that overseers might find useful too:

- Focus on what they can do rather than on what they can't. This will help to promote their independence. [...]
- They may find it hard to remember or concentrate on things, so try to be flexible and patient.
- Put yourself in their shoes – try to understand how they might be feeling and how they may want to be cared for.
- Offer support sensitively and try to give encouragement.
- Make sure they have meaningful things to do, from everyday chores to leisure activities. Do things together if you can.
- Include the person in conversations and activities as much as possible.

(*Alzheimers Society, The dementia guide: Support for carers*; accessed 18.03.2015)

6. Dying, death and bereavement

Many meetings have numbers of Friends in the final stages of their lives and experience the loss of older Friends not infrequently. Untimely or sudden deaths of people who have not reached old age could occur in our meeting too. Each death is sad and stressful, a very personal loss for the community as well as for the family and close friends intimately involved.

i. Offering our support

Dying is a stage in anyone's life that deserves the best care we can offer. Being present and available for someone who is dying is a privilege as well as a challenge and we shouldn't offer our support lightly. <u>Listening will be our main role so that we always take our cues from the dying Friend</u>, and we will similarly support the Friend's relatives and carers – through listening and by being practical, doing small things quietly, acknowledging their spiritual pain. Our care might include arranging meetings for worship in a sick or dying person's home, but we will be sure to offer this with no implication that in some way it ought to happen. The last thing we want is for the Friend or their family to feel 'taken over' by our expectations, or that we need them to care for our feelings in this.

ii. Our own feelings about death and dying

Friends supporting a person facing death or bereavement should take care to support each other as well. Each of us who has lost someone close will inevitably be reminded of it by the experience of caring for another's loss. We must give space for our need without it intruding on the experience of the people we are caring for, perhaps by making time to explore and share with one another in our group, or by asking one person to listen to our story.

- How can we help members of the meeting reflect together on the challenges that will face each of us at the end of life?
- What plans do we have in place for responding to the needs of members with terminal illness?
- Who in our meeting has a particular gift for being with those who are sick or dying? Who has professional experience?
- What resources are available in the yearly meeting or our community to help us respond sensitively and knowledgeably?

(McBee, ed., 2002: p. 165)

iii. Tragic death

Some deaths, especially that of a child, or a terrible accident, murder or suicide will disturb people deeply. Friends and others connected with the loss may have very complicated responses requiring understanding and support we could feel ill-equipped to provide – partly because we too are affected. A common response is for people to avoid those most immediately bereaved such as a parent or partner. A fragmented community coping with grief of this kind may require a whole-meeting approach to care that helps Friends find one another again.

> "When a local child was murdered people began to avoid us in the street. We didn't know this little boy or his family, but the murder happened two doors away from our house. We were obviously too near for other people's comfort. It felt very estranging."

iv. Supporting bereaved children

Children who are bereaved need our special care. Simply being kindly and available signals that the meeting community supports them, no matter what. But we should always access professional guidance to help us understand how we can work with the Friends responsible for children's meeting. Our concern will be for all children at such a difficult time not just those immediately affected.

- ❖ The online resource: **www.quaker.org.uk/tender-hand** includes signposts to relevant publications and organisations.
- ❖ Of particular help will be the organisation Winston's Wish, which provides support, guidance and information from experienced professionals for anyone who is concerned about a child facing the death of a family

member, or who has already been bereaved: **www.winstonswish.org.uk**

❖ *Journeys in the Spirit* issue 82 (December 2013) is focused on the experience of grief, and includes an extract from *The grief of our children* by Dianne McKissock with ideas for times of special celebration and anniversaries (birthdays, etc.).

❖ Guidance is also available from Quaker Concern around Dying and Death (QDD) – a listed informal group of Britain Yearly Meeting: **www.quaker.org.uk/tender-hand**

We have been led to recognise that we cannot truly hear what children and young people need from us if we do not face our own losses with integrity.

We must be ready to acknowledge the intensity of children's feelings and to allow a free expression of those feelings rather than stifling what we, as adults, find too disturbing to listen to.

(Helping children and young people to face dying and death: Minute of QDD Gathering, 21–22 November 2013)

v. Accessing guidance and information

There are many excellent publications that can guide us towards a better understanding of the care needs of dying or bereaved Friends and which will help any Friends address feelings about death.

❖ A list is included in the online resource: **www.quaker.org.uk/tender-hand**

The following three very different angles on approaching the subject might be useful as starting points for discussion in our pastoral group (we would need to select a topic from the first book):

❖ 'Pastoral care for illness and death' in *Grounded in God* (McBee, ed.): Three helpful chapters on how we can respond with our care. The first of these chapters: *Caring for the terminally ill and their caregivers* includes a sound list of advices on 'Visiting Friends who are very ill'.

❖ *The sad book* by Michael Rosen: An eloquent picture book that speaks to any age of reader, this is a moving account of a father's grief at losing his 19 year-old son.

❖ *Dying to know: Bringing death to life* by Andrew Anastasios: An upbeat and pragmatic exploration in images and words on approaching and talking about death.

vi. Planning funerals and memorial meetings

Supporting a bereaved family through the process of planning a funeral or memorial meeting may be part of our role, depending on the wishes of the deceased Friend and/or their family.

❖ **Chapter 6:** *Worship in the life of the meeting* looks at the role of eldership in planning funeral and memorial meetings.

❖ **Chapter 17:** *The Quaker way of right ordering* points towards the full guidance in *Qf&p* Chapter 17 on this subject.

❖ We will find it helpful to be aware of the further insights and advice included in *Funerals and memorial meetings*: *Volume 2 of the Eldership & Oversight handbook series.*

7. Supporting relationships

Just as we are asked to care for all marriages (*Qf&p* 16.07) we will care for Friends in their committed partnerships and in their other significant relationships too. Some of these relationships may not be visible or known to us but they often profoundly affect who people are as whole persons – and therefore as Friends. Relationships of all kinds can suffer strain, sorrow or disturbance, and most meetings will include Friends experiencing one or more of the following examples:

- tensions in a family where only one member is Quaker
- friction and unhappiness in a marriage or partnership, possibly leading to break-up
- discord in an extended family, or parents and children seriously falling out
- breakdown of a close friendship
- dysfunctional relationships at work or a place of study
- loneliness as a single person, whether single by choice or otherwise
- abusive relationship; stalking.

Many of these relationships are between a member of the meeting and others outside it, and can remain hidden for a long time. Elders or overseers may eventually learn of difficulty or sense that something is wrong. When a situation does come to our attention, and it is clear that the Friend(s) concerned are willing for at least some people to know, we should be prepared to uphold Friends in what are nevertheless private matters, perhaps offering confidential listening and other kinds of support without being either intrusive or interfering.

A climate of openness in our community that makes it okay to be known as whole persons allows Friends to support one another in difficulty and to share in the joys. Importantly, we should affirm that the place of the Friend in this community is not affected by whatever is going on in their private life, including when it involves other Friends in the meeting. We don't take sides; we don't ascribe blame.

Three of the circumstances in the above list may be of immediate concern to pastoral care: two because they affect most meetings at some time; the third because behaviours of these kinds are less common but potentially very serious:

    i.   supporting the single Quaker in a family

    ii. responding to relationships under stress

    iii. addressing consequences of abusive relationships or stalking behaviour.

i. Supporting the single Quaker in a Family

The ways a meeting builds community will support many relationships among Friends, especially where both or all parties are members of the meeting. But it will be less the case for relationships where only one partner attends. Sometimes the strength of a Friend's relationship with the meeting is a cause of friction in their partnership, or it could be that commitment to a partnership limits a Friend's Quaker involvement.

These Friends need support that respects their circumstances, while extending a welcome that implicitly includes the absent partner even if we have never met them. A less common situation is where partners worship in different local meetings for reasons that have no reflection on the quality of their relationship. We may or may not know the reason; either way we should recognise that there are likely to be practical and possibly other stresses inherent in the arrangement that could indicate a care need.

> "It is the right decision for both of us, but it's a bit like a bereavement. We are very glad of the support of overseers in both meetings."

ii. Responding to relationships under stress

From the outset we must notice in ourselves any outdated assumptions about people's domestic circumstances. Family structures, partnerships and household arrangements are increasingly varied, and part of the change is that in our meeting, and in society at large, it is easier and more normal to be open about our circumstances now than even a few decades ago.

> Friends who are heterosexual don't assume that everyone else in their community is too. We could be gay, lesbian, bisexual, transgendered; and any of us might be in a first marriage – or single, widowed, divorced, cohabiting or remarried.
>
> Friends who identify themselves in any of these ways may also have children, their own or others'. And these children may have complex family relationships too. We can't tell just by looking at a group of children or young people, who is adopted, fostered or orphaned, or has step-parents or siblings, or is living with grandparents or other guardians.

Each different way of being a partnership, household or family takes its rightful place in society alongside the minority now of lifelong marriages and 'traditional' family structures. Have we caught up with such changes, and are we aware of and okay about the range of relationships in our own meeting? If we have reservations or difficult feelings about this we will need to explore them together in our group. We mustn't let personal prejudice (however mild in our view) compromise our ability to care sensitively and compassionately for any Friend.

When any close relationship comes under stress the help we offer will be much the same as for any other need, in other words, listening and alongside-ness, and if relevant some timely practical support. Perhaps we could suggest a meeting for clearness or mediation, or encourage the Friend to contact Relate (see below).

However, the ending of a partnership is rarely embarked

on lightly and is often the right decision for both people. It can be an opportunity for new beginnings and a transition that holds as much significance for the partners as was their marriage or commitment to each other. In some cases we might receive a request for a meeting for worship to mark a divorce, for example, or we could suggest it. The individual circumstances will speak for themselves as to how appropriate this will be in our meeting, but we should approach this with open minds and guided by loving concern to support both ex-partners.

Children or young people in the meeting who experience discord or break-up of their parents' relationship need our attention and care, however things look from the outside. They may find the loving acceptance of their Quaker meeting a refuge where they can be relaxed and normal for a change, so it might appear that everything is okay with them. On the other hand they may stay away, or be withdrawn and not easy to approach. It will be important for oversight not to be so caught up in the parents' relationship difficulty that we forget to notice how their children may be affected.

❖ Essential reading to help with understanding this intensely difficult time in any child's life will be the booklet *When the wind changes: young people's experience of divorce and changing family patterns*. Published in 2001, this is a collection of writings by children, teenagers and young adults reflecting, anonymously, on their personal experiences. Most meeting libraries will have a copy, or it can be found for sale online.

❖ The Quaker Life leaflet *Clearness* can be downloaded from the Quaker website, **www.quaker.org.uk**. Printed copies are available from the Quaker Centre at Friends House: 020 7663 1030.

❖ Relate is the UK's largest provider of relationship support whose purpose is to help 'people of all ages, backgrounds

and sexual orientations to strengthen their relationships':
www.relate.org.uk, Tel. 0300 100 1234.

❖ *Committed relationships: Volume 6 of the Eldership and Oversight handbook series* provides useful background reading to help us reflect on the nature of partnership.

iii. Addressing consequences of abusive relationships, or stalking behaviour

Though it isn't the business of a meeting to judge the value or health of individuals' relationships, there is an exception in how we respond in the case of a Friend being abusive in their relationship, or engaging in stalking behaviour. Either may be connected with a Friend's mental condition and we may need to access outside support to address a situation. Similarly, we may need advice if a Friend has been or is being abused and seeks our help. We should be prepared to respond in any circumstance where we suspect or learn of someone in the meeting being harmed or who is harming another.

❖ The online resource: **www.quaker.org.uk/tender-hand** includes information on sources of support.
❖ The two Quaker Life leaflets *Maintaining safe communities* and *Maintaining boundaries* might be relevant. The first provides information and guidance for Quaker meetings on dealing with sexual harassment; the second is a guide for individuals on avoiding and preventing sexual harassment.

8. Inclusion of ex-offenders; prison ministry

Friends have a historic concern for offenders, whether in prison or serving other sentences, and for their reintegration into society. Quaker meetings offer a non-judgmental welcome to all people who want to share in our worship.

i. Accepting into our meeting people who may pose risk
These Quaker expressions of witness to equality, and to our belief of 'that of God' in everyone, bring a number of ex-offenders to meetings. Not every meeting is able to offer welcome and care for the ex-offender and ensure safeguards for the community. Nor will attending meeting be the right answer in the case of every released offender. But where it is possible and appropriate it can be an experience with rewards alongside the challenges for a meeting community.

❖ Quaker Life provides an information booklet: *Meetings and (ex) offenders: Guidance on accepting into our meetings people who may pose risk,* which we should refer to for advice on how to respond if our meeting is approached, what we might expect if we agree and what safeguards our meeting will need to put in place: **www. quaker.org.uk/tender-hand**

If the ex-offender was recently released from prison there will be support from the probation service and other agencies. The information booklet suggests that a meeting might appoint a 'receiving group' consisting of the local meeting clerk, an overseer, someone responsible for children and one or two other experienced Friends.

The Receiving Group can act as a contact point for probation officers, social workers, community chaplains, or Quaker prison chaplains who may be aware (or need to be informed) that an ex-offender wishes to attend the meeting... Where a meeting has a Receiving Group it is desirable that they should meet the ex-offender before he or she has any other direct contact with the meeting, discuss their wish to attend meeting and any conditions, appropriate to the risk, which should be observed.
(*Meetings and (ex) offenders,* Quaker Life, 2014: pp. 5–6)

Where an ex-offender has been convicted of a sexual offence the meeting will be advised of relevant safeguards – especially concerning children in the meeting – and the support available. For example, we may be informed of a Circles of Support and Accountability scheme in our area, which the ex-offender might be referred to by the services working with them. This is an ambitious, groundbreaking scheme, which was supported by Quakers and now works independently. But please note that it is not a do-it-yourself option for Quaker meetings.

✤ Full information on the scheme is available on the 'Circles' website: **www.circles-uk.org.uk**

Circles work in partnership with police, probation, local multi agency public protection arrangements and other professionals working in the field of child protection. Circles has at its heart the aim to prevent further sexual abuse, working with the objective of no more victims.

(Circles UK, about circle, purpose and values;
accessed 12.11.2014)

ii. Supporting chaplaincy
One or more Friends in our area meeting may be appointed to serve in the chaplaincy of local prisons; the role of pastoral care will be to support these Friends in what can be stressful and challenging work. They might value having a support group, either in their local meeting or with other Quaker prison chaplains in the area meeting, which could meet regularly for worship, discussion and sharing.

In the event of an ex-offender wishing to attend meeting our prison chaplains could possibly be in a position to provide guidance and information that will aid the meeting's discernment. Or they may be able to act as a link between prison and the meeting before a prisoner's release, with our support for them in what would be a significant role on the meeting's behalf. In this as in all eldership and oversight matters, the fabric of community that sustains our meeting's care for Friends in need is how we work together within agreed Quaker processes, alert to one another's needs and supporting each other.

It can make a big difference to the support we are able to provide our prison chaplains if we take the trouble to become better informed about this service; we can do this very easily by accessing information provided by Quaker Life:

❖ Quaker chaplains can be found in a variety of other settings as well as prisons and secure units. They offer friendship and spiritual advice to people of all faiths and none. Quaker chaplains are supported during their service by Quaker Life: **www.quaker.org.uk/tender-hand**

❖ The publication *A Brief guide to Quaker chaplaincy* brings together the experiences of many Friends working in different chaplaincy settings and provides a resource for all those interested in this valuable form of Quaker service. The guide explains what chaplaincy is and what chaplains do, their times and seasons, and how you might become a Quaker chaplain. There is also a list of publications and links to relevant websites. The *Brief guide* can be downloaded at: **www.quaker.org.uk/ tender-hand**

Queries for reflection, discussion and learning

Chapter 15: Disability, vulnerability and times of stress

Queries for individual reflection

1. Where do I feel my strengths lie in attending to specific care needs. How will I convey this to others in the meeting or in my pastoral group?

2. What needs might I find it hard to respond to? Are there ways I could allay my discomfort or sense of inadequacy? Might I nevertheless feel able to support a Friend who responds to such a need?

3. What are my learning needs on this topic? Are there aspects of care and support I have given little thought to before now?

Queries for pastoral groups

1. How do we prioritise our time and energies in a meeting with a range of different needs – and some we haven't met so far but should be prepared for?

2. Do we need to identify lacks or make changes in our current provision for certain Friends or groups of Friends? How will we go about this?

3. How can we prepare ourselves to meet an urgent care need we are ill equipped to address or which affects us personally or emotionally? How will we ensure that our way of working together is built on sufficient trust to bear stresses when they occur in our group?

Queries for meetings

1. How disability-aware are we as a meeting? How can we be better informed on practical measures we should implement, and about helpful practice to employ in each area of meeting activity?

2. Are there some care needs that predominate in our meeting? How can we ensure that attending to these doesn't overstretch our resources or mean we cannot respond to other less pressing needs?

3. How do we care for the Friends who are giving a lot of service in caring for others?

❖ These pages can be downloaded from the online resource: **www.quaker.org.uk/tender-hand**

THEME 5: Communication

Just as the essential human need to communicate has shaped language, culture and society, so it has shaped the Religious Society of Friends. Quaker structures and processes, form of worship and gatherings of all kinds are simultaneously the ways we open ourselves to the leadings of the Spirit and our means of communicating with each other.

This Theme discusses the many kinds of communication that influence the worship and community life of Quaker meetings and all Friends' outward activity. Meetings differ in the use each makes of some ways of communicating more than others, but every meeting employs a variety of means according to need, habit, accepted practice and increasingly by adopting or experimenting with something new.

Communications in meetings range from purposes to do with business matters and right ordering, through to informal contacts so casual that we can overlook their importance to the life of a community. From the most to the least structured or formal communications, the range in our meeting might look something like this:

> ➢ **Formal** communications in right ordering, that is, communications largely to do with Quaker or meeting business and with the meeting's structures for doing things accountably
>> ➢ **Open** information communicated within the meeting, or to people outside it, including outreach and information we provide to welcome new people

> ➤ **Structured** but informal ways of communicating in groups, such as discussion, sharing and learning activities, threshing meetings and meetings for clearness
>> ➤ **Informal** but planned conversations, discussions or meetings between two or a few individuals, such as for pastoral care purposes or for discussing meeting matters
>>> ➤ **Impromptu** conversations and contacts about matters connected with the work or concerns of the meeting, and which contribute to this in some way
>>>> ➤ **Casual** and everyday conversations by a variety of means that may or may not have anything to do with meeting or pastoral matters.

There is naturally a lot of overlap between these many ways and common threads that run through them all. The following chapters reflect this in an exploration of a subject that is not so much an aspect of Quaker meetings as an essential part of who we are as Friends. Everything that is positive, enriching and vital about our worshipping community is fuelled by good communications. If it is in the doldrums or beset by difficulty, the causes can so often be traced either to poor communications generally or to problems with how some Friends have been in contact with each other.

In tackling a subject of such significance to our meetings the following five chapters positively acknowledge the age we live in now, with all the complications and opportunities it offers us – some that have been with us from the beginning, others very new and constantly unfolding. They invite recognition too of how all Friends are involved to some degree in communicating Quakerism *beyond* their meeting, sometimes intentionally but more often not.

Chapter 16: Communicating as Friends

discusses various factors affecting how well communications across the broad range above work generally in our meeting.

Chapter 17: The Quaker way of right ordering

looks at how right ordering underpins who we are as Friends and therefore influences all our other communications.

Chapter 18: Keeping people informed

considers how one-way communications can be effective, acceptable and a significant element in building community.

Chapter 19: Making connections

explores how Friends connect with one another informally in groups planned for different purposes, reflecting also on individual connections and how these affect a meeting's culture.

Chapter 20: Being in touch in a modern world

reflects on the impact of electronic communications – a strand that runs through every purpose for communicating in meetings.

Chapter 16: Communicating as Friends

~

Pastoral care is concerned with communication because this is how all the responsibilities of eldership and oversight are met. When Friends do things together and get to know one another, when discussions and discernment in the meeting are fruitful, when information is clear and readily available, then everything else is more likely to fall into place.

In most meetings many communications have the positive effects Friends hope for; we are probably also aware of how they fall short at times. If we take a closer look at what might be influencing these different outcomes, it will help us to recognise possibilities for building on the things our meeting does well and learning from what is less effective. This chapter explores ways of becoming more aware of how we communicate and more *intentional* in communicating, and how pastoral practice can contribute to these aims.

There will certainly be more to what is going on in meetings than this exploration can anticipate, so the chapter focuses on factors that commonly have the biggest impact on communications working well – or otherwise. These include:

- caring about how we communicate
- making our intentions clear
- understanding how misunderstandings happen
- the language and content of our message
- how Friends appraise, disapprove or complain.

1. Caring about how we communicate

All communications among and between people in the meeting are linked to a small handful of common purposes:

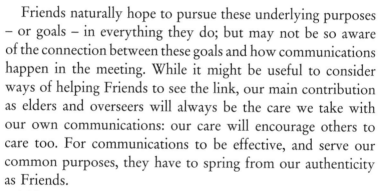

- knowing one another in the Spirit
- caring for one another
- building community
- conducting our business in right ordering.

Friends naturally hope to pursue these underlying purposes – or goals – in everything they do; but may not be so aware of the connection between these goals and how communications happen in the meeting. While it might be useful to consider ways of helping Friends to see the link, our main contribution as elders and overseers will always be the care we take with our own communications: our care will encourage others to care too. For communications to be effective, and serve our common purposes, they have to spring from our authenticity as Friends.

Taking care to communicate effectively means being clear what we want to achieve, and aware of the negative possibilities we really want to avoid. Whatever the means or reason for a particular communication, we hope it will:

convey our message clearly	not carry unintended messages
be received	not be missed, ignored or dismissed
inform and clarify	not misinform or confuse
build bridges	not create barriers
enhance relations	not offend or cause upset

"Communications need regular re-inventing. They have to catch the imagination of the meeting. I think this could be a good role for elders and overseers – not to do the inventing but to encourage anyone to do so and, importantly, to be alive to the new ideas."

2. Making our intentions clear

If I know what I want to communicate, then surely this will also be apparent to the people I hope to reach... won't it? Unfortunately this is often where a failure in communication occurs. Quite certain of our intention we can feel puzzled when the other person gets it wrong or assumes a communication was meant to convey something quite different. Are they being deliberately obtuse? Didn't they listen properly to what we said, or pay attention to what we wrote? It is very easy to believe that other people must be at fault when we have made our purpose perfectly clear. Or have we?

> ➤ Have we implied the purpose instead of stating it? Do we believe people should know without being told?
> ➤ Do we expect the other person or people to do or to see to something? Will they understand that from what we have actually said?
> ➤ Do we want or need a response of some kind? If so, have we said how and by when?
> ➤ Is our message for everyone or are we using a scattergun approach in the hope that the people or person it applies to will notice? Would it be better to address one Friend or a small group? How will the communication affect people it isn't intended for?
> ➤ Are we trying to convey an implicit message without

saying so cleanly? For example, are we using our message to tick people off mildly in the hope that things will change? Should we do that?

➤ Is our communication largely about ourselves rather than what we appear to be saying? Is it about asserting our authority, venting our impatience, or just getting noticed?

➤ Is it more about being seen to be doing something – do we want witnesses to our service, or to be admired for our efficiency or our busyness? Are we perhaps after thanks (and is that such a bad thing)?

Each of these possibilities might present a problem – if only that our communication hasn't achieved its purpose. Lack of clarity is mostly just a nuisance but can have more serious outcomes, such as opening the way for a hostile interpretation (*How dare she imply I would do such a thing?*).

The above queries could help us test our intentions, particularly if we feel at all anxious about a communication we hope to make or if it is vital that our message is properly understood.

> "My co-convener and I both need to email various people on elders' and overseers' business, but we always run them past each other before sending. Ann is very good at spotting if I'm coming on a bit strong over something Friends *should* be doing but don't get round to – like the welcoming rota. I'm better at noticing whether it's clear what we're asking Friends to do."

3. Understanding how misunderstandings happen

A misunderstanding doesn't have to lead to difficulty, but clearly can. So it matters how we deal with it. We might apportion blame and seek redress, or we could try to understand what went wrong and learn from the experience together. It's possible to learn from second-hand experience too. The causes of some misunderstandings are so common that just being observant of the fixes that others get into may help us spot misapprehensions early on in our own contacts with people – and do something about it. Some of these common causes include the following examples:

i.   making unhelpful assumptions
ii. remembering and recalling inaccurately
iii. withholding or misreading different perspectives
iv. failing to get our message across.

i. Making unhelpful assumptions

> "The first item on the overseers' agenda just went on and on. There was a lot of talking but very little communication – until it began to dawn on Friends that we were actually all in agreement on what several had assumed would be a matter of serious dissension. We had to get through half an hour of people struggling to defend their positions against non-existent opposition, before we finally arrived at a minute of unity."

People make assumptions about others all the time – it's a necessary part of functioning as human beings. We assume a friend will arrive on time or else phone to say they have been delayed; we assume another of our friends will simply turn up 15 minutes late as usual. And we will probably be right in both cases, because that's our personal experience of these friends.

But we could be basing our assumptions instead on what we *think* we know about others – sometimes from hearsay, sometimes by drawing wider conclusions from very little 'evidence'. An assumption can be strengthened when a few people talk among themselves, confirming a shared belief about what others think, or have done, or intend to do. Whenever we make assumptions in these ways about others it pays to check and with a genuinely open mind. Perhaps we were right. If we discover we were wrong, we now have an opportunity to avoid a misunderstanding.

Where our assumption reflects badly on someone in any way we have an absolute responsibility to check this. Checking means asking the person concerned rather than asking other people about them. It means we have to speak to the person, which might not be at all easy to do.

ii. Remembering and recalling inaccurately

"Two Friends in our meeting fell out over a stupid misunderstanding. One said she remembered perfectly well agreeing to get rid of the hydrangea (so she dug it up); the other claimed they'd agreed to cut it back. Actually, they were both wrong, I remember them deciding it should be moved away from the path. These Friends now won't speak to each other and both have given up looking after the garden."

If we recall a conversation we had yesterday, and again in a week's time, each account will be a bit different but on neither occasion will it be literally accurate. No matter how good our memory we will have filtered details during the conversation based on what we wanted, needed, expected – or feared – to hear. During any conversation each person will lay down different inaccurate foundations for recalling exactly what was said.

In most circumstances exact details are irrelevant. Both parties share a good sense of what took place, which they can work with. But when details are an issue – and we have not thought to check them – we may find our different recollections amount to a significant misunderstanding. Having different recollections is not about being untruthful but about being human. It's such a common experience that people usually find ways of putting right anything problematic; a sense of humour and willingness to take responsibility for having made a mistake are hugely helpful.

But sometimes it won't be that easy, perhaps especially where antipathy or ill feeling already exists. People in these circumstances are sometimes responsive to help through mediation, which elders and overseers might consider suggesting.

❖ **Chapter 14:** *Conflict and difficulty in the meeting* looks at various approaches that enable people to give their own account of an issue and to hear one another.

iii. Withholding or misreading our different perspectives

How do people communicate when they know, or believe, that they differ on some fundamental issues? Our ease with silence can mask discomfort with speaking about the things that matter most to us: we may say nothing rather than take a risk. But not saying is also risky. When we do get round to voicing what's been bothering us it may be from a point too far on in an unspoken conversation, the conversation we should have had but didn't. What we say at this point may simply not make sense to the other person; we haven't been enough in touch to communicate properly now.

> "We knew there was tension in the meeting over vocal ministry, so we did some creative listening after meeting for worship to share our concerns. One Friend said she never ministered because she was sure her non-theist views would upset people. Another said he didn't minister because he knew his Christian beliefs would be unacceptable in this meeting. I said, 'I think you two need to have a conversation!'"

Another common source of misunderstanding can be triggered when something a Friend says appears to signal they hold attitudes their listener has felt threatened by in the past. An alarm bell goes off – and there is nothing like an alarm bell for fixing a moment in the memory. Recalling the conversation, this is the one detail that seems significant – about the conversation and about the Friend.

As elders and overseers we aren't expected to bring the insights of counselling to misunderstandings between Friends, but at times may have to consider the possibility that an issue is not all it appears. What we do with that possibility is another matter. We won't patronise anyone with our belief that their reactions are linked to past experience. If this is happening only the person themselves can intuit it.

But there is a lot we can do to help different perspectives to co-exist creatively as well as peaceably – so that there is less of the silence that masks unsaid things and more of the silence that connects us. Two other chapters in particular explore the aim of enabling disagreement without estrangement:

❖ **Chapter 14:** *Conflict and difficulty in the meeting* suggests approaches to building a peaceable meeting.
❖ **Chapter 19:** *Making connections* offers insights into how Friends connect with one another in groups and as individuals.

iv. Failing to get our message across

"I needed to know which Friends were currently appointed to roles, so I asked our clerk of nominations, who pointed out an A4 sheet in small print lost among a scattering of unrelated notices. She was clearly annoyed that I seemed to be implying the information hadn't been made available, when they were so careful to maintain an up-to-date list. It was always pinned to that board and obviously I'd failed to look for it properly."

There are at least two parties in any communication – those who want to convey a message and those it is intended for. Things can go wrong at either end and in the space between them too, any of which can lead to a misunderstanding that puzzles both parties.

When we initiate a communication we can easily lose sight of the fact that what occupies our attention – because it is our job or a 'hot' issue from where we are standing – may not be everyone (or anyone) else's priority. As the recipient we can do the same thing. We can forget that our attention is also needed elsewhere than on the matters currently occupying us, and either ignore a message on another matter or give it scant attention. Between these two 'ends' are the means used to communicate and the nature of the message (e.g. how long it is and how much of other people's time it will take up).

Failure to get a message across can easily lead to misunderstandings. A little more awareness of one another's point of view is sometimes all that is needed to ensure a message receives the attention it deserves. Our communication is more likely to succeed if we empathise with the other people involved – if we put ourselves in their shoes:

> ➤ This is what we want to tell them; but what do they want or need to know?
> ➤ This is *our* priority concern; but do others have priorities we should be alert to?
> ➤ This is the way we prefer to communicate our message; but which is the most likely way of reaching the people we want to receive it?

4. The language and content of our message

i. Inclusive and exclusive ways of communicating
> ➤ Do we refer by name – without further explanation

– to people who some in the meeting know/knew well but who are strangers to others?

➤ Do we give out a notice that is unintelligible to a newcomer?

> AM is at Thatton next Saturday – see Judith if you'd like a lift. Bob is giving his Sufferings report and Linda will speak in the afternoon about EAPPI

> What is AM and where is Thatton? Who are Judith, Bob and Linda? What is Bob suffering from? What is E-yappy?

➤ Do we assume that people recognise Quaker terms, acronyms and references or that everyone is familiar with the Christian tradition and biblical stories?

➤ Do we over-use God language or strenuously avoid it?

➤ Does the language we use come from assumptions about people – such as that everyone is middle class, partnered, university educated, okay financially, etc.?

➤ Do we assume everyone is more or less aware of how things work in the meeting, what is going on, what went on before, what is being planned?

Inclusive communications needn't be contrived to cover every possibility of who might receive them, but it is important to check we are not carelessly excluding some people in the meeting or making it hard for them to feel part of what is going on.

"We want people to feel really welcome, whether they've been coming for years or this is their first time. So we try to notice who's there and make sure no one gets left out of conversations over coffee. We don't use acronyms in notices and we always explain what happens at area business meetings, even if there are no newcomers that week. That way we don't forget when new people turn up."

ii. Quaker terms and language

Quaker language and turns of phrase are part of our sense of community, and for that reason may feel excluding to non-Quakers and newcomers. This is not to say Friends should avoid some of our best-loved language, just a caution to avoid being clannish with it. People will meet this language naturally in ministry and in Quaker literature, and it might be that terms such as 'waiting in the light', or 'speaking truth to power' will arouse people's curiosity, inviting questions or conversation.

Although language naturally changes over time Friends value Quaker terms for their accepted and usually historic meaning. They connect us to our roots. It may be useful for a meeting to reflect together on using Quaker language so that it fits our current purposes, but not so that we degrade it or find it no longer has meaning for us.

A way of using this language worth noting, and perhaps questioning, is when Friends employ Quaker terms to add weight to a point they want to make, or to claim authenticity that puts it beyond challenge. If we spot this way of cloaking ordinary secular impulses, we will need to act tactfully to respond to the real message. Common examples include:

Concern: e.g. 'I have a concern.' A Quaker concern is always tested in the group. The Friend usually means they are concerned about something. And sometimes it is simple enough to reframe it in those words without causing offence.

Leading: e.g. 'I have been led to do this or say this.' Often the Friend who claims this sincerely believes they are responding to a God-given leading, and it might be true. The outcome or the anticipated effect is one way of knowing. If it causes needless hurt or upset, is it likely to be a Spirit-led inspiration? The Quaker way is to test leadings as we do with concern, which is to submit them to questioning.

Speaking truth: This is mostly associated with the phrase, 'Speaking truth to power'. But it is sometimes offered as 'I'm speaking my truth', meaning, 'This is what I want to say, it's how I see things and I want you to hear me out.' We can note any implication that the person's truth is therefore *the* truth without needing to engage with it. It is usually more helpful to respond to the real message rather than to question the choice of word. If someone wants to be heard our response should be to listen.

> "I asked an overseer, who lived nearby, if she'd be able to visit a Friend who was poorly at home. And she said she'd rather not, because visiting wasn't 'her ministry'. What she meant was she didn't want to do it and didn't want to tell me why. I can accept that, but I wish she hadn't dressed it up to make it sound like a spiritual reason. If everyone only did things that were 'their ministry' there's an awful lot in meeting that wouldn't get done at all. Sometimes it's our ministry to do the thing that isn't our ministry."

Discernment: e.g. 'I have discerned the right way forward', which can be another way of saying, 'I have thought about the matter and this [it seems to me] is what we should do next.' There are many instances when we undertake our own discernment in order to make a decision for ourselves. But we cannot discern on behalf of others and we shouldn't confuse our own clarity with the clarity of a group we are part of. Corporate discernment is a cornerstone of Quaker practice, which all Friends need to become familiar with.

❖ **Chapter 17:** *The Quaker way of right ordering* looks further into the Quaker decision-making process.

5. How we appraise, disapprove or complain

It is rarely an easy thing to offer someone a response to their actions or words – unless our words are wholly approving. Whatever we say is unavoidably about the person and how they 'performed' rather than an objective view of the matter itself. So it *is* personal to them. It is also personal to us. This is our perspective and we hope that sharing it will be useful (otherwise, why are we offering it?). Whether or not a response is received positively will depend a lot on the care we take to look at the matter from more than one angle. The most important other angle is that of the person concerned: we enquire; we listen; and only then do we offer them our thoughts. It matters too what we do with views other than theirs or ours. Circumstances might require us to:

- retain an open mind about anything we are told about someone by others
- reflect on the matter with other elders or overseers to discern the best approach
- consult others, such as relevant role holders in the meeting.

i. Thanking and praising

Before looking at the challenge of communicating disapproval or criticism of what someone has said or done (or we believe or are told is the case), it is worth reminding ourselves that the point of all 'feedback' is to encourage Friends in the positive contributions they make in the meeting.

The most effective way of doing this is to express genuine appreciation – in other words, to thank people. This simple act is easily overlooked, which can leave people feeling disheartened. Accepting a role or agreeing to undertake a task need not imply that we are okay about being taken for granted; it can make a big difference to how motivated we feel to carry on with demanding work when someone thinks to thank us, and is specific about what they have noticed.

"As Area Meeting Clerk I felt every meeting had gone badly, but without fail, somebody (not the same person) would say quietly 'well done'. That's enough to keep you going."

"Friends are really good at not giving negative strokes, which is great! But positive strokes that acknowledge the unique qualities and contribution of a person are an enlivening, nourishing and important part of human relations. I haven't quite fathomed out why Friends don't do this generously, because they are generous in so many other ways."

The traditional habit of not thanking Friends for their ministry or their service is based on the Quaker view of ministry (including all kinds of service) as prompted by God and given to God. Friends were thankful that the individual was faithful to their calling, but thanks and praise were due only to God.

This habit has largely fallen into disuse, to the regret of some Friends, it must be said. It is now common to record a formal minute of thanks for Friends' service and for Friends to thank one another for ministry that they appreciated. Our current practice therefore varies, which can leave Friends who are not thanked believing they have therefore done a poor job or that their ministry was unwelcome. If Friends are in two minds about this, perhaps discussing it as a whole meeting would be useful.

"We make an end-of-year concluding minute thanking Friends for their service to the meeting in that 12-month period – '*in roles appointed by the meeting and in many other ways*'."

"In our meeting people thank one another for their ministry in a personal way, e.g. 'Thank you for your ministry, Dave. I found it very helpful' – or – 'It really spoke to me'. Some Friends prefer to say something along the lines of, 'Thank you, Friend, for responding to your leading to minister'."

In the same vein, 'Always start with the positive' is sound advice for anyone seeking to draw a Friend's attention to an action of theirs found wanting in some way. A while spent in reflection will usually reveal the good or the positive in a situation. There is no hypocrisy in offering our observation of this when discussing the difficult matter, as long as we don't deceive the Friend about our main purpose.

ii. Plain speaking and speaking 'in love'

Speaking to someone 'plainly' about what (we think) they do wrong – in order to help them change – may not be either wise or effective; we have to think very carefully about our intention and our choice of how to achieve it. Telling someone they should change is rarely much help to them; we cannot change anyone except ourselves, and that's hard enough. Questioning our intention more closely may help us recognise that it could be partly about getting something off our chest. We also have to be aware that naming someone's faults is likely to make them feel bad, rather than encouraged to see our point of view.

> Joe, can we have a word? When we speak in meeting it isn't helpful to use obscure theological terms that not many will recognise. Also, people do find that you tend to go on rather too long.

> Thank you for your ministry, Joe. It was very interesting, though I did get a little lost in the bit about 'parousia'. It would be good to have a conversation some time about these ideas and how Friends offer spoken ministry.

Sometimes criticism is conveyed with the message that it is done in love, is offered lovingly for the person's own good. We should be very wary of invoking love to explain our action – we do not hurt or offend someone out of love.

The meaning of Quaker plain speaking is often misunderstood. Plain speaking in fact means to have a real engagement with the other person, in which we might both be changed. The positive Quaker intention is to put our relationship with someone else on a more real footing. In all things to do with communications between Friends, relationship is at the heart of the matter. And a relationship always goes both ways.

> **Some phrases to watch**
>
> I'm sorry but...
> I hope you won't take this the wrong way...
> I didn't like to say anything before...
> I feel bad telling you this...

iii. Third party complaint

Am I conveying a message of disapproval or complaint that I imply comes from other – unnamed – people as well? A communication of this kind is unlikely to lead to a positive outcome. It indicates that the Friend has been discussed and found wanting, which might be the case, but it doesn't take much to imagine how we would feel if we were the subject of such discussions. We want our message to make a positive difference not arouse feelings of humiliation and hurt. If it's important to speak to a Friend about a perspective shared by others (perhaps Friends in our pastoral group) we must say that cleanly. It may be necessary to pass on that these Friends have received complaints from others in the meeting, in which case we must speak to those others and ask their permission to name them.

> It's not just me, there are others who feel this way, but I can't say who they are – it's confidential.

> *Who thinks this way – is it people I thought were my friends? How long has it been going on? Why didn't they say anything to me?*

It will be important to pursue every avenue that allows openness first. There might be an exceptional circumstance that justifies a complainant's anonymity (e.g. in cases of suspected bullying or where abuse has been reported), but we have to be aware of the possible consequences, and be prepared to meet them. We should be particularly watchful of electing to speak on behalf of the 'victim' on the grounds that they lack the courage or the ability to speak for themselves. It is quite possible that we may in fact be doing this – perhaps unconsciously – as a way of expressing our own grievance or hurt.

Another kind of third party complaint can make for even bigger problems. If someone complains 'confidentially' to other people about a person's actions or attitudes, and everyone withholds from speaking directly with the person concerned, that accused person may get wind of it but is unable either to address the complaint or to respond from their understanding of what is going on. The silence on the matter can have a negative power, and when it erupts out of harboured ill feeling it carries disproportionate weight.

Third party ways of communicating disapproval, complaint or criticism can cause havoc in a meeting community. If we spot them happening, or find that we as elders or overseers are implicated, we will need to take action early on to avert the most difficult consequences.

❖ **Chapter 14** *Conflict and difficulty in the meeting* offers guidance on the kinds of intervention that might be helpful.

iv. Checking our facts
When called to intervene in a complaint we must be scrupulous in checking facts. It is our responsibility to both parties in a matter of contention to be certain of what really happened and what was actually said or written. It isn't a matter of challenging a Friend's truthfulness but simply acting fairly to ask:

❖ Who else saw this happen or heard this said?
❖ Can you show me any letters or emails that confirm your account?
❖ Was there anything you said or did that might have triggered this?

Exaggerating details of an incident in order to explain how we feel is common; it can help to describe the truth of feelings but it will be at the expense of the truth of the facts. If as elders and overseers we take such an account at face value we will not find a truth that is shared with all the people concerned – which must surely be our goal.

One point of view is that feelings are also facts and should therefore always be taken seriously, even if there is dispute about what was said or done. But the strength of someone's feelings is no proof of events. We can attend to a Friend's feelings separately from our efforts to find out what actually happened. How a person feels can be more to do with personal life experience than with any facts of the matter, but it is often a more available answer to hold someone else accountable for our strong feelings than to consider this possibility.

Summary

The issues touched on in this chapter are of course not an exhaustive list. They are included as examples and an introduction to the significance of communication to our common purposes as Friends, and therefore to the work of pastoral care.

If they seem to emphasise the problematic nature of communications in meetings, we have to keep in mind that at the heart of this exploration are positive principles that are mostly second nature to Friends. These are the underlying principles of our Quaker faith that prompt us to behave as Friends should – honestly, fairly, peaceably, straightforwardly and with care for one another. It's when there is a problem that we realise how very important it is to hold to our principles as Friends.

> Maintain that charity which suffereth long, and is kind; put the best construction upon the conduct and opinions one of another which circumstances will warrant. Take heed ... that the enemy produce no dissensions among you; that nothing like a party spirit be ever suffered to prevail. Let each be tender of the reputation of his brother; let every one be earnest to possess the ornament of a meek and quiet spirit. Watch over one another for good, but not for evil; and whilst not blind to the faults or false views of others, be especially careful not to make them a topic of common conversation. And even in cases in which occasion may require that the failings of others should be disclosed, be well satisfied, before they are made the subject of confidential communication, either verbally or by letter, that your own motives are sufficiently pure.
>
> (*London Yearly Meeting Epistle,* 1834)

Queries for reflection, discussion and learning

Chapter 16: Communicating as Friends

Queries for individual reflection
1. 'Our main contribution as elders and overseers will always be the care we take with our own communications: our care will encourage others to care too.' When I am communicating with or to others, what does it ask of me to be aware that I am setting an example?
2. How do I feel when people offer me their genuine thanks for something I've done? Do I make a habit of thanking people when I appreciate them? What difference does it – or might it – make?
3. If I am angry or upset by someone, what is the next thing I tend to do? What do I need to take into account when considering the timing or nature of my response? What do I want my response to achieve?

Queries for pastoral groups
1. How clearly do we communicate to Friends about the work of eldership or oversight? Are there things we assume Friends will take for granted? How will we check that everyone understands what we intend?
2. How can we encourage Friends to be aware of the importance of inclusive communications, and the problems and discourtesies associated with excluding some people, however inadvertently? What actions can we take?

3. What can we do to support helpful and effective communications among Friends? Is there a need for discussion in the meeting about how communications affect the life of our community? How might we go about this?

Queries for meetings

1. How good are we as a meeting at taking care with our communications? Are we sufficiently conscious of how each careful, or careless, communication affects the ways we work together as a community? What does it mean to 'take care'?

2. What do we understand by the term 'plain speaking'? How is it a helpful concept to us in our meeting? When might it be unhelpful or possibly cause difficulty?

3. How good are we (individually) at accurately recalling things we are told? Are we aware of times when getting things wrong has caused a problem – for ourselves or other people? How should we take people's naturally flawed perceptions into account in the ways we communicate as Friends?

❖ These pages can be downloaded from the online resource: **www.quaker.org.uk/tender-hand**

Chapter 17: The Quaker
way of right ordering
~

I am so aware that it is easy to imagine a Society that runs in a happy and spontaneous way with no clutter of bureaucracy – and I know that in real life it is the hard work of unselfish people behind the scenes that makes things happen.

(Welton, 2007: p. 7)

Friends' typical dislike of bureaucracy and hierarchy is sometimes expressed in a general antipathy to 'being organised'. As we say of ourselves, self-mockingly (but with a certain pride), organising Friends is like herding cats. It is easy to see how this can be linked to the Quaker testimonies to simplicity and equality, but Friends also need to recognise that without agreed structures, processes and practices we wouldn't have a Society. George Fox's founding inspiration included the insight that a discipline such as came to be known as 'Gospel Order' would be necessary. Early Friends might not have survived as a coherent body without it.

Today our Quaker ways of doing things can still be traced to an early statement of that insight made by the Elders of Balby in 1656. Their epistle 'unto the brethren in the north' comprised twenty 'advices', which were the first detailed directions to Friends about what they should do in particular circumstances and how they should conduct themselves. It ends with a much-loved postscript, tempering these detailed directions with a reminder of why they are needed and how they may be fulfilled:

> *Qf&p* 1.01 Dearly beloved Friends, these things we do not lay upon you as a rule or form to walk by, but that all, with the measure of light which is pure and holy, may be guided: and so in the light walking and abiding, these may be fulfilled in the Spirit, not from the letter, for the letter killeth, but the Spirit giveth life.

This chapter looks at aspects of a meeting's life that Friends agree to attend to in disciplined ways, in 'right ordering', and in that same light, so they 'may be fulfilled in the Spirit'. Quaker processes emphasise our responsiveness to divine guidance and to each other. We seek to give space and opportunity for discerning together in the light, to take time and care with recording our decisions, and to keep Friends and others properly informed.

These are creative processes that also require some exactness. Fruitful discernment depends on agreeing how and when Friends speak and the way we listen for guidance and to one another. Written communications will only serve their intended purposes if they are clear, unambiguous and factually accurate. However, the ways Friends communicate for matters that depend on right ordering don't have to be stilted or experienced as distancing on that account. We bring ourselves to all our Quaker business and procedures, together with our sense of humour, our warmth and our real personalities. Being real together in the Spirit is in fact how our Quaker processes work.

At the heart of this chapter is the importance of good communications to matters of right ordering. The matters included here are those especially relevant to eldership and oversight and they are each addressed from the perspective of this Theme: Communication. Chapter references indicate where these topics are covered more fully or from another angle, and in some cases other publications and resources referenced in the chapter are the first places to look for fuller information.

1. The right holding of meetings for worship
2. Local and area meetings for worship for business
3. Pastoral care meetings; minutes and written records
4. Children and young people's work; safeguarding
5. Marriages and funerals
6. Nominations business; roles and appointments
7. Legal and financial responsibility; the meeting as an employer
8. Responsibilities of oversight for financial matters
9. Local and area meeting address lists; membership matters

Right ordering – the correct manner of doing things, in keeping with Quaker tradition and practice. A body of wisdom and insights that has evolved over three hundred years of seeking the guidance of the Spirit, and partly captured in the Book of discipline.

(www.ealingquakers.org.uk/jargon_buster; accessed 7.5.2013)

1. Right holding of meetings for worship

Our manner of silent worship has the longest history of any of our practices and is at the heart of right ordering. Meetings for worship need to be rightly held both to foster our gathered stillness and to ensure Friends' practice stays recognisably Quaker. The responsibility of eldership for the right holding of meetings for worship includes helping people understand what is going on in Quaker worship, so they can participate from the start and more fully as they continue to attend.

> Both eldership and oversight are essential for
> communicating our tradition and current practice – to
> newcomers and to everyone in our meeting. We
> communicate by example, by how we explain things,
> in written communications and by making opportunities
> for people to do their own exploring.

Approaches to vocal ministry have changed over time. Our
current conventions are mostly unspoken and unexplained,
yet Friends come to recognise them as part of right ordering.
Vocal ministry is a form of communication that needs our
attention and our support just as much as other practices
'peculiar' to Quakers.

❖ **Chapter 4:** *Meeting for worship* and **5:** *Vocal ministry*
discuss in some depth the role of eldership in supporting
Quaker worship and vocal ministry.

❖ *Quaker faith & practice* Chapter 2 provides guidance
from many generations that will help our understanding
of how meetings for worship are rightly held.

2. Meetings for worship for business and the Quaker decision-making process

Corporate discernment is a central tenet of Quakerism with
a history almost as long as our manner of worship. Eldership
seeks to help Friends understand the spiritual basis of corporate
discernment and the disciplines observed in meetings for
church affairs (*Qf&p* 12.12 e.), and oversight encourages
participation in these meetings, also known as 'meetings for
worship for business' (*Qf&p* 12.13 b.). This section is largely
concerned with meetings for worship for business – sometimes
shortened to 'meeting for business' – held by local meetings

(LM) and area meetings (AM). They are at the core of our community life, binding us in common purpose through the distinctive practice of the Quaker business method. As experienced Friends we can do much to support others in their Quaker journey by encouraging their attendance. *Qf&p* 3.10 suggests that we invite newcomers to come with us: 'Help them to understand the business and to get to know the membership'.

> *Qf&p* **3.02** ...We have a common purpose in seeking God's will through waiting and listening, believing that every activity of life should be subject to divine guidance.
>
> This does not mean that laughter and a sense of humour should be absent from our meetings for church affairs. It does mean that at all times there should be an inward recollection: out of this will spring a right dignity, flexible and free from pomp and formality. We meet together for common worship, for the pastoral care of our membership, for needful administration, for unhurried deliberation on matters of common concern, for testing personal concerns that are brought before us, and to get to know one another better in things that are eternal as in things that are temporal.

Elders have an active role in seeing that meetings for business are conducted in right ordering. It is helpful for one or two elders to serve at each meeting to uphold the clerks and, if needed, to remind Friends of the discipline. Everyone present needs to be aware of 'the onerous task laid upon the clerk' (*Qf&p* 3.10) and the elders' task includes helping Friends' recognise their own part in enabling the service of clerkship. The presence of elders signals too that this is a meeting for worship and that contributions are offered as ministry. Elders who serve at a meeting for business are not always currently appointed elders; for example, any experienced Friend might be asked to serve in this capacity in a local or area meeting where elders aren't appointed, or on an occasion when no currently appointed elder is present.

"The elder is rarely involved in active 'eldering' at our AM but mostly provides a presence which seems to be reassuring to the Clerks. Elders meet with the clerking team in December or January to discuss how we can best support them during the coming year."

Attenders are usually welcome at meetings for worship for business, by permission of the clerk, but may be asked to leave the room briefly during certain confidential items or matters for the discernment of members only. It is good practice for a member – often a Friend in a pastoral role – to accompany anyone asked to leave. When we accompany an attender for this purpose we include them in being part of right ordering; it offers an opportunity to say something to that effect and to explain what is happening in their absence.

Meetings have to undertake their own discernment on the question of which items of business are confidential or for members only. The guidance in *Quaker faith & practice* is very brief, offering only one example: 'It should be borne in mind that some matters, particularly membership, are confidential and cannot easily be discussed with non-members present.' (*Qf&p* 4.08)

Many area meetings routinely exclude attenders from all membership matters, including the reading of visitor reports and sometimes from hearing letters of application too. Here is one attender's account of how that experience affected her (the area meeting has since changed its practice to admit attenders for all membership business, unless otherwise guided by the clerk):

Area Meeting (AM) is responsible for matters of membership so that is where I hoped to gain knowledge and experience of the process of becoming a member.

Generally my attendances at North of Scotland AMs have been a part of my growing relationship with, and understanding of, the Society, but in this case far from enlightening me, AM seems to draw a veil over the whole membership process. Attenders are excluded from matters of membership, not merely prevented from participating, but actually required to leave the room.

So I ask myself what happens in the application for membership procedure that is so confidential that only members who have been through the process themselves are allowed to have knowledge of it? Alarm bells are going off in my head because somehow this feels like some sort of secret. Oh dear! For me this isn't good.

(Affleck, 2014: pp. 25–30)

Increasingly area meetings now recognise that enabling attenders to hear membership applications and reports can be a powerful way for them to learn about the process and meaning of membership. In some meetings attenders are asked to leave during discernment and decision on membership *after* an application or report has been read out; in others the meeting is asked whether it wishes attenders and visitors to leave or to be present; and in others Friends make no distinction between attenders and members for these items of business.

A meeting's discernment on what they consider to be in right ordering could be necessary in many instances where we believe that explicit guidance exists, when in fact it is largely a matter of habit – the effects of which on the community or on certain Friends may not have been sufficiently considered.

❖ **Chapter 6:** *Worship in the life of the meeting* looks at meetings for worship for business as part of an exploration of Quaker worship.

❖ The online resource: **www.quaker.org.uk/tender-hand** lists a number of very readable publications on the Quaker decision-making process.

❖ *Qf&p* Chapter 3 gives us the full guidance we need to understand the purpose and practice of meetings for worship for business (meetings for church affairs).

3. Pastoral care meetings

The Quaker business method is applicable to any group or committee convened for conducting Quaker business, which in most meetings will include pastoral groups. It gives Friends the confidence that they are working accountably, and everyone, including anyone new to the group, knows where they are. However, the nature of pastoral issues may involve us at times in working more freely together and communicating in less formal ways than are usual in meetings for business, which raises questions about how we can keep to the spirit of corporate discernment (see the reference to Chapter 3 below).

Minutes and records

Maintaining records is an important part of pastoral practice. We are advised to keep minutes (*Qf&p* 12.12 and 12.13) and other documentation tends to accumulate, such as reports, paperwork on financial matters and significant correspondence. There is no need to keep everything, but we will find it useful to have a record of matters that recur, and prudent to keep records of contention or conflict.

> Newly appointed conveners or clerks of pastoral care groups will find well-maintained records invaluable for building on previous practice. When we compile our records it is helpful to be aware that we are communicating our experience and learning to future role holders.

❖ **Chapter 3:** *Grounding our practice* looks in more detail at pastoral meetings and business, including flexible approaches within right ordering. It addresses questions of confidentiality and how minutes are passed on, disseminated and stored. It also looks at the implications of data protection legislation on keeping records of sensitive or contentious issues.

4. Children and young people's work; safeguarding

Quaker Life provides resources and information on every aspect of children and young people's work, including guidance and documentation on safeguarding procedures. *Meeting Safety* should be familiar to all Friends working in eldership and oversight. This short document issued by Quaker Life gives an overview of safeguarding within Quaker meetings and includes an introduction to other organisations Friends work with in this area. Elders and overseers have a role in ensuring our meeting works within the policy and procedures drawn up by area meeting trustees, who have responsibility for safeguarding. We should be in touch with the area meeting safeguarding coordinator and know how to raise concerns or take action.

Written or verbal communications with all adults working with children and young people must make clear the meeting's intentions and expectations. We cannot risk misunderstandings about the meeting's duty of care, nor should we let children and young people down with provision that disregards good practice. Where a local meeting lacks a written policy on children's work and care of children and young people, elders and overseers might consider initiating a process of discernment in the meeting leading to the drafting of a policy.

Elders, overseers and Friends working with children and young people might jointly raise awareness of the importance of these and other issues concerning the younger members of the meeting. There is much for a meeting to think about creatively and gladly – beyond agreeing the details of our procedures – if our meeting aspires to become a truly all age worshipping community.

❖ *Meeting safety* can be downloaded from **www.quaker. org.uk/tender-hand**

❖ Example policy documentation is available from Quaker Life: **safe@quaker.org.uk**

❖ Guidance on all matters to do with children and young people can be accessed online: **www.quaker.org.uk/cyp**

❖ **Chapter 10:** *All age community* discusses children and young people from the broader perspective of the role of eldership and oversight in their care, nurture and support.

5. Marriages and funerals

Friends participating in arrangements for these occasions will work closely in one case with the area meeting registering officer, and in the other with the Friend(s) our area meeting has agreed will advise on funeral arrangements, see *Qf&p* 17.07 and 17.14–15.

❖ **Chapter 6:** *Worship in the life of the meeting* considers elders' responsibility for meetings for worship on special occasions. It discusses the significance of these occasions in the lives of individual Friends and for the worshipping community.

i. Marriages

A Quaker wedding has to be approved by the area meeting for business (AM) and is usually arranged by the AM too – though this responsibility can be discharged to a local meeting in certain circumstances. The registering officer meets with the couple at an early stage and will be available to guide local Friends in all practical and formal matters well ahead of the event. Elders will need to uphold and support the registering officer, who might be working with a non-Quaker partner in the couple and non-Quaker parents. Non-Quaker partners and family may have a clear idea of how they would like the wedding to be but less aware of what is appropriate or inappropriate in a Quaker wedding.

Elders undertake certain responsibilities in the preparation and conduct of meetings for worship for the solemnisation of marriage, and both eldership and oversight may have a role in planning and taking part in meetings for clearness where these are held. In some cases the registering officer might refer the matter of whether to allow a marriage according to the usage of the Religious Society of Friends to the AM for decision. A meeting for clearness may then be arranged with the couple, which can be invaluable in helping the AM reach a decision. Naturally, the discernment process on allowing a marriage will be a delicate matter to address, with implications of care for the couple and others, both during and after the meeting's decision.

Remarriage of divorced Friends is one such sensitive issue in a meeting. AMs have discretion on whether to grant permission and may ask for a meeting for clearness to be arranged with the couple, enabling confidential matters to be discussed in a supportive setting away from the meeting for business itself.

While the remarriage may be allowed, some Friends could still feel uncomfortable with the idea, especially if the local meeting experienced first hand the breakdown of previous relationships, or if ex-partners belong to the same meeting. There may be a need for pastoral work to support Friends in their difficult feelings.

❖ *Qf&p* Chapter 16 discusses marriage in all its aspects as they concern Quaker meetings. Friends should only use the current version of Chapter 16, which can be accessed to read online: **http://qfp.quaker.org.uk**

❖ Elders and others supporting the registering office may find it useful to become better acquainted with the subject by accessing the *Handbook for registering officers for marriage in Britain Yearly Meeting of the Religious Society of Friends* on the Quaker website: **www.quaker. org.uk**

❖ **Chapter 19:** *Making connections* looks at meetings for clearness from the broader perspective of ways Friends connect with each other.

❖ **Chapter 15:** *Disability, vulnerability and times of stress* looks further into caring for Friends in their relationships.

ii. Funerals

Often elders and/or overseers will be asked by AM to make arrangements for advice and support to be provided and made known to all local meetings. *Qf&p* 17.15 advises on drawing up AM guidance notes as a way of pooling and sharing local experience. Guidance is usually a welcome support to Friends, who are naturally concerned to bring sensitivity, compassion and care to their contacts and arrangements. These will include ensuring communications are clear and accurate, leaving no room for the intrusion of misunderstandings or of details being neglected.

❖ *Qf&p* Chapter 17 addresses all matters concerning funeral and memorial meetings.

❖ *Funerals and Memorial Meetings: Volume 2 of the Eldership & Oversight handbook series* covers many aspects of right ordering in connection with these events.

❖ **Chapter 15:** *Disability, vulnerability, and times of stress* considers the responsibilities of eldership and oversight for care of the dying and the bereaved.

6. Nominations, roles and appointments

i. A concern of eldership and oversight too

Communications about roles and appointments affect many aspects of meeting life. Nominations committees and meeting clerks seek to ensure that communications on these matters are conveyed helpfully in agreed ways. Where pastoral care appointments are concerned, elders and overseers may participate in some of these communications, for example in welcoming new appointees and providing information and guidance about their role.

Local and area meetings bear responsibility for the way nominations and appointment procedures are conducted, and for how appointments work out, both from the perspective of the meeting and of the serving Friend. In practice, eldership and oversight will support Friends in all things to do with belonging to a meeting community, which in most cases includes their service.

ii. How Friends know about the work of their meeting

Communications connected with roles and appointments flow in a number of directions starting with information about the various roles in the meeting, which ideally will be available for anyone to consult, not only the nominations committee. The information might consist of role descriptions compiled into a booklet and perhaps accessible electronically too. But it is important not to see role descriptions as fixed. Roles change and develop, sometimes quite rapidly, and meetings should be able to respond to that process.

> If our meeting lacks such a resource, we could make a start by asking everyone in post to describe their role in a simple format that ensures essential information is included. There are some excellent examples available on meeting websites that could help us build our own resource.

Another common lack will be apparent where people are relatively unaware of which Friends are appointed to roles and what they do. There is a lot to be said for raising awareness of who is serving the meeting. One reason is that Friends need to be supported and upheld in what can sometimes be onerous as well as rewarding work. In a large meeting Friends will know who the clerk is, and perhaps the treasurer, but may not be aware of who serves on the Nominations or Property and Finance committees, or who convenes the Children's committee. Upholding the work of the meeting or a committee in a general way is not the same as noticing that Hannah, whose son broke his leg on Tuesday, has several meeting commitments in the next couple of weeks.

A further reason Friends need to know about the work of the meeting is that in one way or another we are all involved, and any of us might be approached to consider service we will otherwise have given little thought to. The following are some suggestions offered by meetings for raising awareness of roles:

- Friends introduce themselves after meeting and briefly describe their role.
- Children interview a Friend about their service and write or speak about it.
- Short articles appear in a regular slot in the newsletter.
- Committees hold open meetings from time to time, for anyone to come and experience that area of work in progress.
- A 'Roles & Service fair' (like a careers fair) with short presentations is held, followed by opportunity to visit 'stalls' to ask questions or gather information sheets.

And Friends serving in eldership and oversight must be sure to act on the advice in *Qf&p* 12.06, bringing imagination and creativity to the task. Our ability to undertake our responsibilities depends on ease of contact with Friends and on accurate perceptions and understanding of how pastoral care in our meeting works.

Qf&p **12.06** Elders and overseers (where appointed) will only be able to serve well if they are known and accessible to Friends and attenders. Care should be taken that members of a meeting know which of their number are serving for the time being in each capacity

iii. Caring for Friends at key points in their service

Care before appointment

The accountable nature of communications about roles becomes clear as soon as a Friend is approached to consider service. The approach will no doubt be friendly and exploratory but there will already have been a lot of discernment by the nominations committee about the name and the role, which will be reflected in the letter or conversation inviting a response. In subsequent communications, a role description conveyed at the beginning takes on the nature of a 'contract' – at least in the way a Friend perceives what they have agreed to in accepting nomination. There must be no big surprises after appointment.

Should a Friend feel misled by unclear communications earlier, we shouldn't be surprised if there are problems, including the Friend being unable to serve in the way expected, unhappiness and perhaps withdrawal from the meeting, or resignation from the role. Any of these outcomes are pastoral concerns, which will involve speaking with the Friend, and perhaps also with others implicated in a misunderstanding, to see what might be learnt.

Care at the start and end of a term of service

A formal (and friendly) letter of welcome sent to appointed Friends is a detail of care whose importance can sometimes be overlooked. The letter should include the start and end dates of the period of service and essential information needed to help the Friend settle into their post, including who in the meeting can provide guidance on the role.

This first contact may be followed up by a more personal welcome, perhaps from the convener of a committee, with further information such as details of training events and the funding arrangements for these.

At the end of a Friend's term of service, the meeting's care will often include a personal letter of thanks. Meetings see to this variously, sometimes with a letter from the clerk, sometimes from the clerk or convener of the relevant committee. Thanks are usually also included in the minute recording the end of a term of service.

Where a Friend has come to the end of a three-year term and the nominations committee decides not to invite them to consider serving a second term, this must be approached with sensitivity and care. The worst way is to leave the Friend to learn about the decision on the appointment of someone else to the post. A note of thanks at that stage may not be enough to prevent a natural response of feeling disregarded and, importantly, not trusted to understand or accept the reasons for the decision. It may not be easy to initiate a conversation about this *before* the nomination of another person is brought to the meeting for business, but it really must be done.

If elders and overseers find this is not happening we have a responsibility to advise the convener of Nominations about the consequences for Friends, and naturally with sensitivity and respect for their appointed responsibility.

❖ **Chapter 8:** *The meaning of community* explores the significance of service to how Friends feel included and valued in their meeting community.

❖ *Quaker faith & practice* 3.23–25 covers nominations and appointments.

7. Legal or financial responsibility; the meeting as an employer

Some roles carrying the burden of legal or financial responsibility will need particular support from the meeting. These roles include treasurers and trustees, registering officers (in England, Scotland and Wales) and committees responsible for employees such as wardens, caretakers, cleaners, etc. Friends have to be aware of the importance of clear communications in these areas of a meeting's business, and of agreed lines of contact being observed in every case – for example, between pastoral groups and trustees, treasurers or clerks.

> Meetings do, unfortunately, get into difficulties when Friends take short cuts in what seems a simple matter, such as confirming arrangements or making promises that should rightly be discerned and agreed at a meeting for business. And we should not overlook the possibility of impropriety or fraud, which is not unknown in Quaker meetings.

Friends may find it useful to read '*A vulnerable victim?*', the report of a meeting's experience of the discovery of fraud. It offers insights into what could go wrong in any meeting, given an unfortunate coincidence of opportunity, human frailty, flaws in the system, and a very Quaker reliance on trust rather than checks. This is the vulnerability the judge in the fraud case referred to. There are no easy answers, but the report makes clear that lax procedures not only render a meeting vulnerable, they could invite malpractice in someone who would otherwise have been deterred from stepping over a boundary, and the meeting will have failed in its responsibility to care properly for that person too.

- ❖ *A vulnerable victim? A report for North Somerset & Wiltshire Monthly Meeting*, by John Welton. Quaker Stewardship Committee, May 2007.
- ❖ Guidance on all matters to do with Quaker meetings as employers is available from Quaker Life: 020 7663 1000. *Qf&p* 15.19 discusses trustees' responsibility for the employment of staff.
- ❖ Reading *Qf&p* Chapter 14 would be a useful way to get a sense of the responsibilities our treasurers and trustees bear.

8. Responsibilities of oversight for financial matters

These can be some of the more daunting tasks we undertake, especially if we are approaching them for the first time. *Qf&p* 12.13 m. and n. ask us (i) to be aware of Friends' circumstances so we can be sure they don't receive requests for financial contributions they would find it hard to meet, and (ii) to respond to Friends who either request or might need financial assistance. Financial circumstance is a very sensitive area of anyone's personal life. How do we go about these tasks without intruding on people's privacy, or offending them, or allowing our embarrassment to inhibit us from doing what is needed?

i. The annual appeal (formerly the schedule)

> *Qf&p* **14.09** Treasurers of local meetings may consult overseers for advice on which members and attenders should receive contribution schedules. Some meetings have found it more convenient for the treasurer to appoint an assistant or collector to prepare schedules and send them out, and to manage the contributions.

An approach to this task could perhaps include inviting all Friends generally, and lightly, to let an overseer know in confidence if they cannot contribute financially – which they may or may not choose to do. Overseers might anyway be sufficiently aware of some Friends' financial circumstances to advise appropriately; with others it is probably better to let the Friend receive the request to contribute to the annual appeal along with everyone else than to probe for information. Our guideline will be that if we need to know something as sensitive as this about a person we will ask them directly, not others about them. If we don't feel able to enquire directly, we will have to act without that information. Making discreet enquiries might feel a benign, even loving, thing to do, but in fact it infringes a person's rights to privacy and to be consulted on matters that affect them.

ii. Financial assistance

Agreed local and area meeting policies will be our guide on providing funding of any kind to Friends. If our meeting lacks written guidance maybe we should consider drafting guidelines in our oversight group in consultation with the treasurer or trustees. Being fully aware of established practice in our meeting will enable us to discuss matters clearly with an applicant.

> Overseers should make it known in the meeting that people can claim routine expenses, and that discretionary funding and grants of various kinds for other things might be available. Some Friends may be reluctant to ask for 'charity' and we should keep a lookout for people who may need to be encouraged to accept financial assistance.

Routine expenses

It is often an agreed meeting policy to pay for roles training, for conferences and courses Friends are appointed to attend, and to reimburse necessary expenses incurred by Friends in carrying out roles, including stationery, travel, etc. Overseers are not usually involved, but we can remind people that this is routine and not related to financial need, and advise on how to claim from the local or area meeting treasurer. Some meetings encourage people always to claim expenses, even if they feel they can afford not to, so that no one who really needs to do this feels awkward or exposed. If Friends want to donate money reimbursed, this is done as a separate transaction.

Discretionary funding

Meetings may also agree to meet or contribute towards the costs of Friends attending courses or events, such as those that support their service or their Quaker understanding or spiritual development. Discretionary funding for these purposes may or may not be related to need. For example, a meeting may have a policy of subsidising all new members to attend a course of their choice at Woodbrooke. We need to become familiar with our local and area meeting funding policies so that we can advise Friends with confidence.

Clear guidelines will support our task, but it remains our responsibility to have the confidential conversations needed for assistance to be approved. The first piece of advice therefore is to have other conversations first – with the treasurer and with others in our oversight team. Overseers may need to take requests for discretionary funding to a meeting for business for decision, or they may have their own budget, which they have full authority to administer.

> Meetings often fund costs in part; in which case we might ask an applicant how much they feel they could afford to contribute to the total. Our yardstick for arriving at a fair decision might be to ask whether a grant would make the difference between someone attending an event or not.

Discernment on an application involving financial need will mean at least one overseer having a confidential conversation with the applicant to clarify that this is the case. But it is better for negotiations on the matter not to involve only a single overseer with the applicant – to avoid possible difficulties and misunderstandings. Information about applications might be shared among overseers, but should otherwise be kept confidential. Overseers should discuss a request as a group before deciding whether to endorse it, and they might need to consult local or area meeting treasurers, elders, the nominations committee, or other role holders. Generally the overseers' role will be as an advocate for the applicant.

iii. Other sources of funding

Some area and general meetings have trust funds they can draw on. These will often have very specific terms attached, which overseers should check before taking forward a request for financial support further.

❖ The *Directory of Quaker and Quaker-related grant-making trusts* is an essential resource available to overseers on request from Friends House, on the understanding that it is not generally circulated but kept within the Quaker fold. You can request a copy from **resources@quaker.org.uk** or by phoning 020 7866 1030.

❖ Examples of meeting policies on payment of expenses and discretionary funding are available in the online resource: **www.quaker.org.uk/tender-hand**

9. The local and area meeting address lists; membership matters

❖ *Qf&p* Chapter 11 details the administrative requirements on all these matters, emphasising that procedures need to be simple and flexible enough to reflect individual and local circumstances. Options for meetings to consider are explained in outline and further guidance can be obtained from Communications & Services Department at Friends House (020 7663 1000). Always refer to the most recent version of Chapter 11 – accessible online: **http://qfp.quaker.org.uk**

i. Address lists

The practice of maintaining local and area meeting lists of members and attenders has several implications for how Friends communicate or publish the information they contain:

- the requirement for each area meeting to maintain an official register of members
- the requirement to keep a list of attenders and children not in membership
- the difference between maintaining lists for the record and making lists available in printed or electronic form
- the legal requirements of data protection
- Friends' wishes regarding information to be included and for what purposes
- the need to maintain security and confidentiality by limiting availability of published lists.

It is often a responsibility of oversight in local meetings to bring all these factors together in compiling a contact list, which is then passed on for inclusion in a published area meeting list. The local list may also be published separately and disseminated to local Friends only. But the same requirements of data protection, permission, security and confidentiality apply however and wherever Friends' details are made available.

Friends need to be aware of how much the world of data and information storage and retrieval has changed since the guidance in *Quaker faith & practice* was written, and of more recent guidance on protecting children and young people. For example, it is now recommended (*Qf&p* 11.39) that birthdates of children and young people under the age of 18 should not be included in published/disseminated forms of a meeting address list, and some meetings choose not to include children's names either.

> Clarity about practice within the meeting is important to reassure people that Friends undertaking these tasks take issues of security and confidentiality seriously and are mindful of the risks of information falling into the wrong hands. So we will advise on not leaving printed lists lying around in our meeting venue and we will ask Friends to safely dispose of old lists.

ii. Membership

Communications to do with membership should naturally be unambiguous and conveyed in right ordering, but this should not inhibit us in our informal conversations with Friends about membership and how they might apply. In fact the more we do this the better. We want to be accessible and responsive *and* we need to make the Quaker way clear. The right ordering of membership matters is covered in detail in *Quaker faith & practice*. The subject of membership of the Quaker community is addressed more fully elsewhere in this book:

- ❖ **Chapter 9:** *Belonging and commitment* considers the meaning of membership. It also discusses how eldership and oversight can support Friends in their discernment, and how each contributes to the right ordering of membership processes.
- ❖ *Qf&p* Chapter 11 explains membership procedures and other membership matters in full. Area meetings have the freedom to alter the process of applying for membership so long as the principles in *Quaker faith & practice* are followed.
- ❖ For a clear digest of the main points in *Qf&p* Chapter 11, refer to the Quaker Life leaflet *Membership: principles and*

processes. This is available to download: **www.quaker.org.uk/tender-hand,** or in printed form on request from the Quaker Centre, by email: **quakercentre@quaker.org.uk** or call 020 7663 1030.

❖ *Moving into membership: Volume 8 of the Eldership and Oversight handbook series* was revised in 2011 with a preface explaining that the revision process was necessarily limited and that some details will therefore be out of date. The handbook is useful background reading, but for current guidance on process elders and overseers should refer to the latest edition of *Quaker faith & practice* (available online: **http://qfp.quaker.org.uk***)* or the above leaflet.

Queries for reflection, discussion and learning

Chapter 17: The Quaker way of right ordering

Queries for individual reflection

1. What do I understand by the term 'right ordering'? Where do I notice this positively influencing the work of the meeting? What is happening when it works well?
2. Have I ever noticed a lack of right ordering? What might be causing neglect of right ordering in a meeting matter that needs it?
3. In what circumstances might my actions or my presence – or absence – be part of right ordering? To what extent do I feel I am an essential part of the meeting's formal structures and processes?

Queries for pastoral groups

1. What is our role in the right holding of meetings for worship for business? What does this ask of us, both during meetings for business and at other times?
2. How do we respond to the idea that we have a part to play in supporting Friends in their appointed roles and other Quaker service? How might we go about this?
3. Our group has formal communications links with others who are involved in a number of matters that we also have a responsibility for, such as meetings for worship for special occasions, financial matters, children and young people's work, etc. Can we map

the formal links we are aware of, looking for areas that we are less sure about, and areas that need our particular attention?

Queries for meetings

1. 'We bring ourselves to all our Quaker business and processes, together with our sense of humour, our warmth and our real personalities. Being real together in the Spirit is in fact how our Quaker processes work.' How do we establish a habit of being this real with one another in our meeting?

2. What is the spiritual basis of our practice of corporate discernment? How can our meeting embody and express the spiritual foundations of the Quaker decision-making processes?

3. How do we fulfil our legal and moral responsibilities in matters of employment or finance? How do our Quaker testimonies influence our conduct and communications in these matters?

✤ These pages can be downloaded from the online resource: **www.quaker.org.uk/tender-hand**

Chapter 18: Keeping people informed

~

This chapter is concerned with all those occasions and circumstances when anyone in our meeting provides information for a wide audience. A flow of information is essential for keeping people in touch with what is going on in the meeting and beyond, and for making our presence known to people outside our meeting. Communications of these kinds are largely open for anyone to see or to receive, and invariably one-way: 'This is what we want you to know or to be aware of and we are choosing the way it is conveyed.' As with all communications, the most important part of the process is how information is received. Is it reaching the people the information most concerns? Is it having the intended effect?

> How Friends convey information can be a sensitive area of a meeting's life; eldership and oversight may need to be active in promoting sufficient and helpful ways and ready to respond to the effects of lacks or unhelpful practice.

1. Disseminating information in the meeting

Providing people with information contributes significantly, sometimes hugely, to community building. We feel included when we know what is going on and how our meeting works, and we learn a lot about Quakerism this way too. The meeting's 'business' is of course a lot more than the matters and processes described in **Chapter 17:** *The Quaker way of right ordering.* When Friends disseminate information in the meeting it is likely to be a mix of those kinds of business and much more informal matters. For example, our newsletter may contain the minutes of the local meeting for business, a report from our Quaker Peace & Social Witness representative and dates of events and meetings for a range of purposes, together with a Friend's account of their trip to New Zealand, a recipe for ginger muffins and perhaps a crossword.

Identifying some matters as more 'formal' than others doesn't mean we have to keep things neatly separated – even in our minds. Quakers see the whole of life as sacramental and that naturally includes all our business and all our contacts with others. But we do have to be clear what our communication is for and what we want it to achieve. This will help us be aware of relevant boundaries and whether right ordering should influence our approach.

We also need to hold in mind two groups of people who may be affected by our communication: those we are addressing, and everyone else who will receive it or learn of it. We have to be aware of each of these groups when we communicate information to many people at once:

> When we display a notice about all age worship, do we think of all the people who will read it, including:
> - the children
> - the parents
> - other users of the building
> - adults who have reservations about the idea?

When we announce an event on the subject of death
and dying, are we aware of people present who might
be:
- bereaved
- terminally ill or caring for someone who is
- receiving treatment for life threatening illness?

Different ways for different needs

Not everyone is able to attend meeting for worship regularly
enough to access all the information they need on the occasions
they are present. If verbal announcements and noticeboards
are the only means a meeting uses to convey information, just
missing a single Sunday may exclude a Friend from essential
connections. These days most meetings make information
available in several ways to accommodate Friends'
circumstances:

i.   **Announcements** or 'Notices' after meeting for worship.
     These have to be intelligible, at least in essence, to anyone
     who happens to be there. For example, if we refer to a
     person by name, perhaps we also invite them to stand to
     show who they are; we should watch our use of acronyms
     and Quaker terms for what might baffle, offering a brief
     explanation; we can indicate that further information is
     included in a printed version of the notice; and so on – all
     of which is basic good manners and just needs a little
     imagination. This is not a family gathering but an open
     house that welcomes guests by making sure they feel at
     home too.

ii. **Noticeboards** are often used as a way of gleaning
     information by newcomers or anyone who is not yet on
     a circulation list (and for something to do in an unfamiliar
     lobby with no one to talk to…) They are also our shop
     window for other users of a meeting house. Do they

represent us well? Do they show us caring about how we present ourselves as well as what we say? Do we look like an interesting and welcoming group of Friends?

"We use email a lot, but noticeboards, a flip-chart outside the meeting room on Sunday mornings and notices after meeting for worship all help towards getting news around."

iii. **Printed copies** of notices and other communications can be useful to supplement spoken announcements, though clearly we should try not to produce more paper documents than necessary. There may be a need for paper copies of circulated documents to be posted to Friends unable to receive them electronically and we should remember to invite Friends to request print in large font.

iv. **Newsletter.** Most meetings produce some form of regular newsletter, programme of events or diary sheet. This might be disseminated by email or made available electronically by one means or another as well as in paper form. Meetings should regard these publications as public documents and check that they are accessible to any reader, that their content reflects Quaker principles, and that they serve us well in the impression they give of who Quakers are. There may be a need for audio versions of newsletters and other printed material.

v. **Electronic means.** Various communications can be circulated effectively and quickly using an email circulation list or web-based contact group. Meetings use these means for communications such as weekly notices and for longer communications such as reports and minutes. Information from outside our meeting might be passed on similarly, including the monthly mailing to clerks from Friends House. Any Friend can in fact receive this mailing directly on request, but some meetings find that more people read it when it is circulated internally. A Facebook closed group for our meeting might be welcomed by people who would find it more accessible than other means of receiving disseminated information, bearing in mind that this will become increasingly the case among Friends.

Where minutes are circulated to everyone on the address list, it is helpful if they come with a brief explanatory sentence or two about 'LM' or 'AM' (the same applies if minutes are displayed). Not everyone on our circulation list will have attended a meeting for worship for business and may not know they would be welcome to attend, or which Friend they should speak to about this.

> "To reduce the number of notices we have developed email interest groups Friends can sign up for on topics such as 'Sustainability', 'Peace', 'Animal Welfare', etc. and the clerk ensures that notices relating to these matters are sent to targeted Friends."

❖ **Chapter 20:** *Being in touch in a modern world* discusses email and other electronic communications in further detail.
❖ Information about audio versions of printed material is available in the online resource: **www.quaker.org.uk/tender-hand**

2. Contacts with external organisations – Quaker and non-Quaker

Our meeting is in contact with other local and area meetings, and with Britain Yearly Meeting, Woodbrooke Quaker Study

Centre, various Quaker organisations, and perhaps with Quakers elsewhere in the world. Meetings receive many communications – including appeal requests – from non-Quaker organisations, and often have contacts with local churches and various other groups in the local community. They may use the media for outreach as well or have a presence on social media such as Facebook or Twitter.

> Use of social media by meetings is growing as Friends experience its advantages over more conventional means. A meeting Facebook page, for example, can connect us in an immediate and responsive way with other groups in our community and further afield.

Whenever Friends are in touch with an outside organisation, Quaker or otherwise, we convey something of who we are, both as a meeting community and as Quakers. Not all of these will be communications to do with meeting business, but where such matters are communicated externally it is important that Friends use the agreed channels and that the Friends who need to know – in our local or area meeting, or nationally – are kept informed. We will want to make sure our communication has a good chance of fulfilling its purpose and that where possible we make real connections with the potential for a life beyond this moment.

> Each contact is an opportunity for engagement that can enrich our meeting. Where these contacts are with non-Quakers they are also part of our outreach, including when this is not one of our intended purposes.

From time to time world, national or more local events will arouse the concern or interest of Friends such that our meeting wishes to make a public response from a Quaker perspective. There are various ways of going about this including contacting the local press, using social media, writing to our MP, etc. If a response is urgent Friends will of course act quickly, but not alone. Friends would need to discern prayerfully a course of action and could do so with each other by phone or electronically in very little time if need be.

> "The morning after 9/11 Friends from across our monthly meeting (as it was then) gathered in a public green space and stood silently in worship. No one spoke; no one explained. Passers by stopped – mostly a little way off – and held the silence for a while. Some joined the circle, put down their bags and just stayed."

❖ The Quaker Life *Outreach handbook* includes helpful advice on working with the media, and guidance is also available from staff in Quaker Communications & Services Department (020 7663 1000).

3. Making ourselves known

Members and regular attenders in small meetings will probably know each other reasonably well. In any medium-sized or larger meeting some Friends will be better known than others, and some by only a few people they are especially connected to. Looking around at the start of worship most Friends in these meetings are likely to spot some people they recognise without being able to recall their names.

"I worry when I welcome on the door that I'll ask someone if this is their first time, only to be told they've been coming for the last two years, and that they at least know who I am!"

Irregular attendance, transfers between meetings and frequent new arrivals combine to make Quaker meetings very different from the stable and constant communities that were previously the norm. Friends are missing that background climate of familiarity and knowledge of each other, which in former times Quakers took for granted in their meetings. So this is something eldership and oversight might need to work at.

We cannot turn the clock back, but we can aim to increase Friends' ease with each other and to enable those whose connections with the meeting are looser – or who have only recently arrived – to feel more included in the community.

Common approaches to informing people about our community and raising Friends' awareness of one another include the following:

i. **Introducing ourselves by name** when we stand to speak for any reason. This can be done in a friendly and informal way, for example, 'I'm Ruth Cook and I serve as an elder in this meeting. I'd like to draw your attention to a meeting planned for...' The only time when it isn't appropriate to give our name is when we minister in meeting for worship. It isn't Friends' practice to refer to others by name in ministry either, including the Friend whose ministry has prompted our own.

ii. **Sharing news after meeting for worship**. A regular opportunity for sharing news openly can make a real contribution to the ways Friends find fellowship. Used well a space for this after meeting for worship offers small openings that anyone might pick up on in conversation later. Brief guidance at the start on what is appropriate for the context is helpful to anyone unfamiliar with the practice. This might include an invitation to share our own significant news, as well as news of others – when we are clear they would be happy for us to pass it on.

iii. **'Afterword'**, or **'Afterwords'**. This practice varies; in some meetings it is introduced as a space at the end of meeting for worship in which to share thoughts that might have been offered as ministry, in others as an opportunity not dissimilar from sharing news. But the basic principle is the same, Friends speak in the group about something that feels important to share with others, and everyone listens and learns about one another. Both sharing news and Afterword benefit from being 'held' by the presence of eldership to ensure that the experience feels right following straight on from worship.

"We use 'Afterword' for anything Friends would like to share. It might be something that was 'not quite ministry', a thought about world events or personal news. We listened tenderly to a Friend who asked to be upheld by the meeting in a serious family difficulty, and with spontaneous laughter to an account of a crushing embarrassment."

"After worship we share 'Joys and Sorrows', then we have news of absent Friends, then notices. These are part of the way we care for people. Should we have a caution about news of absent Friends? Are we sure this news is for passing on? I think we have to trust that Friends will use the opportunity appropriately."

iv. **Photographs of people in the meeting,** or perhaps just those in key roles, displayed somewhere prominently.

> "We rent our premises and we haven't got a noticeboard. So we display photos of everyone in an album and prop it open at different pages each Sunday. Our album gives the impression of a large meeting full of children, and in one sense we are. Families have moved on, but they changed our meeting – they are an important part of who we are as a community now."

This is a lovely idea, but meetings may want to consider issues of child protection (safeguarding) before displaying photographs of children, or of vulnerable adults, especially if names are attached. Personal safety implications – perhaps for anyone – will be more of an issue where displays are on a fixed noticeboard and if the display is in a building used by other groups or is open to the public.

v. **Name badges.** Some meetings find these work well; others have experimented for a while and then discontinued because use has been patchy and it takes quite a lot of organising. Name badges are most useful in meetings with many visitors or a shifting population. Even if not everyone chooses to wear a badge, those who do signal their willingness to be known and their interest in knowing others. It isn't only newcomers who find it easier to take the initiative in a conversation when they know a person's name. A meeting might consider doing this just once a month in a simple way, such as providing sticky labels on the day and offering marker pens to write with so the name will be clearly legible. Again, safeguarding might need to be taken into account in some circumstances.

vi. **Welcoming with information.** One element of our

welcome will be to make information available at the right moment. A leaflet rack kept up to date with a supply of the many available Quaker leaflets is a good start. Some meetings compile a 'Welcome pack' that includes a selection of these leaflets together with a homegrown leaflet about the meeting and perhaps a copy of *Advices & queries* too. An attractive cover rather than a plain envelope turns our pack into a gift anyone would feel pleased to receive. It helps if someone in the meeting agrees to keep these packs replenished and, importantly, up to date – especially if they include information about meeting arrangements or roles, both of which can change quite often.

❖ **Chapter 19:** *Making connections* emphasises that welcome is a great deal more than providing information.

vii. **Reaching out.** Eldership has a responsibility for encouraging links with the local community (*Qf&p* 12.12 k.) and both eldership and oversight are concerned to meet the needs of enquirers (*Qf&p* 12.12 j. and 12.13 d.) – which begins with how they find out enough to prompt that first enquiry. So we will encourage Friends to make use of the most up-to-date resources available and to be responsive to ideas tried by other meetings.

In order to welcome people in they first have to arrive at the door. For anyone who has not been before, and especially if our meeting hopes to attract passers by, we will want to make sure that the meeting venue is identifiable from the outside and that our welcome is apparent before entering the building. This may not be straightforward if our venue is tucked away down a side road or we are constrained by the fact that it is rented, but there may yet be things we can do to address 'invisibility'. It can be an enlightening exercise to actually go down the road, head towards the building and ask ourselves:

➤ Can I *easily* spot the place where the Quaker meeting takes place from the directions I was given or found on the website?

➤ Is there anything about this building that puts me off going in?

➤ Is there a notice *outside* the building giving the time of meeting for worship?

➤ Is the entrance door clearly marked? Is it open?

❖ **Chapter 19:** *Making connections* looks at what happens next – once a newcomer feels okay about crossing the threshold.

❖ An essential resource for all meetings, the *Outreach handbook* offers insights and practical suggestions to help us inform people in our wider community about Quakerism and about our meeting.

Queries for reflection, discussion and learning

Chapter 18: Keeping people informed

Queries for individual reflection
1. Do I make a habit of introducing myself by name when I make an announcement? What other things can I do to avoid mystifying or excluding some people?
2. How aware am I of the people I'm addressing when I convey information and of others who might receive it? How can I check that the information I give is being received and understood in the way I intend?
3. What information and communications do I find helpful or unhelpful? What effect does information overload have on me?

Queries for pastoral groups
1. 'Eldership and oversight may need to be active in promoting sufficient and helpful ways of keeping people informed, and ready to respond to the effects of lacks or unhelpful practice.' How might we approach each of these tasks?
2. What can we do towards informing visitors and enquirers effectively about Quakerism and the kind of worshipping community our meeting is? What do we feel needs to be changed or developed in our meeting's current practice?
3. How do we make sure other people in the meeting know who we are, what we are here for, how we can

each be contacted or approached, and who or where else to go to for pastoral needs?

Queries for meetings

1. Are verbal notices, noticeboards, our newsletter, and other ways of disseminating information, serving their purposes effectively in keeping people informed? What areas of providing information could we develop and improve?

2. How do we ensure that all our contacts with external organisations convey an accurate impression of the Society of Friends? How might we raise awareness in the meeting of the range of connections and the part they play in our outreach?

3. In the exercise of approaching our building as outsiders, we each ask ourselves:
   - Can I *easily* spot the place where the Quaker meeting takes place from the directions I was given or found on the website?
   - Is there anything about this building that puts me off going in?
   - Is there a notice outside the building giving the time of meeting for worship?
   - Is the entrance door clearly marked? Is it open?'

   What first impression will visitors have before they even enter our building? What could we improve? Are there other ways we could consider of conveying information beyond our meeting, which might prompt people to give us a try?

❖ These pages can be downloaded from the online resource: **www.quaker.org.uk/tender-hand**

Chapter 19: Making connections

~

Communications among Friends when they meet together for any purpose, including for the formal business of the meeting, are what oil the wheels of our community. This chapter explores the many other defined purposes for which Friends meet in groups, and also considers the contribution to community and pastoral care of informal communications between Friend and Friend or with people outside the meeting.

❖ **Chapter 17:** *The Quaker way of right ordering* addresses the more formal processes and procedures of meeting business.

❖ Section 3 in **Chapter 8:** *The meaning of community* looks at how Friends build community through groups convened for a variety of purposes, including purely social gatherings.

1. Engaging together in groups

It scarcely needs saying that if we want connections in our meeting to flourish there must be opportunities for Friends to come together other than for worship and for business. Social occasions play a significant part, but Friends value engaging with each other in more structured and/or focused ways as well. These might include groups planned for sharing and discussion, for learning and exploration of our Quaker faith, as well as those organised for pastoral care purposes.

Friends not only build community whenever they come together in groups, this is how the life of worship in the meeting is nurtured too. People naturally bring connections and insights from these other activities into the stillness of worship where they become part of our experience as a whole meeting.

> "We hold a monthly meeting for learning before meeting for worship. On these Sundays, worship is noticeably deeper and more gathered."

Our participation in groups likewise helps support meetings for business and the work of committees and pastoral meetings. Friends hear others speak from viewpoints they may not share, but which they come to understand better through listening, reflecting and responding in a structured setting.

Structured ways of being together in groups are designed to facilitate and encourage good communication. Variety of approach is important to meet different needs, and each approach has a useful purpose. Worship sharing will fit some purposes and not others; discussion is harder to organise well but is needed from time to time; on occasion the particular discipline of a threshing meeting will work best.

❖ The online resource **www.quaker.org.uk/tender-hand** includes explanations of a range of different methods for working in groups and guidance on how to facilitate them. This information can also be found in publications you may have in your meeting, including *Spiritual reviews*: *Volume 3 of the Eldership and Oversight handbook series*, which has an appendix listing other publications on the subject.

Most groups we participate in as Friends don't require us to be 'good at' communicating but are opportunities for us to find both our voice and the substance of what we want to say. The real discipline we learn is to become good at listening. All the following examples of group settings ask as much or more of the listeners as of anyone who contributes by speaking:

    i.   groups for study and learning, and for sharing our stories or spiritual journeys

    ii. threshing meetings; meetings for learning

    iii. meetings for clearness

    iv. caring circles or other groups for sharing care

i. Groups for study and learning, and for sharing journeys

There is an abundance of published and often free resources for Friends to choose from including study packs on a range of topics, and most meetings will have a collection of such material. An easier way of going about this is for a meeting to subscribe to *Being Friends Together*:

❖ Developed jointly by Quaker Life and Woodbrooke, the resource *Being Friends Together* provides simple online access to over 1,000 activities and resources for use by groups of Friends in their meetings. For details of how your meeting can subscribe, go to **http://together. woodbrooke.org.uk**. A fuller reference to this resource is included in **Chapter 9**: *Belonging and commitment*: 4. Learning together.

In whatever ways we approach it, any choice of activities or learning programme will be influenced by a number of factors including Friends' interests, the needs of the meeting as a whole, and what will be practical and possible in our meeting's circumstances.

If the answers to any of these aren't clear we may need to undertake discernment as a meeting. *Being Friends Together* includes a simple step-by-step discernment process that will help meetings with this stage of planning learning activities. Alternatively, arranging a varied programme of one-off sharing or learning sessions might enable Friends to discover what they would like more of – and maybe to appreciate the value in nurturing good communications among Friends through engaging together in groups. At the time of writing a selection of activities can be accessed on the *Being Friends Together* website without subscription and anyone in the meeting could do some initial searching for possibilities.

A meeting would be unlikely to entrust the job of choosing activities to one person alone, so Friends would need to agree how to go about deciding what activities or programmes to select, perhaps by appointing a small group to look into this and to make recommendations. As well as choosing a resource or planning their own approach, Friends need to take into account a number of other considerations in order to get learning or sharing groups off the ground:

> **Who is the opportunity for?** Is it of general interest or will it appeal to certain Friends who share a special interest? Is it specifically for newcomers or for people with more Quaker experience? Is it for all ages or adults only? Meetings need opportunities of all these kinds and we should check that different opportunities are offered, say, over the course of a year, to reflect the range of perspectives, interests and needs in the meeting.

> **Will the group be closed or open?** Open groups allow people to try something out, but a group can achieve more depth when people commit to being together for the duration of a course or to ensure confidentiality among Friends sharing personal journeys. Committing

to turn up because we recognise that our presence is needed by other individuals and by the whole group is an important part of what it means to belong to our local meeting too.

➤ **Who will coordinate a programme or facilitate sessions?** Are there Friends in the meeting with facilitation skills? Is there a need for training? Often meetings repeat a formula that feels easy, such as someone giving a talk followed by questions. This can be a useful contribution to a programme of learning and sharing but Friends also appreciate opportunities to engage with their own journeys and experience. Working from a resource or study pack with clear directions for conducting activities is a very accessible way to learn new skills.

➤ **What do we know about Friends' availability?** This is often the hardest issue to resolve, but Friends organising activities must make the attempt to avoid excluding certain predictable groups of people – for example, those in work, or studying, or with children, or with accessibility needs, or who live some distance away. Again, a range of opportunities may be what our meeting should aim for, varying the venue, times and frequency of group meetings.

➤ **How can we anticipate group dynamics?** We will want to ensure as far as possible that participating in a group can be a positive experience for everyone. People who feel confident in their own ideas and their ability to express themselves tend to use groups well (though they might dominate groups too). Some people feel anxious in group settings and find them bruising experiences, especially if dominating behaviour is present. Experience of leading groups is the best preparation for handling such tensions and caring for participants, so we may need to look for opportunities to learn these skills and encourage others to do so as well, perhaps by working alongside a more experienced Friend.

❖ Guidance to help Friends facilitate groups so that these feel safe as well as liberating is available online at **www. quaker.org.uk/tender-hand**
❖ **Chapter 9:** *Belonging and commitment* includes further discussion of the importance of learning together in building community.

ii. Threshing meetings and meetings for learning

Occasions sometimes arise when discernment on an issue will benefit from the whole meeting considering it outside the context of a meeting for business. A matter might need to be discussed first in a much more exploratory way, and sometimes this will reveal that the issue is not one that should come to a meeting for business, or not yet.

• It might be at a stage of questioning rather than making proposals.
• In order to move forward there may be a need for Friends to understand the issue more or to engage with new or complex information. The meeting could be helped by an opportunity to discuss and question information or proposals made available beforehand.
• Where there is contention on a matter Friends might need space and the opportunity to express this in a setting that can be safely held within an agreed discipline.

Sometimes a meeting for learning held in a spirit of amicable exploration will be right for the first two of these scenarios. Depending on the size of the group and the time available, techniques such as brainstorm, SWOT analysis (of strengths, weaknesses, opportunities and threats), small group discussion, etc. can be part of how Friends work with each other on the issue. Whatever way it is organised a meeting for learning needs to be carefully led to enable effective communication.

If an issue is likely to generate strong opinions and differences, the discipline of a threshing meeting – appropriate to the third scenario – should be used. There is guidance to help Friends plan and clerk a meeting of this kind in the Quaker Life leaflet *Threshing meetings,* which describes the process more fully. Be sure to arrange for skilled clerking.

❖ Further information on these and other ways of exploring issues is available online at **www.quaker.org.uk/tender-hand**

iii. Meetings for clearness
A Quaker Life leaflet with the simple title *Clearness* provides similarly helpful guidance. It describes the process and explains when a meeting for clearness is an appropriate process to use and when not. Briefly, it can be used for individuals or couples, but not for groups or whole meetings. In appropriate circumstances, and when thoughtfully conducted, a meeting for clearness can be a powerful means of helping someone to articulate an issue and to find clarity that helps them move forward.

Friends need to be aware that elders and overseers cannot impose a meeting for clearness on anyone; the initiative must always come from the Friend seeking clearness. The only exception is when an area meeting requires a couple to engage in a meeting for clearness in preparation for marriage. In this case the meeting for clearness has a dual purpose: to help the couple find clarity on whether it is right for them to marry, and to enable the area meeting to decide whether it is right for the couple to have a Quaker marriage.

❖ The use of meetings for clearness in preparation for marriage is explained in **Chapter 17:** *The Quaker way of right ordering.*

iv. Caring circles or other groups for sharing care

These may be set up in meetings having very different pastoral care systems, including separate elders and overseers, joint eldership and oversight, or corporate systems of eldership and or oversight. In traditional systems they replace overseers' lists, enabling a defined group of Friends to be in touch with each other and to offer the kind of informal support that comes just from being better acquainted. In meetings with partly or fully corporate eldership and/or oversight, the groups will be the basic unit of contact and support for pastoral care.

Where a meeting is large enough to warrant subdivision for pastoral care purposes, circles replicate the circumstances in many smaller meetings. Rather like the 'house' system that some older Friends will recall from their school days, it creates smaller communities in which Friends have a better chance of forming the bonds we all need to support one another. Often there are further 'mechanisms' to ensure good communication between group members and to enable mutual oversight.

'Linked' systems

In a linked system each Friend is connected to the people on either side of them in a circular 'chain'. They sustain those links with regular contact and by generally keeping each other in mind. Newcomers and people less connected with the meeting might be included in the system as 'spurs', i.e. someone in the circle is responsible for staying in touch with them, but there is no expectation, yet, of a reciprocal relationship.

When and how caring circles/groups meet is usually for them to organise, and might range from a regular discussion evening to shared meals or outings arranged around the needs of children in the group. Groups might contribute as a team to the work of the meeting as well. Whatever other learning, sharing, social or practical activities groups meet for, the underlying purpose is for group members to get to know one another, to be there for each other and to be available to respond to need.

Among Friends meeting together informally there will naturally be plenty of talking, and the listening they do will be a large part of the care they provide. They will agree on how to observe confidentiality and should know where support is available for needs that cannot be met from within the group. Leadership, which might be by appointment or by agreement, will play a significant role in how the group gels and what Friends are able to gain from being members of their group.

A wide variety of communications among Friends in a caring circle or group will cover most of the ways explored in this Theme, including conveying information, engaging as a group and connecting informally; in other words, very much akin to the range of communications in the whole meeting community. Here is one (large) meeting's example of how it works for them:

"Our meeting is divided into six geographically-based caring and sharing circles of between 20 and 30 people. Each circle is responsible for the pastoral care of its members and they do this in various ways – through meetings, social events, telephone trees, shared meals, link-people. Circles take it in turn – for a month at a time – to provide helpers for the children's class, and also to set up the meeting room for meeting for worship, act as doorkeeper and read from *Advices & queries* during worship. Each circle has a convener and the conveners meet together every two months to share ideas and to support one another."

❖ **Chapter 2:** *Ways of working together* explains differences and similarities in the wide range of pastoral care systems found in local meetings.

❖ **Chapter 21:** *Leadership among equals* discusses leadership as an essential service Friends provide for each other, which doesn't seek to dominate but supports initiative and participation in groups.

2. Informal connections between individuals

Informal contacts might appear to have little influence on the life of our meeting, but they are never *just* about personal friendships. All friendships between people in the meeting contribute to community life and this is also how Friends transact a lot of meeting 'business', exchange ideas, accomplish practicalities and care for one another. Each of us is likely to be making connections in the following ways:

i. planned or chance meetings, conversations and contacts on meeting matters
ii. everyday conversations and connections to do with anything at all
iii. 'caring' contacts within the meeting
iv. friendly and welcoming exchanges with visitors, enquirers and people outside our meeting.

Oversight practice should include noticing how such connections are essential to the fabric of our community so that we can build on that – especially by encouraging positive connections of these kinds with people who are less involved in the meeting, and between generations. We may need to discourage unhelpful informal contacts between Friends too. For instance, we will want to avoid the problems that can ensue when people talk about others rather than with them, and the excluding effects that strong connections between a few people can have on others when played out repeatedly in the meeting.

i. Planned or chance contacts on meeting matters

These include all those instances when we (and many others) want to catch up with someone, say on eldership or oversight business, outside the context of a formal meeting. Informal contacts and conversations for these purposes contribute to the work of the meeting by picking up on things in a timely way and by being part of the background to our discernment when we are together as a group. We use them for transacting matters that only a few 'need to know', for consulting more widely than our pastoral group, for checking our actions with each other and for mutual support. And they are helpful to people who lack confidence speaking in groups, as opportunities for sharing ideas, thoughts and feelings.

"There always seems to be meeting stuff we need to talk about on Sundays. I get a better chance of a decent conversation with local Friends when I bump into them at Yearly Meeting or Woodbrooke!"

"A couple of us (this year's and last year's clerks) phone each other relatively often to chat things through."

There are possible drawbacks as well, which we should be alert to:

• We could be side-stepping proper discernment procedure by failing to involve everyone concerned.

- 'Busyness' of this kind can occupy us to the detriment of our availability to Friends in other ways.
- Private conversations going on in corners to preserve confidentiality *will* be noticed and can look excluding.

ii. Informal and everyday conversations

Very often, and happily, conversations and connections between Friends are about many things other than matters to do with the meeting. Chatting around the table at a shared lunch, over coffee or in each other's homes, or exchanging emails and phone calls, are just what we do as Friends because we are interested in each other.

"We make a priority of nurturing a friendly atmosphere during coffee after meeting for worship and making sure people aren't left out. The result is lots of good conversations which support relationships and build community."

All Friends in the meeting will connect with at least some others in these ways, but as Friends serving in eldership or oversight we could both practise and model the art of approaching people we don't yet know, or know well, and opening up a friendly conversation.

Most people enjoy personal attention but may feel uneasy if it appears that this is only the overseer doing his job. So our conversation needs to be genuinely two-way – we will be sharing something of ourselves as well as taking a real interest in the other person. This need not be difficult, people *are* interesting, and it is often remarkable how little Friends know about the life stories or current circumstances of people in their meeting.

iii. Caring contacts

Many contacts between individual Friends will be in the nature of active caring. They might well include being sociable and conversational but will often have an element of confidentiality (see **3. Confidentiality** below) and certainly sensitivity to circumstance and need.

How are our communications affected when their main purpose is to provide care? Essentially, however informal and friendly our contact, we are responding to a pastoral care need and doing what we can to attend to it. So we are accountable for our actions and will act advisedly, that is, under the guidance of our pastoral group and subject to the group's discernment. In that spirit, our caring communications are enabled to be loving and helpful and we can avoid the kind that are ill-informed or ill-judged. Even a simple gesture such as a sending a card will be better done when it comes out of a thoughtful process of considering together how this communication might be received.

"We keep a stock of really nice cards suitable for different occasions, so there's no delay when we want someone to know we're thinking of them."

"Phoning someone we haven't seen for some time feels awkward if we don't know them well, it might put them on the spot. We send a card for the first contact. It's a friendly gesture they can respond to if they choose."

"One Friend who is an artist produced a special card design for the meeting. We send these cards to people who are sick, away or who might just need friendly contact."

❖ **Chapters 11** to **15** explore a broad range of caring contacts in some detail.

iv. Communicating with visitors and enquirers

Welcoming people who arrive at our meeting is something that happens in the moment – a person turns up and a Friend is ready to offer their hand with a friendly and personal greeting. Some people lack the confidence to do this in a responsive way and it is not uncommon for newcomers to be directed immediately to a leaflet rack or to be simply handed information. We can't script a more responsive encounter, and it would sound odd if we did, but it can help to think of our welcome as four steps to a connection:

1. *Greet* – 'Welcome, Friend. I'm Jake.'
2. *Enquire* – 'Is this your first visit here?'
3. *Listen* – 'Hi, I'm Sandy. Yes, but I've been to meeting a few times before, when we lived in Devon.'
4. *Respond* – 'Which meeting was that?'

The four steps are simply an opener to a conversation and to sense how much of that a newcomer will find useful or comfortable. It's missing the point to see welcome as a matter of providing information; it ignores the fact that most people who want information about Quakers or about this meeting can find it on the internet and will have done just that before deciding to come at all.

The information a visitor needs now is what it feels like to be here. If we offer real and responsive engagement (which includes leaving them be if that is what we sense they need) they are more likely to feel at ease and truly welcome.

> ### 'Show' rather than 'tell'
>
> It isn't our job to tell people what a friendly meeting we are; it is to *show* them. So our conversation with a visitor will include what any thoughtful host would remember to do, e.g. point out the loo and where they can leave a coat or umbrella, which door leads to the meeting room, and a brief assurance that they can sit where they like and read a leaflet during worship if they would like to.

Similarly, after meeting we should see it as our job to ensure newcomers are not left stranded with no one to talk to. Welcome is a process of continuing alertness and appropriate attention lightly offered for as long as the newcomer is present that day, and which might be followed through in subsequent contact.

Nor should we see caring for the needs of enquirers and attenders as a separate activity from our care for other Friends. It is just one part of our wider responsibility for welcoming and including everyone and at its best when it feels natural and uncomplicated. We can make welcome our habit in simple and regular ways, such as looking around during coffee to see who is on their own while others are in conversation. That person might be a newcomer – or they might be the Friend who doesn't come to meeting very often, or the attender without a role, or who is otherwise less well connected. They could be someone in a key role, perhaps even the clerk, who Friends don't approach because they assume this busy Friend will have other things on their mind.

3. Confidentiality

Confidentiality affects much of our work of eldership and oversight; each Theme in this book includes discussion of how it applies to various aspects of our roles.

> Confidentiality is particularly relevant to our thinking about the many informal communications involved in pastoral care – there will be occasions when we learn of things we shouldn't pass on and we'll share things we wish others to keep to themselves.

As elders and overseers we are in a position to help the meeting 'consider our understanding and practice of confidentiality within the Quaker tradition of openness and plain speaking'. This is the purpose of the Quaker Life leaflet *Confidentiality* – an essential resource for every meeting. Elders and overseers might consider providing copies to all Friends engaged in pastoral care and to members of committees, caring circles and other closed groups. We must also ensure it is readily available for anyone in meeting who might find themselves entrusted with information that isn't intended to be generally available to others, which will be each of us at different times.

Our practice should include raising awareness and understanding of confidentiality issues – which are an important part of how we build a resilient community together and how we forestall some very common causes of upset and conflict. We could, for example, use the leaflet as the basis of a meeting for learning. Taking this action may become necessary when a difficulty or conflict arises, but will be more useful in the context of our meeting being a place where Friends learn together about all manner of things that support the life of the community.

...how can we be open without betraying trust? How can we share without slipping into gossip? Suppose, however, that some knowledge is hard to bear, or we feel that someone is at risk: is there a limit to confidentiality?

(*Confidentiality*, Quaker Life leaflet, 2011: p. 1)

❖ Each of the leaflets noted in this chapter – *Clearness, Threshing meetings* and *Confidentiality* – can be downloaded from the Quaker website, **www.quaker.org.uk**. Printed copies are available from the Quaker Centre at Friends House: 020 7663 1030.

Queries for reflection, discussion and learning

Chapter 19: Making connections

Queries for individual reflection
1. What kinds of positive contribution do I make when working in groups? What are my less helpful habits? How can I support the positive contributions of others?
2. How often do I use informal or chance conversations for transacting meeting business? What safeguards should I observe to ensure these are helpful and in right ordering?
3. How do I feel about welcoming newcomers to meeting and engaging in conversation afterwards? How can I do this in ways that make genuine connections? Recalling an occasion when I felt uncomfortable arriving somewhere for the first time, what should I do differently for a newcomer here?

Queries for pastoral groups
1. How do we ensure a range of learning and other group activities that allow everyone in meeting to have choices that will work for them? Which Friends find it hardest to attend groups or are least inclined to? How can their needs be accommodated too?
2. What are our own training or learning needs regarding working in groups? How might we introduce less familiar approaches to learning and sharing into the

meeting and help Friends develop skills and confidence, including in setting up and leading groups?

3. How can we encourage more informal connections among Friends, including people who are less involved in the meeting, and between generations?

Queries for meetings

1. What is going on that enables visitors, and all of us, to experience our meeting as welcoming and friendly? How can we build on connections that work well and create more fruitful connections where we find lacks?

2. What opportunities exist for people to share their stories, spiritual journeys, reflections or experience? How could we involve more Friends in such activities and make them a more regular part of the life of our meeting?

3. What part do all our informal connections with one another play in our community? How can we encourage the positive life in these interactions and ensure they don't exclude certain individuals or groups? What more can we do as a meeting to encourage conversation and friendly contacts between individuals?

❖ These pages can be downloaded from the online resource: **www.quaker.org.uk/tender-hand**

Chapter 20: Being in touch in a modern world
~

Advices & queries 7 Be aware of the spirit of God at work in the ordinary activities and experience of your daily life. Spiritual learning continues throughout life, and often in unexpected ways. There is inspiration to be found all around us, in the natural world, in the sciences and arts, in our work and friendships, in our sorrows as well as in our joys. Are you open to new light, from whatever source it may come? Do you approach new ideas with discernment?

Thinking about communications in Quaker meetings can take us only so far before we need to note how *all* our lives are affected by electronic communications of many and different kinds. This process is not entirely new – it has been with us since the invention of the telephone. But the increasing speed of change since the emergence of the internet in the 1980s, with such a radical expansion recently in the range of media or 'platforms', means that this is no longer a side issue. Nor is it a one-off shift; living with technological change is, and must be, a continuing part of principled Quaker thinking about communication.

That unavoidable fact can make for complications in Quaker meetings, which mostly include a mix of Friends who take 'new' technology in their stride and others who feel somewhat alienated by much of it. Friends try to be open to new light from wherever it might come, but can also feel concerned by what this means in practice and seek the safe ground of familiar ways.

1. Facing or embracing change

Friends may feel an element of resistance and antipathy to change itself, along with a practical wariness about technologies whose histories are still very young, which are still proliferating, and whose implications we cannot yet assess. Even so, as a Society we aspire not only to move with the times, but to be often ahead of them – not for the sake of it, but because our enduring principles lead us there. A little perspective can help us see why this is important:

i. Friends have come a long way in recent memory

Quaker meetings have moved on significantly from when – not so long ago – the main ways Friends communicated with each other were face-to-face encounters, meetings, phone calls, letters and paper records. Meetings have been routinely producing their own printed material for many years now, but Friends who go back a bit further will remember the hand-written minute books, kept largely as a record rather than as information Friends might access. Most Friends will not regret taking the step of displaying or disseminating minutes, enabling everyone in our meeting to have a reminder of what has been agreed. That innovation was a natural outcome of Friends who owned computers and printers just using them in the service of their meeting. So our practice changed and Friends adapted to a new way of being better informed about their community.

ii. We can feel emboldened by our history

To put reservations about the influence of new technology on our Society into perspective, we should note the activities of early Friends who enthusiastically embraced the communications technology of *their* time – the printing press. The message of 17th-century Quakerism was everywhere in a steady stream of tracts and pamphlets, many of which are still available for us to read – and to connect with our roots.

> From the early 1650s, Quakers contributed voluminously to the growing mass of controversial religious writings. They published their answers to the questions that were in the air. They denounced what they perceived to be corrupt customs and false doctrines, exhorted magistrates, ministers, and people to repent, and rebutted publications they disagreed with, including many that were directed against the Quakers. Pamphlet wars were waged, in which disputants quoted (and misquoted) each other and replied point by point in a manner not entirely unlike modern Internet flame wars.
>
> (Kuenning, 2003: p. 1)

iii. Our Quaker community is all age and our meeting is not alone

We can be tender with the feeling of Friends who are not ready to relinquish the idea that the old ways will go on serving us well enough, but Friends cannot afford to neglect the task of making digital technology work for our Society – at every level, including our local meetings and the everyday interactions between Friend and Friend. We should particularly not overlook how attitudes might influence the presence or absence in meetings of young people, the 'digital natives' who have grown up with this technology and who use internet and social media platforms more easily even than any Friend – young or old – might make a phone call. There is nothing new about a gap between the worlds of the young and the generations ahead of them. But today we risk a gulf in understanding if our meetings lack a proportion of not-so-young Friends who are making digital communications a significant part of their world.

2. Email

At the time of writing email is the electronic medium most commonly used by Friends to connect with each other. Meetings increasingly use email for disseminating information such as minutes, reports and newsletters, for consulting Friends, say on proposals or draft papers, and for making arrangements and agreeing dates. Using email for such purposes works well for meetings on the whole, and with fewer Friends these days not online there are fewer objections to it being used routinely – as long as alternative options for being included are available.

Friends will be aware of several advantages their meetings have experienced as this way of communicating has become more usual:

- Communicating is quicker and therefore tasks get done sooner.
- The way Friends fulfil roles in the meeting is changing. It has made a big difference to how we carry out essential business.
- Connections have opened up – both within the meeting community and with Friends in other local meetings. It has influenced how area meetings develop a sense of community that includes Friends who rarely attend area meetings for business.

In our eldership and oversight practice we must nevertheless bear in mind those unable personally to contribute to or gain from these advantages. These Friends may sense that others see making special arrangements for their benefit as irksome, or they find that alternatives happen sometimes and other times get forgotten. We should see that Friends in the meeting who often circulate information are aware of the need for workable and regular alternative arrangements.

> A workable arrangement will include Friends without email not receiving absolutely everything by post. As long as our arrangement is clear and inclusive we can expect individual Friends to play an active part in the solution that works for them.

Friends are well aware that communicating electronically is not without its drawbacks or its detractors. As a medium it has to be used wisely and with care or our meetings risk running into trouble. The following suggestions might help elders, overseers and others approach some of the issues that can arise.

i. Meetings where few Friends use email

> Such meetings need strategies that make it possible for email to be *part* of how Friends communicate within the meeting community – anticipating that access to email, and other electronic media, will steadily become more common.

Meetings need to be able to receive emails from other meetings and Friends, and to have access to electronic communications from yearly meeting and elsewhere. Some meetings appoint an email link person – not necessarily anyone in a clerking team – who prints off emails and passes them on or posts them. Larger meetings often devolve this responsibility to pastoral care groupings (e.g. circles), and some messages might be passed on by phone.

ii. Email overload

> What really needs to be sent and to whom? This is an ongoing and fine judgment – Friends complain about receiving too much information and also about not being told enough.

Things can come to a head with people asking to be removed from circulation lists, and others individually requesting to receive certain pieces of information but not the rest.

This might on the face of it seem a simple request, but it comes from a misunderstanding of how addresses come to be grouped in a list. While Friends will hope to avoid sending unwanted emails, it makes sense to use and re-use a circulation list for disseminating essential information rather than to add each recipient individually. The problem of balance is not easy to resolve and everyone needs to be part of finding the answer. Rather than a few people incurring extra work, it might be better if Friends can see that a compromise might be needed, which includes recipients agreeing to glance at and delete anything of no interest to them and senders always checking that their message is essential.

iii. Circulating to everyone

> Before circulating information on a particular subject to every address on our list, we have to ask whether this is the best way.

Are Friends circulating something because they always do? Has there been any discernment on what should be circulated by email and what might be disseminated in other ways? Do we make appropriate use of an email group or online discussion board (which people choose to join or not), the newsletter or a website?

iv. Blind carbon copy (BCC)

When we circulate an email to a number of Friends, should we use BCC or have all addresses shown?

If being inclusive and open in our relations with one another is important to us, we will mostly choose not to conceal who else is receiving a message we send. This preference is usually fine as long as Friends have given permission for their email addresses to be shared. We can probably assume permission if each Friend concerned has formally agreed for their email address to be included in the published meeting address list. If not, the first time we send an email to a group of Friends (e.g. all elders and overseers in the area meeting) we should use BCC and ask people to respond giving permission, or otherwise, for their address to be shown in future mailings.

However, BCC is sometimes used as security against various mishaps or misuses, including an email being forwarded by a recipient to others it is not intended for. Whether BCC is effective for these purposes appears to depend on a number of factors to do with the email system of either the sender or the receiver of the email; we cannot even be certain that recipients will not be able to see, or to access, the other addresses.

Where the purpose of circulating an email is for the recipients to be in touch with one another, then they do need to be able to include everyone in their reply and to see what other Friends are saying. Consulting Friends between meetings on a matter that needs immediate attention (not unusual in eldership and oversight) is an example of this way of being in touch. Another way of enabling this – while guarding against accidental forwarding or addresses being harvested by hacking – is to send emails by BCC and to include in the body of the email (or an attachment) the list of email addresses in a form that can be copied and pasted into the 'To' field of a reply.

❖ Information in this section is based on a Wikipedia article, 'Blind carbon copy', accessed on 1 August 2014.

v. Privacy and confidentiality

Do we assume our private and confidential email will stay private? We can never be certain about that, and if it does go further, it could go very far and wide indeed.

With that caution in mind, the advice to treat every email as if it were a public document makes sense. We should therefore check that we would be happy for anybody we mention in our email to read it. This also ensures we are thinking about them and caring for their feelings, whether or not they will ever read what we say. We may need at times to refer in an email to the existence of a confidential pastoral matter, but discussion or detail must wait until we can speak in person. We should only include what it would be possible for anyone connected with the confidential matter to read without causing difficulty or hurt.

We have to bear in mind as well that the law, currently the Data Protection Act, applies to how Quaker meetings store and retrieve information (including electronically), as it does to any other organisation, and that this includes storing emails too. This means we have to be clear that it would not present a problem to be asked to provide a copy of anything we have written about someone to that person.

❖ Guidance for meetings on data security can be accessed on the Quaker website: **www.quaker.org.uk/tender-hand**

vi. Tone

> It is much harder than people mostly assume to get the tone of an email communication right so that it reflects our true meaning and doesn't carry an unintended message or cause offence.

We can be feeling perfectly friendly as we dash off an email in between other tasks, but to the recipient it appears abrupt or dismissive. We can ask what seems a straightforward question and come across as critical or accusing. This aspect of email communications is well recognised and yet still a bit of a puzzle. It is tempting to think of email as just an electronic letter, but in fact people do write very differently in electronic communications, treating them more like phone conversations.

Without the more considered approach people tend to bring to writing a letter, or the immediate two-way clarifying of a message possible in a phone call, email can and does lead to misunderstandings and sometimes trouble. Part of the problem may be precisely connected with the advantage of being able to reply swiftly. Many of us have come to rely on rapid exchanges as essential to the way we plan our time and commitments, but sometimes waiting before giving our response will be the wiser course.

vii. The right medium?

> Are we choosing to say something difficult in an email instead of speaking in person – face to face or on the phone? If so, we really have to examine that choice from the recipient's perspective.

Email may give us the chance to have our say without being interrupted, but where does that leave the person at the other end? Will they hear us or will they just be angry at our presumption – and blast off a lengthy riposte? Conflict arising from email exchanges often starts this way. It is far too easy to react with our annoyance or our certainty about someone else's action or intentions by immediately opening up an email. If we need to do this – and sometimes the urge is very strong and we cannot let it go – it is a good idea, a useful discipline, to write our message in a document rather than an email. We can then leave it, preferably overnight, before deciding what to do with it. Often just putting it into words eases our tension and might clarify what we really want to say.

If we still believe it must be sent by email, the next thing is to discuss our intention with someone else and to share what we've written. We must give as much attention to how our message will be received as to what we want to say. Do we want our message to chasten someone, to put someone in their place, even to hurt someone who has hurt us? Will they take it lying down?

viii. Email abuse

This is not common, but regrettably does happen. When feelings run high between Friends, they can sometimes get completely out of hand and one person or another might resort to sending a hurtful email – or several – in their anger or frustration.

It is very difficult to stop someone who chooses to use email in this way. We can each decide not to open emails from such a person, but we cannot stop them copying in others who may well read what is being said to or about us. Clearly if something of this kind comes to the attention of eldership or oversight, action has to be taken immediately. The sooner it is addressed the more positive the outcome is likely to be. As with most difficulties in meetings, waiting for things to blow over is rarely an effective strategy, and meanwhile Friends who have been hurt can feel abandoned. Email can exacerbate a conflict, but it is essentially a conflict that needs our attention in the same ways as any other kind.

> ❖ **Chapter 14:** *Conflict and difficulty in the meeting* includes guidance on actions to address this kind of problem.

ix. Good practice and ground rules

> Web-based email groups and online discussion boards are often moderated to guard against misuse of a site and to ensure a safe place for people to exchange views and information.

Usually a set of ground rules operates for these platforms, which members agree to and moderators apply. 'Netiquette' goes a step further in describing the need for common courtesy and respecting other's views. Personal emails are not public in a way that needs moderating by anyone else, but the same principles of courtesy and care for others should naturally apply, as in all our communications.

> For online community and discussion to work, it is very important that everyone feels welcome, safe and listened to. In some ways we have to use more care and creativity when we meet online than face to face. This involves careful consideration both in what we say and in how we 'listen' to the contributions of others, seeking to hear what is behind the words. It is easy to be misunderstood and hurtful online. Please use humour with care and avoid irony and judgemental statements.
>
> (*Woodbrooke guidelines for online learning and 'netiquette'*, 2013)

A meeting that has run into trouble through email accidents or misuse might consider discussing good practice in electronic communications and agreeing to certain boundaries. In addition to clarifying what Friends find problematic or unacceptable in the content of an email, discussion might include what we feel free to do with an email we receive:

> ➤ Is it okay to forward it without the sender's permission?
> ➤ Is it okay to reply and to include additional recipients, who might also receive the whole email string?
> ➤ Is it okay to pass it on in an edited form?

These and other very available possibilities are often done with the best of intentions but can have unfortunate, sometimes disastrous, consequences.

❖ Examples of online ground rules and netiquette guidelines are included in the online resource: **www.quaker.org.uk/ tender-hand**

3. The wider picture

This chapter has so far focused on email as the communications platform currently of most concern to eldership and oversight. But we need to be aware that Friends use a variety of other platforms as well, and will do so progressively.

Less than ten years after its founding in 2004, Facebook was reported by the *Wall Street Journal* to have a billion active users. Twitter had maybe half that number, but generating hundreds of thousands of individual messages per day. These figures are just an indication of the scale and the swift pace of growth and change of social networking media.

Social media are now essential to the fabric of modern communications. For instance, rapid electronic messaging is used both by governments and protest groups worldwide, not only relaying but actually helping to make our daily news. At the same time individuals use these media for the most fleeting of personal interactions.

In between those extremes they offer free and fast forms of contact for interest groups of all kinds. Type the words 'Quaker' or 'Britain Yearly Meeting' into the search box of Facebook and you will become aware of a web of connected sites; use Google to search for any Quaker topic at all and you will gain access to blogs by individual Friends, interest groups and meetings who use them to spread messages or news and to write about issues that concern them; and by registering as a blogger on a page that looks interesting you can be part of the discussion. More and more people make first contact with Friends through links like these.

i. What are the implications for pastoral care?

Social media will become increasingly for many a natural way of maintaining contact and exchanging information. We shouldn't assume that it is only the young who are web-savvy or only older people who are unaware both of the power and the pitfalls of these media.

> Elders and overseers must face their own misgivings, if they have them, and recognise their role in seeing that Friends who use social media can do so to the advantage of the meeting community.

We will have to give these areas the same level of careful attention as described above for email communications. Friends forming interest groups on Facebook have to know confidently just which communications become public to what circle of people. It is now practical to forge networks worldwide at great speed, with corresponding cautions about how such networks are maintained as safe environments. At the level of local or area meetings, Friends might see the advantage of setting up a Facebook group, but immediately have a choice to make as to whether this should be a *secret* or a *closed* or *open* group. (In the first, only members know the group exists; in the second only members see its messages.) The same principled considerations we bring to any other interaction, face-to-face or electronic, will need to apply.

ii. Keeping pace with change

Significantly for how Friends use communications in Quaker meetings, we must be prepared for social media to continue changing rapidly, and to live in a world in which we cannot make assumptions about the means by which any individual is happiest to communicate. Instant exchange of ideas, information and plans becomes possible with social media, but this very facility brings a danger of excluding some people who choose not to use a particular medium. Being a non-user may not be lack of confidence or know-how, but simply a matter of not having time. Paradoxically, these ultra-fast media are notoriously time-consuming.

"My grandson in Australia doesn't use email these days, it's all Facebook, which – he says – is so *EASY*. I plucked up the courage to ask a teenager in our meeting to show me how. Thank you, Ella!"

Pastoral care has had to adapt to the effects that these developments are already having on meetings and the activities of Quakers everywhere, and our practice will no doubt continue to respond appropriately as new platforms and new technologies emerge in the coming decades. We needn't feel anxious about this. The enduring principles Quakers live by in all the ways we communicate with each other will go on being applicable to whatever the future holds, although it may take careful discernment to see just *how* they are applied in each newly emerging medium. Eldership and oversight in meetings can serve to ensure that this discernment happens and that Friends are supported in adapting to change.

> We have to look at our world of proliferating and emerging technology as opportunity, not threat. We live in an exciting age that brings challenges for modern Quakerism that will affect whether we flourish or decline. And yes, we might need a steadying hand at times to meet those challenges. If we can find the steadiness we need in our local Quaker meetings, so much the better for the furtherance of our Religious Society.

Queries for reflection, discussion and learning

Chapter 20: Being in touch in a modern world

Queries for individual reflection

1. What is my relationship with electronic communications? Where can I seek support and encouragement if I lack confidence? How could I support and encourage others if I am more skilled or at ease than they are?

2. Have I – or other people I know – had experience of unfortunate consequences arising from email use or misuse? How did this affect my emailing habits, and what advice would I give to other users of email?

3. How would I contribute to a review of communications in the meeting? Am I prepared to move with the times, or even eager to do so? What might be the consequences of Friends resisting change?

Queries for pastoral groups

1. How can we facilitate learning and help Friends develop confidence with 'new' technologies? What could we do to encourage intergenerational support?

2. 'Social media will become increasingly for many a natural way of maintaining contact and exchanging information.' How do we respond to this idea? How can we become more aware of the implications for pastoral care and be part of raising awareness in the meeting?

3. How effectively are we using electronic communications

to conduct eldership and oversight business? How will we develop this aspect of our pastoral practice?

Queries for meetings

1. Are we making good use of electronic communications as a meeting? Have we got a well-maintained, attractive and informative website, which encourages enquirers to want to see for themselves? If we need help with this or other electronic communications, where will we turn?

2. Do we need to discuss good practice in electronic communications as a meeting, perhaps agreeing to certain boundaries and drawing up guidance? How should we go about this?

3. How do we respond to the increasing use of social media, both in the culture around us and by the Society of Friends nationally? What might this ask of us in our meeting?

❖ These pages can be downloaded from the online resource: **www.quaker.org.uk/tender-hand**

THEME 6: Leadership

Qf&p **12.02** To be without an ordained clergy is not to be without either leadership or ministry. The gifts of the Spirit to us include both. For us, calls to particular ministries are usually for a limited period of time, and those gifts pertain to the task rather than the person. In one lifetime a person may be called to a number of ministries.

(London Yearly Meeting, 1986)

There is more to this extract from the opening passages of *Quaker faith & practice* Chapter 12 than might first meet the eye. This is the only explicit mention of 'leadership' in the whole of Chapter 12, which makes it significant for elders and overseers wanting to understand the place of leadership in how they carry out their responsibilities.

In fact leadership is little discussed anywhere in *Quaker faith & practice*, perhaps reflecting the foundational claim of Quakerism that Friends were led by God, by the Spirit, not by human leaders. Friends' historic stance against hierarchical leadership is still a characteristic of our faith tradition that continues to attract new attenders, just as it did in the 1650s.

But like any organisation, the Society of Friends – and each Quaker meeting – has a structure. Whatever form an organisation's structure takes, its purpose is to make it possible for its members to act cooperatively rather than randomly or on whim, and some people will be needed to take a lead in how that comes about. Our book of discipline may not dwell on leadership but it is rich in examples of Friends whose ministry lays in showing the way for our Society.

Similarly, *Qf&p* 12.02 indicates that leadership will be implicit in much of Chapter 12. We see this most clearly in the responsibilities listed in 12.12 and 12.13, which describe how elders and overseers ensure active pastoral care largely by *enabling* the actions of others.

> *Qf&p* 12.12 and 12.13 advise us:
>
> *to guide... foster... promote... ensure... support... respond... consider... make opportunities... discern... see that... check... arrange for... remind... listen... advise... explore... etc.*
>
> The verb that occurs most frequently is *encourage*.

The lists of eldership and oversight responsibilities describe practical things we can do to nurture the meeting's spiritual life and build community. While they are unmistakably what we understand as service, few are simply things we do for others; many more depend on us taking a lead in enabling aspects of our corporate life to work well and meet people's needs.

This is the sense in which a meeting needs leadership as well as service. Friends could decide something should happen, and then just wait and see. If nothing happens it will be because no one took the initiative. As soon as one or more people set things in motion – by making arrangements, encouraging others, creating an opportunity, involving people in exploring possibilities – leadership is present. In essence leadership is that simple. It is also that essential: effectively, leadership is a form of service a community cannot do without.

Qf&p 12.02 also serves as a reminder that Quaker witness to 'the priesthood of all believers' is significant to how we approach the responsibility of leadership:

- Friends serve in every aspect of the life of a Quaker meeting, including leadership.
- Any of us might be called to a number of these ministries over time.
- A meeting's need is not for especially gifted people but for ways to achieve tasks with the help of Friends who are willing to serve and to lead – for a while.

So we understand leadership in Quaker meetings to be a form of ministry not reserved for a few specially appointed leaders, but a skill, or a potential skill, which any of us might be called to develop and put to the service of our meeting community. Importantly, Friends don't invest leadership in certain individuals who are then seen as indispensable to the running of our meetings. Friends serve in a role for a time only, but leadership is a continuing process.

The two chapters in this Theme explore how a Quaker understanding of leadership is expressed in the practice of eldership and oversight.

Chapter 21: Leadership among equals

examines 'servant-leadership' for its relevance to our responsibilities, looking particularly at the purpose of leadership in pastoral care and how Friends other than those appointed to roles might be involved in taking a lead in our meetings.

Chapter 22: Leading with discernment

considers how the Quaker process of discernment relates to 'being responsible for' aspects of the meeting's life, and reflects on questions of authority in the ways Friends provide leadership.

Chapter 21: Leadership among equals

~

> Let's not be shy about lifting up the importance of human leadership, while at the same time expecting that it will be informed by the presence of the Spirit in the life of the leader, rooted in the spiritual understanding of the community. God has no hands but ours.
>
> (Larrabee, A. M., 2007: p. 11)

It is not uncommon for Friends to see no need for leadership in meetings, possibly because they were drawn to Friends at the start by what appeared to be an absence of leaders in Quaker organisation. If we invite people who are sceptical about Quaker leadership to see it as equally necessary in a Quaker meeting as in any community, what will they find that is different from their experience in other areas of life or in a previous church?

This chapter begins by introducing servant-leadership, a very Quaker approach to leadership that is especially relevant to eldership and oversight. Servant-leadership is not alone as a principled and effective style of leadership – in some instances or in some parts of our Quaker structures other approaches can be more applicable. But here it provides the essential background for exploring leadership in pastoral care.

1. Servant-leadership

> Then a feud broke out among them over which of them should be considered the greatest. He said to them, 'Among the foreigners, it's the kings who lord it over everyone, and those in power are addressed as "benefactors". But not so with you; rather, the greatest among you must behave as a beginner, and the leader as one who serves. Who is the greatest, after all: the one reclining at a banquet or the one doing the serving? Isn't it the one who reclines? Among you I am the one doing the serving.'
>
> (Luke 22: 24–27, (*The Complete Gospels: Annotated Scholars Version*, 1992))

Friends may have encountered servant-leadership as a model inspired by the example of Jesus, perhaps also as the way Quakers have expressed leadership since their beginnings. Friends tend to be less aware that the term 'servant-leadership' has a relatively short history.

In 1970, Robert Greenleaf published his first essay to come out of research into how organisations achieve their goals through leadership. 'The Servant as Leader' described a non-authoritarian model of leadership based on a number of challenging principles that appeared to turn more usual approaches to organisation and management upside down. Servant-leadership calls for ethical and caring behaviour, places a high value on cooperation and community, and promotes the sharing of power in decision-making. Above all it stresses the importance of service over any other function of an organisation or the people within it.

❖ **Robert K. Greenleaf,** a Quaker and retired director of management of AT&T, one of the largest business organisations in the United States, wrote a number of influential books on the subject of servant-leadership. Some of these are available to borrow from the Quaker libraries at Friends House and at Woodbrooke.

i. Being a servant first

The idea of *The Servant as Leader* came out of reading Hermann Hesse's *Journey to the East*. In this story we see a band of men on a mythical journey... The central figure of the story is Leo who accompanies the party as the *servant* who does their menial chores, but who also sustains them with his spirit and his song. He is a person of extraordinary presence. All goes well until Leo disappears. Then the group falls into disarray and the journey is abandoned. They cannot make it without the servant Leo. The narrator, one of the party, after some years of wandering finds Leo and is taken into the Order that had sponsored the journey. There he discovers that Leo, whom he had first known as a *servant,* was in fact the titular head of the Order, its guiding spirit, a great and noble *leader.*

(Greenleaf, 1977: p. 7)

Greenleaf's key insight was that non-authoritarian leadership depends on us being primarily motivated to serve, on service expressing our true nature so that we are *recognised* as servants first. We need to be a servant who is also a leader, rather than a leader who is also a servant. This insight sparked Greenleaf's post-retirement career of writings about servant-leadership, which organisations of all kinds – from big business to schools and churches – found both compelling and workable.

The influence Greenleaf's writing had on the Society, at the time and since, has been more tangential. Friends recognised how servant-leadership was already embedded in Quaker practice and that it had been there from the beginning in the inspiration early Friends drew from Jesus' example.

Christ took not upon him this kind of greatness, nor did exercise this kind of authority; but he was a servant; he made use of the gift of the Spirit, of the power of life wherewith the Father filled him, to minister and serve with. He did never lord it over the consciences of any of his disciples; but did bear with them, and pity them in their infirmities... he did not hold forth to them whatever he knew to be truth, requiring them to believe it; but was content with them in their state, and waited till their capacities were enlarged, being still satisfied with the honesty and integrity of their hearts in their present state of weakness. Nor did he strive to reign over the world...

> (Isaac Penington, 1660, in Keiser and Moore, 2005: pp. 161–2)

Friends also saw that Greenleaf's work could help us appraise and develop our distinctive way of Quaker leadership, that is, leadership among equals.

❖ Further information about the writings of Robert Greenleaf and other authors exploring the same fundamentally good idea can be found in the online resource: **www.quaker.org.uk/tender-hand**

ii. 'Patterns and examples'

Servant-leadership tells us that when we serve people's needs effectively we are able to be more effective leaders too. In supporting the well-being of Friends and the community – which is the essential job of eldership and oversight – our service provides a model of the very thing we hope to encourage in others. It is how everyone learns the way things are done in this community – from taking part in meeting for business to gathering quietly before worship, from supporting a Friend in distress to chipping in with the washing up. A

Quaker meeting therefore needs a core of Friends who habitually reflect the Quaker way, who know the ropes and are seen to be behaving as anyone might expect a Friend should: in the Quaker phrase we are being 'patterns and examples'.

> "For me, one key part of the leadership role has been in listening to and talking one-to-one with Friends, and also trying to deepen my own sense of worship so as to contribute more fully during meeting."

We model leadership similarly. Our leadership doesn't have to be so consistently subtle – like Leo's – that nobody actually notices. There will be times when serving effectively means providing confident and visible leadership. But the same principle applies: we have to practise a way of taking a lead that anyone could learn from and employ, should the need and opportunity arise.

In all the ways we attend to the responsibilities of eldership and oversight, our actions and attitudes model both Quaker service and Quaker leadership. So we need to stay alert to the influence on others of our example. We will observe servant-leadership practised by other Friends, such as local and area meeting clerks, clerks of committees and other role holders, and Friends guiding the meeting in witness and faith in action. Friends have a lot to learn from one other.

By making it a habit to reflect on our own practice and to learn from example, we may also spot the difference between an enabling style of leadership – which trusts other people to have competence and ideas of their own – and 'micro-management'. George Fox is seen bordering on the latter here in a typical instance of practical brilliance, yet he remains well aware that he has to let go and trust. There is no record of whether Fox's son-in law took his detailed advice to him in that spirit!

> And as concerning the meeting place itself, whether the barn or the house, I shall leave to you. But the barn will do better, if you could make it wider, maybe it may be better, because then there will be the house to go into... And the yards are low which may be raised and laid dry, and if you have stones enough, and poor men to get them... And I would have all the thatch pulled off all the houses and laid in a heap to rot for manure to be laid upon the close... But these things I leave to you.
> (George Fox: an unpublished letter to Thomas Lower)

2. Leadership in eldership and oversight

George Fox is an unusual and therefore not especially helpful example to us of how leadership can work in Quaker meetings. On the whole Friends aren't looking for such exceptional charisma, drive and certainty in their leaders – although, like most organisations, we gain from the presence of inspirational people who have gifts of leadership and vision. Britain Yearly Meeting employs a Recording Clerk who may be called upon to be a leader of this kind. (The Recording Clerk is also a servant of the Yearly Meeting and contributes a huge amount of service.)

Inspirational leadership might arise in our meeting or it might not. Either way our sense of purpose doesn't depend on it. Rather, we arrive at this through inspiration shared and discerned corporately. A Quaker meeting needs an idea of what it aspires to, and the direction it wants to move in, and any number of Friends might contribute to discerning that 'vision'.

Leadership comes into the picture when the example of a few Friends taking the initiative – or just getting on with things in agreed ways – both clarifies how the meeting's vision can be expressed in practice and encourages others to pursue it. These or other Friends may also help the meeting discern its direction and purpose at the outset, perhaps through a spiritual review.

> Good leadership works by drawing something out rather than putting something in. It offers other ways of seeing and opens up opportunities for movement and change.

Helping the meeting engage with its vision is the essence of all eldership and oversight practice; it requires Friends offering leadership in pastoral care to be:

- **Observant** – We listen to Friends, we notice opportunities, energies and needs in the meeting, and we reflect these so that others notice them too.
- **Self aware** – We are conscious of our example in how we respond to what we notice or what we hear, and in discerning the way forward through Quaker process.
- **Active** – We are prepared to take the initiative in what happens next; we act to get things moving; we show the way.
- **Enabling** – We encourage and support the leadership of other Friends who provide impetus or direction.

Friends newly appointed – and perhaps daunted by the prospect of fulfilling these expectations – should bear the following in mind:

We share leadership

Eldership and oversight require the kind of leadership just described, but this will be met mostly by the group rather than by individuals. It is elders and overseers jointly, and/or as separate groups, who are expected to take a lead in guiding the meeting community.

We learn along the way

Most people will understand very well that anyone new to eldership and oversight needs time to grow into their role. It is everyone's job to uphold Friends who serve the meeting – in the knowledge that we are all learning, including those who have been around for many years.

And we should remember that while our responsibilities are broad, our leadership is mostly needed in just two ways:

i.   leading the way in conveying the Quaker faith
ii. leading the way in nurturing fellowship.

i. Leading the way in conveying the Quaker faith

A duty to transmit the essentials of Quakerism, including our history and evolving tradition as a Society, is 'laid upon elders' as a thread that runs through most of the listed responsibilities of eldership. Implicit in the responsibilities of oversight is the importance of promoting Quaker learning through encouraging Friends to participate in Quaker process and to experience Quaker practice.

This learning may well happen irrespective of anything elders and overseers do to encourage it, but equally it may not be happening sufficiently or in ways that we would hope.

Our leadership is needed to enable good openings and opportunities for Friends to learn about Quakerism, to promote regular experience of worship and other Quaker practices 'in right ordering', and to convey the Quaker faith by our own example.

> "We have to have a strong spiritual foundation to our work in the world, and that is helped by ensuring that in all we do we are well grounded in our spiritual practice, which includes all our ways of working together. Elders have a leadership role in helping this happen."

ii. Leading the way in nurturing fellowship

Our ministry as a meeting to build community is the principal responsibility 'laid upon overseers'. Through one means or another, many of the responsibilities of both eldership and oversight are connected with helping us work well together and to grow in community. In his essay 'The servant as religious leader', Robert Greenleaf offers a wry comment on why we have to take leadership seriously in this respect:

> In an off the record discussion, a high level church executive, a sensitive and thoughtful person, made this observation in all seriousness, 'I have come to believe, after long experience in my job, that an important passage of scripture should be rewritten as – When two or three are gathered in my name, there is bound to be a fight about something'.
>
> (Greenleaf, 1982: p. 185)

Friends are not faced with the complication of needing to agree on points of religious doctrine, but as communities incorporating diversity of many kinds, Quaker meetings too are prone to disagreements that can affect how we work together in the Spirit. Communities need effective leadership that helps people discover, value and nurture what they share while respecting – and learning from – how they differ. This is how different energies among Friends in a meeting are able to combine in support of a creative and self-sustaining community. And when that comes about, leadership will still be needed but may be as scarcely noticeable as Leo's.

> "Several times in a Quaker situation I've felt for the first several minutes 'Who's in charge here?' Then realised we all were."

❖ **Chapters 8** to **10** explore this subject further.

3. Openings for leadership

i. Leading and following

An essential skill of leadership is having a good sense of when the right thing to do is only to *see that* something is done. For instance, as elders and overseers we will want to encourage fellowship, but might recognise that we neither *need* to be the Friends who initiate or organise events or activities, nor even *should* be. This will be because we understand the importance of enabling leadership in others: our aim is a resourceful community in which Friends have opportunities to gain skills and to contribute their experience.

Quaker leadership is very much a fluid arrangement in which Friends sometimes lead and other times follow as different tasks or roles call for different gifts. Triennial appointments depend on Friends undertaking a range of service, which means that many Friends, perhaps most, will experience leadership at some time. Following the leadership of others is the majority experience for all Friends, and often this will coincide for individual Friends with when they are taking a lead in another matter.

> "I think of our meeting's way of working as a 'dance of leadership' – like a folk dance with different dancers active in turn. When two come to the centre for some moves, others stay back, then these dancers drop back allowing others to come forward. There are no 'head dancers' – all in the formation are equal and play a leading role at different times. All the dancers are listening to the same music."

ii. Making room for contribution

Various circumstances and attitudes in our meeting might influence whether or not leadership is, or can be, a shared experience:

- In meetings large enough to find it essential to spread the load it is common for people to be called upon to take a lead as needs or opportunities arise.
- There may be resistance to the idea that Friends not appointed to pastoral roles could contribute to this service. Resistance may come from role holders or from others in the meeting; either way, we do need to address it. Friends might need encouragement to contribute – perhaps within clear boundaries.
- A small meeting may have too few Friends to appoint to pastoral roles, so a natural sharing of responsibility emerges – and often works rather well.
- Elders and overseers can feel that they should invariably undertake every initiative, that it is their job to do so. Other Friends may be happy with this assumption and encourage it – but this doesn't mean it is a good idea.

- In some meetings a few key Friends stay in post as elders or overseers for many years, often beyond what they or the meeting would wish. In others the same few Friends rotate through three or four essential meeting roles every six years. The longer either of these situations continues, the harder it is to imagine alternatives.
- Elders and overseers can fail to encourage leadership within their own groups, or to agree how that works between a group of elders and a group of overseers.

"We have very widely shared forms of leadership with initiatives for social events, political actions, spiritual activities, etc. coming from many different groups and individuals. Elders play an important role by not 'squashing' Friends' enthusiasm and by encouraging a distributed sense of responsibility."

Sharing responsibility, including leadership, is a necessary part of corporate systems of eldership and oversight, which may or may not include appointed roles. Where leadership is allowed to arise naturally in response to a leading, the meeting has the option of testing that leading in the usual way – through corporate discernment. Meetings with more traditional systems might well do the same; we shouldn't assume that only Friends appointed to roles have gifts of leadership to offer, or that those gifts cannot be used outside an appointed role.

We have to look beyond the 'problem' of how to get jobs done and see the importance of nurturing gifts available to our community. This includes leadership, which is a gift more widely spread amongst us than we often give room for. Do we look further than the same very able Friends? Do adults think of children and young people as also capable of taking a lead and being trusted to do so?

"We give our children responsibility in various ways, e.g. once a term they choose the appeal and speak to it. When we have all age worship children serve as elders, doorkeepers and welcomers. They also choose the theme, organise the planned part of the worship and introduce it. They like being appreciated for this and don't feel patronised."

❖ **Chapter 2:** *Ways of working together* considers various possibilities for how responsibility in eldership and oversight can be shared.

iii. Supporting initiative

Friends feel more able to take a lead when they know that contributions are welcomed as a significant part of a shared enterprise. We can support this understanding through our own example as elders and overseers, such as the ways we seek to:

- encourage Friends to take on responsibility – and support the development of skills that grows from this
- make no assumptions about who might offer leadership based on age, disability or lack of experience
- facilitate collaboration between Friends with different or complementary gifts
- practise a cooperative and collaborative style of leadership.

When it is working well pastoral care is unremarkable and often scarcely noticed. Friends meet, worship, make others welcome, socialise, study together, undertake service and witness, and people feel good about their community. Meanwhile, elders, overseers and others underpin initiatives that make things happen through frequently unseen but significant actions. Perhaps we offer a bit of practical support that helps a group get off the ground, or we spot an opportunity for separate initiatives to work more effectively together. Sometimes our support might be no more than sensing and articulating what is already happening so that Friends feel motivated to carry on. Enabling people to be active and contributing members of their community is both an expression of our leadership and the most valuable service we can give.

> When my son… was in kindergarten, I was asked to coach his soccer team. Not knowing much about the game, I invited Mike Xu, … a friend, to co-coach the team with me. … After Adam Arterbury scored our team's first goal with a kick of over 20 yards, Mike pulled Adam out of the game and asked him to name the two members of his team who were closer to the goal than he was … Over the next several years, the teams coached by the mantra of 'an assist is as good as a goal' could not be stopped; they were unbeatable! …I have often wondered how our world would be different if the principle of assisting or serving others was viewed equally with that of scoring or gaining for one's own.
>
> (Gardiner, 1998: p. 122)

Elders and overseers depend on the support of others in exactly the same way – it is no different for anyone in the meeting. Our common aim is to encourage a climate in which the abundant giftedness among Friends can be nurtured and shared for the benefit of everyone. Being able to develop our gifts is good for us as individuals and essential for the health of our community.

4. Skills for a thriving meeting

The story of Leo (p. 387) only partly works as a model of servant-leadership – from a Quaker perspective. Leo gave the narrator important insights, but arguably at the expense of fulfilling his role as leader of the journeying group. If Leo had been an effective servant-leader he could have left the travellers when he did knowing they would manage without him – because he would have served their *long-term* needs by helping them develop leadership skills. In this more Quaker version, when Leo left, another servant-leader would have emerged to ensure the group stayed together and completed their journey. (But it wouldn't have made such a good story!)

George Fox, on the other hand, did exactly that. With structures and processes he established to ensure the early movement would work as a corporate body, the Religious Society of Friends was able to survive the repeated incarceration of its leader and eventually his death. Meanwhile other leaders began to emerge, enabled by George Fox's founding inspiration to respond with openness to new light. The religious movement, the structures, the style of enabling leadership and that inspirational story are still with us.

As Friends we want our meeting to survive, but more than that, to thrive (as George Fox did too). This chapter has offered a way of thinking about leadership that should support that aim – with an invitation to reflect on our own practice and the way things work in our meeting, and to tussle with the questions our reflections raise. We might gain fresh insights to help us with some of the more taxing aspects of our roles, or find new ways of being a community that works well together in the Spirit. Even if we are simply mindful of the principle of leadership through service it will prompt us to:

- temper any urge to organise others for their own good by remembering our responsibility to listen well and respond sensitively to what we hear
- avoid busily being the person who does everything ('serves' everyone) at the expense of enabling others to gain experience and share responsibility for their meeting – which is also hard work, but of a different and more essential kind
- recognise that we could be called to offer our leadership in circumstances we least expect or would wish for, and that we can meet the challenge of this necessary and valuable form of ministry.

Hazel's anxiety and the reason for it were soon known to all the rabbits and there was not one who did not realize what they were up against. There was nothing very startling in what he said. He was simply the one – as a Chief Rabbit ought to be – through whom a strong feeling, latent throughout the warren, had come to the surface.

(Adams, Watership Down, 1972: p. 196)

Queries for reflection, discussion and learning

Chapter 21: Leadership among equals

Queries for individual reflection

1. How aware am I of exercising leadership in my meeting – through a role or in other ways? What am I looking for in the things I do that will help me to notice and reflect on how I serve in this way?
2. What contribution do I make to the two main ways leadership is needed in our meeting: leading the way in conveying our faith, and leading the way in nurturing fellowship?
3. 'An essential skill of leadership is having a good sense of when the right thing to do is only to *see that* something is done.' How do I respond to this idea? How easy do I find it to let go of the reins and encourage others to take the initiative and do things in their own way?

Queries for pastoral groups

1. 'Enabling people to be active and contributing members of their community is both an expression of our leadership and the most valuable service we can give.' In what ways do we actively welcome and support shared responsibility for worship, building community and caring for one another? And how can we enable this without over-supervising people?
2. How do we, and others in the meeting, learn about

leadership? What opportunities are there for each of us to experience taking a lead and to learn from more experienced Friends?

3. How do we avoid busily being the people who do everything ('serve' everyone)? What is pushing us in that direction, and how can we address it?

Queries for meetings

1. How are Friends in the meeting engaged in both leading and following? Are some of us doing more of one than the other, and is that okay? How do triennial appointments affect this? What do we personally feel about the ways leadership is shared in the meeting?

2. 'We want our meeting to survive, but more than that, to thrive.' What part can leadership play in helping our meeting community to flourish?

3. Do we need leadership? Could we manage just by sharing responsibility and all of us pulling our weight? What do we feel is the downside of leadership? What does 'leadership among equals' actually mean?

❖ These pages can be downloaded from the online resource: **www.quaker.org.uk/tender-hand**

Chapter 22: Leading with discernment

~

This chapter looks at the connection between leadership and leadings – how we lead and how we are led. At the heart of this relationship is discernment, a process that underpins everything we do as a worshipping community, and which is the source of the authority anyone in meeting has to undertake a task or a role.

> The distinctive Quaker practice of corporate discernment is how we arrive at decisions and agree on actions by seeking together the guidance of the Spirit. It is also how we define our structures, and the roles and processes through which our structures work. We can refer to *Quaker faith & practice* for some of the guidance we need, but our own discernment as a meeting will interpret that guidance and find the ways that work for us. This is how it comes about that meetings vary, often markedly, in how they provide for pastoral care.

1. Discerning responsibilities and roles

When we take responsibility for an aspect of the meeting's life – for example, meeting for worship or the needs of children and young people – are we fully aware of what to 'be responsible for' means in practice?

> ➤ What boundaries, or limits, apply to our responsibility? Are Friends in the meeting clear about these?
> ➤ What connection does responsibility have with authority to decide things and take action? How do we know what is within our remit to act on and what not?
> ➤ Is authority, in this sense, attached to our role, to the responsibility, or to the task?
> ➤ How does responsibility for certain tasks or duties work when Friends are all equally responsible for care – as they might be in a corporate system?

The answers to such questions will depend a lot on how a meeting provides pastoral care. Arrangements will usually include appointing some Friends to roles: as elders or overseers; to joint or shared roles named in other ways; as conveners in a corporate system; or perhaps in a small meeting there might simply be a contact person. Depending on how our role is defined, we accept varying degrees of responsibility for seeing that pastoral care works in the ways our meeting has discerned.

Often Friends take the pastoral care system in their meeting 'as read', rather than as a matter for the meeting's discernment, including how roles within the system are defined. This is more likely to be the case where elders and overseers are appointed separately, on the assumption that *Qf&p* 12.12 and 12.13 provide all the information needed.

There is a difference between responsibilities and roles. While the listed responsibilities guide our eldership and oversight practice, Chapter 12 does not define our roles for us. The responsibilities can be met in any system, however differently roles are described, and whether appointments are made or not.

Most local meetings will benefit from discernment to clarify pastoral roles – as Friends intend these to be fulfilled in their meeting. The area meeting may also need to be involved in this discernment (*Qf&p* 12.15). Thinking it through together helps everyone become aware of what they are asking serving Friends to be responsible for, and what authority they give them to act on the meeting's behalf. If there are questions or uncertainties about these things, the most helpful way to address them will be through discernment that at some point is brought to the gathered meeting.

When roles are clearly defined we know at least where our service fits in the meeting's 'map'. Further discernment in each pastoral group will be needed to add the detail: the ways and means of undertaking responsibilities and providing leadership. This discernment has to negotiate a balance between:

- noting what the listed responsibilities indicate eldership and oversight should address
- responding to the needs of this meeting in these circumstances
- being realistic about our resources.

A need for compromises will no doubt emerge, but we will have thought them through together and agreed on priorities. Our leadership role will become clear too through this discernment, which will include addressing the less straightforward aspects of the queries offered above on responsibility, boundaries and authority.

❖ **Chapter 2**: *Ways of working together* discusses different systems of eldership and oversight in meetings.

2. Discernment on questions of authority

Friends understand the one true authority to be the leading of the Spirit, as may be discerned and tested in the gathered meeting. Whether it is useful to apply the word 'authority' to our dealings with each other is another question and might be one of the reasons the word doesn't appear in *Qf&p* Chapter 12. In exercising care with how we use the word 'authority', we should be aware too that leadership and authority are not the same thing: they are related but different aspects of how our Quaker structures work.

i. Appointed or delegated authority

Much the greater part of the way we express leadership in pastoral care draws on goodwill, cooperation and the contributions of others. And from time to time we will need to make decisions and to take action on the meeting's behalf – on the meeting's authority.

> We should be clear that our authority to take actions doesn't come from what it says in *Quaker faith & practice* about our responsibilities. We cannot pick up the table copy to meet a challenge with, 'I'm sorry, Friend. But it says in here that I can.'

We can only act on our appointed or delegated authority by recognising that we are answerable to the corporate discernment of the gathered group. Authority might appear to be implicit in the responsibilities listed in *Qf&p* 12.12 and 12.13, but it is actually given to us by the meeting. In other words, the Friends we serve give us *permission* to serve them.

- In most systems of pastoral care this permission starts with the AM (area meeting for business) appointing people to serve in roles defined by the meeting, and each local meeting discerns how the roles should work in their circumstances, giving Friends the authority to serve the local meeting specifically in those terms.

- In corporate systems the AM may also appoint some roles, such as convener or facilitator, or the LM (local meeting for business) might do this. While everyone has explicit permission to serve their meeting in oversight and/or eldership, and are trusted to do so, local discernment may lead to delegating some tasks to individuals, groups or committees, giving them further authority to carry out these particular tasks.

> When a meeting appoints anyone with the authority to carry out a role or task, it both gives its permission for them to serve as asked and trusts them to do so. Seeing the authority we are given as *permission* and *trust* reminds us that asserting our authority will rarely be a good idea.

ii. Discerning a leading

A question about authority that can exercise Friends concerns 'eldering' someone for inappropriate or disruptive vocal ministry. Only exceptional circumstances require an intervention during meeting for worship, but they do occasionally arise. We are aware that taking action could make matters worse, but feeling the weight of our responsibility we may believe it is expected of us. This is an example of where it is more helpful to think about responding to a leading rather than acting on our authority.

> "I once eldered someone who rose to speak for the third time. I wasn't an elder at the time, but I happened to be the experienced Friend who spotted the right moment and the kindly thing to say. No one questioned my authority to take that action. It was clear I'd responded to a leading to help restore the right holding of our worship."

This Friend did have the authority to act, but not through being appointed to a role. It came from his leading, which – as it turned out – he discerned rightly would serve the meeting. This is not to suggest that it will be okay for anyone to intervene whenever it seems right to them. Discernment about what to do in such an event will be part of eldership practice so that Friends are prepared to respond appropriately.

But this Friend's example does help us see that we each have to bring our own discernment, our sense of where we are led, to how we serve. Being faithful to our leadings is the source of the *spiritual authority* we need to take action. Should elders question the action of such a Friend, hopefully they would focus on whether his leading was rightly discerned rather than his lack of *appointed authority*.

He might have been right to sense the moment and what to say, but mistaken to judge that he was the right person to act at the time. But he could have been right about that too. There will be occasions when no appointed Friend is present, or perhaps able, to respond to a need of one kind or another. In any system of pastoral care, authority rests with the meeting's discernment, and there might be times when this means responding in the moment and checking our leading with others later.

> Whatever the circumstances in which we respond to a leading, we have to be clear that checking, or testing, our leadings is an essential part of how we agree to work together as Friends.

❖ **Chapter 5**: *Vocal ministry* discusses this subject more fully.

3. Discernment as testing

Appointment to a role encourages us to offer leadership, but that alone is not enough. The reality is that we only lead when others agree to 'follow' – by being willing to cooperate or join in. We cannot expect this to happen unless our leadership is responsive to what individuals and the community need, which means we have to both find this out and be aware of how the needs we discover might be met. We can go about this in various ways:

- reflecting on a question to see where we are led
- talking informally and frequently with many different Friends of all ages and listening well to what they are saying
- being observant of how Friends receive the ways we respond to need
- consulting others with eldership or oversight responsibilities informally
- accessing advice or information available from a number of sources
- discerning together in the pastoral meeting
- bringing a matter for the discernment of a meeting for worship for business.

These ways fall into three interlinked means by which we can test how we might respond with our service and leadership:

i. testing through listening
ii. testing through guidance and information
iii. testing through Quaker process.

i. Testing through listening

Listening for the guidance of the Spirit grounds all our discernment and is where we naturally start. We can do this alone, in worship or with our pastoral group. We must also listen to Friends' experience, insights, concerns, ideas and hopes – informally and in more structured settings, such as the discernment process of a meeting for business. This will be the key to how we are able to offer leadership; our own sense of being led, individually or as a group, can only take us so far.

> By being fully present, being open in mind and body and heart, listening unconditionally, one can model the new leadership that places service above self... Authentic listening, focused attention, is at the heart of the essential transformation.
>
> (Gardiner, 1998: p.124)

When it is clear that we are truly listening, Friends are more likely to recognise that we are motivated by an intention to serve, not by misguided notions about our status in the meeting.

❖ Various Quaker ways of testing through listening, both structured and informal, are described in **Chapter 19:** *Making connections.*

ii. Testing through guidance and information

Our faith tradition is a complex inheritance of struggles and clarity, fallow times and renewal, which has shaped our modern Society; fresh insights are continually part of that tradition too. *Quaker faith & practice* contains a distillation of this past and contemporary wisdom and is often the first place we will look for guidance. We should be aware as well of the existence of an abundance of relevant Quaker literature and other resources available to help us in our discernment.

"I see my particular leadership role in helping people to be more aware of how the Society works nationally – not as a 'weighty' Friend but definitely as seasoned by my experience, which is broad as well as long."

Guidance might be available from more experienced Friends in our local and area meetings, and at times it could be important for the group to take advice from staff at Friends House. When we have discovered what seems to be the way forward from accessing the guidance or information we need, we must then remember to sit with this, to turn it around in the light – often as part of group discernment – before we pursue it further.

iii. Testing through Quaker process

From time to time or in particular circumstances, our pastoral group may need to send a minute to a meeting for worship for business for the discernment of the whole meeting. Examples might include a question of a different way of working, a proposal to conduct a spiritual review or a residential event, or perhaps a matter of difficulty or conflict.

Even where a delegated responsibility includes taking action on behalf of the local meeting, circumstances might lead the group to check this is what the meeting wants them to do by taking it to the local meeting for business. Alternatively, our local group might refer a matter to the area meeting pastoral committee, and on occasion, that group might refer the matter for consideration by the area meeting in session by sending a minute to AM.

❖ **Chapter 17:** *The Quaker way of right ordering* looks further at corporate discernment and processes in right ordering.

4. Discernment as learning

Testing our leadings allows discernment to transform our service from the business of getting things done into Spirit-led actions that have the potential to empower the meeting in pursuit of its vision. And we will inevitably meet challenges in the process that test *us* too.

i. What if we get it wrong?

Spirit-led discernment doesn't mean there is always a perfect solution – Spirit works in an imperfect world and through imperfect people. In a meeting for business that has laboured overlong to agree the precise wording of a minute, a Friend might propose that it is 'a good-enough minute' – and it usually is.

We may strive to do our best in carrying out our responsibilities, and also have to accept that sometimes what we are able to do, although not wrong, will be less than we wished and *only* 'good enough'. This can feel quite hard, especially where we hope to make a real difference – for example to a Friend's circumstances, to resolving conflict, or towards building community. Perhaps what we need to do in these circumstances is to be kind on ourselves in our disappointment, while staying attentive to need and keeping other possibilities open.

There will be times when what we do might actually be a mistake: we make the wrong decision or act without sufficient care or forethought. If we are lucky our mistake will have only temporary negative consequences: we can put it right as far as possible, learn from it and resolve to be more careful in future.

> "I got it dreadfully wrong telling someone what I thought about her upsetting another Friend. Obviously I should have asked her what happened before wading in, because what I'd been told turned out to be less than half the story."

And we must support one another when these things happen; blame and scapegoating are often very available but have no useful place in how we respond to human error. We have to keep our attention on minimising harm in *every* direction, and maximising the potential for moving forward.

Occasionally a mistake has more far-reaching consequences. Many meetings can give examples of even quite small errors of judgment having devastating effects, for example on individuals who suffer hurt and are never seen in meeting again, or on a whole meeting that finds itself in a turmoil of escalating difficulty. We can hope to avoid such effects by staying alert to the experience of others and placing their needs above our own confusion or embarrassment. But if the worst does happen, eldership and oversight have a crucial role in mending the hurts, making amends and rebuilding community.

❖ **Chapter 14:** *Conflict and difficulty in the meeting* addresses approaches that will help in instances of this kind.

ii. Trusting the process

> Discernment is a continual cycle of reflection and seeking guidance, considering possibilities, deciding what to do, taking action, and reflecting again to review how it went. This is much the same process when we undertake it alone in a matter that needs acting on immediately, or when a whole meeting works to find the right way forward on a complex issue that could take months to resolve.

As elders and overseers we need to be aware that right answers might not be easily available, and cautious about being too readily persuaded by what appears to be a good idea. But we have to trust the process, recognising that, historically and in our own experience, being open to leadings of the Spirit does repay our trust. Thinking things through pragmatically with as much information as we can glean goes hand in hand with trusting, and sometimes being inspired.

We could hope to feel inspired and certain more often and more reliably, but that is not how it works, which is probably just as well. A particularly Quaker balance of trust in leadings and conscientious testing produces the dynamic form of decision-making that at its best distinguishes Friends. In all the thinking we do about leadership in eldership and oversight, the bottom line is whether we are open to leadings *and* open to learning from where we are led.

> In many instances discernment of our gifts lies very closely to discernment of our leadings – but not always. In keeping with God's mystery and unpredictability, it can happen that we are led into areas of weakness or disability. This may assist us in learning humility; it may help us be clear that credit for successes does not belong to us personally; may uncover and develop unsuspected abilities; may be an exercise in obedience, or function in ways that never become clear.
>
> (Loring, 1992: pp. 12–13)

Queries for reflection, discussion and learning

Chapter 22: Leading with discernment

Queries for individual reflection

1. How do I recognise when an urging to do something is a true leading or coming from somewhere else within me? What is the difference between a Spirit-led action and a simple compassionate response?

2. What is my role in the discernment process of our pastoral group? How can I aid that process, and how might I possibly inhibit it?

3. How do I deal with feelings of not having done enough or of having got something badly wrong? Am I able to review my part in what happened and learn from it? What would support my ability to grow from such an experience?

Queries for pastoral groups

1. How aware are Friends that they collectively give us authority to take actions and make decisions, within a role that the meeting also defines? How clear are we that Friends permit and trust us to exercise authority on their behalf?

2. How do we identify and agree on our priorities within the broadly defined roles we are appointed to?

3. In what ways do we test or check that our leadership is responsive to what individuals and the community need? How do we respond when we find out that we have been getting it wrong?

Queries for meetings

1. How do eldership and oversight roles or delegated duties fit in the overall 'map' of our meeting? Do we recognise the authority of appointed Friends to take actions on our behalf? How is that authority conferred in our meeting? Are there limits to or boundaries around that authority?

2. 'Discernment is a continual cycle of reflection and seeking guidance, considering possibilities, deciding what to do, taking action and reflecting again to review how it went.' How well embedded are our meeting practices in this cyclical process? Are there any stages we tend to miss out on?

3. How thoroughly do we engage with the parts of our processes that require us to become well informed – with factual and other information, and by consulting Friends with skills or experience? How can we make good use of people and resources so that our discernment is conducted as fully in the light as possible?

❖ These pages can be downloaded from the online resource: **www.quaker.org.uk/tender-hand**

Epilogue

At the end of 22 chapters on the work of eldership and oversight, which also pose so many questions, perhaps we are left with a feeling that, really, it is all too much to think about and clearly all too much to take on.

So this is the moment to put things into perspective with a reminder about the book's purpose as a toolkit for discernment – in our pastoral group or in our meeting. And it starts here with each of us personally deciding what feels okay in what we read and what doesn't, what is more useful and what less, when to lay the book aside and when to open it again.

Personal discernment on the service we 'signed up' for is even more important. As the section on self-care in **Chapter 12**: *Receiving care* suggests, we really should see looking after ourselves as an investment that will benefit our meeting and our service, as well as being entirely the right thing for us.

The service of eldership and oversight can be very demanding; there is no doubt about that. But with a sense of proportion and a habit of sharing the load, we can each find that 'the responsibility of eldership and oversight will bring its own rewards' (*Qf&p* 12.10).

Qf&p **21.22** There is, it sometimes seems, an excess of religious and social busyness these days, a round of committees and conferences and journeyings, of which the cost in 'peaceable wisdom' is not sufficiently counted. Sometimes we appear overmuch to count as merit our participation in these things... At least we ought to make sure that we sacrifice our leisure for something worthy.

True leisureliness is a beautiful thing and may not lightly be given away. Indeed, it is one of the outstanding and most wonderful features of the life of Christ that, with all his work in preaching and healing and planning for the Kingdom, he leaves behind this sense of leisure, of time in which to pray and meditate, to stand and stare at the cornfields and fishing boats, and to listen to the confidences of neighbours and passers-by...

Most of us need from time to time the experience of something spacious or space-making, when Time ceases to be the enemy, goad-in-hand, and becomes our friend. To read good literature, gaze on natural beauty, to follow cultivated pursuits until our spirits are refreshed and expanded, will not unfit us for the up and doing of life, whether of personal or church affairs. Rather will it help us to separate the essential from the unessential, to know where we are really needed and get a sense of proportion. We shall find ourselves giving the effect of leisure even in the midst of a full and busy life. People do not pour their joys or sorrows into the ears of those with an eye on the clock.

(Graveson, C. C., 1937)

References

Publications referred to in this book

Authors and editors appear under surname. Publications that are authored by organisations are entered under titles. This list includes only items quoted in the text. For full resources see the online resource: **www.quaker.org.uk/tender-hand**

Adams, Richard (1972). *Watership Down*. Harmondsworth: Puffin Books.

Affleck, Pamela (2014). 'A plea from an attender' in *Scottish Friend*, May. Published by Quakers in Scotland.

Anastasios, Andrew (2010). *Dying to know: Bringing death to life*. London: Hardie Grant Books.

Ashworth, Timothy, and Alex Wildwood (2009). *Rooted in Christianity, open to new light: Quaker spiritual diversity*. London: Pronoun Press in partnership with Woodbrooke Quaker Study Centre.

Becoming Friends: Living and learning with Quakers (2010). Developed for Quaker Life and Woodbrooke Quaker Study Centre by Ginny Wall. London: Quaker Books.

Being Quaker, doing Quaker: A learning resource for meetings (2012), leaflet. London: Quaker Life.

Being ready for children in your Quaker meeting (2012), leaflet. London: Quaker Life.

Bible: *New International Version* (2nd ed., 1998). London: Hodder & Stoughton.

Bieber, Nancy L. (1998). 'Depression: The invisible problem' in *Pastoral Care Newsletter*, Philadelphia Yearly Meeting Family Relations Committee, January.

Brief guide to Quaker chaplaincy (2014). London: Quaker Life.

Clearness (2011), leaflet. London: Quaker Life.

Committed relationships: *Volume 6 of the Eldership and Oversight handbook series* (revised reprint, 2007). London: Quaker Books.

Confidentiality (2011), leaflet. London: Quaker Life.

Conflict in meetings: Volume 4 of the Eldership and Oversight handbook series (2005). London: Quaker Books.

Connecting as a community (2010), special issue of *Journeys in the Spirit: Youth edition*. London: Quaker Life.

Dealing with difficult behavior in meeting for worship: Meeting the needs of the many while responding to the needs of the few (2002), by a task group of the Friends General Conference Ministry and Nurture Committee Philadelphia: Friends General Conference.

Directory of Quaker and Quaker-related grant-making trusts. London: Quaker Communication & Services Department.

Duncan-Tessmer, Christie (2008). 'Weaving children and adults into full meeting life' in *Pastoral Care Newsletter of Philadelphia Yearly Meeting,* January.

Durham, Geoffrey (2013), *Being a Quaker: A guide for newcomers* (2nd ed., revised and updated). London: Quaker Quest.

Epistle (1834). London Yearly Meeting of the Religious Society of Friends.

Finding our way into meeting for worship (2011), leaflet. York: Friargate Meeting elders.

Fox, George, unpublished letter to Thomas Lower. Tuke 2/5/1/1/2, Borthwick Institute for Archives, University of York.

Funerals and memorial meetings: Volume 2 of the Eldership and Oversight handbook series (2nd ed., 2003). London: Quaker Books.

Gardiner, John J. (1998). *Quiet Presence: The Holy ground of leadership,* in *Insights on leadership* (ed. Larry C. Spears). New York: John Wiley & Sons.

Gorman, George H. (2007). *The amazing fact of Quaker worship*, (first published as the 1973 Swarthmore lecture). London: Quaker Books.

Greene, Jan, and Marty Walton (1999), *Fostering vital Friends meetings: A handbook for working with Quaker meetings*. Philadelphia: Friends General Conference.

Greenleaf, Robert K. (1970). 'The servant as leader' in *Servant leadership* (1977). New York/Mahwah: Paulist Press.

Greenleaf, Robert K. (1982). 'The servant as religious leader' in *The power of servant-leadership*, (ed. Larry C. Spears, 1998). San Francisco: Berrett-Koehler Publishers. Reprinted with permission of the publisher. All rights reserved. www.bkconnection.com

Guidelines for overseers dealing with mental health issues (2013). Manchester and Warrington Area Meeting.

Journeys in the Spirit: Children's edition. London: Quaker Life.

Keiser, Mel, and Rosemary Moore, eds. (2005). *Knowing the mystery of life within: Selected writings of Isaac Penington in their historical and theological context*. London: Quaker Books.

Kuenning, Licia (2003). *Publishing old Quaker texts*. Glenside, PA: Quaker Heritage Press, qhpress.org/aboutqhp/oldtexts.html

Lampen, John (1985). *Twenty questions about Jesus*. London: Quaker Books, 1985 (in *Quaker faith & practice* 27.03).

Larrabee, Arthur M. (2007). *Leadership and authority in the Religious Society of Friends* (J. Barnard Walton Memorial Lecture, no. 44). Melbourne Beach, FL: Southeastern Yearly Meeting.

Larrabee, Margery Mears (2007). *Spirit-led eldering: Integral to our faith and practice* (Pendle Hill Pamphlet 392). Wallingford, PA: Pendle Hill.

Loring, Patricia (1992). *Spiritual discernment: The context and goal of clearness committees* (Pendle Hill Pamphlet 305). Wallingford, PA: Pendle Hill.

Mace, Jane (2012). *God and decision-making: A Quaker approach*. London: Quaker Books.

Maintaining boundaries (leaflet). Quaker Life, 2012. Previously titled *A delicate balance*.

Maintaining safe communities (2012), leaflet (previously titled *Sexual harassment*). London: Quaker Life.

McBee, Patricia, ed. (2002). *Grounded in God: Care and nurture in Friends meetings*. Philadelphia: Friends General Conference.

Meeting safety (updated regularly). London: Quaker Life.

Meetings and (ex) offenders: Guidance on accepting into our meetings people who may pose risk (2009, reprinted in 2014), information sheet. London: Quaker Life.

Membership: Principles and processes (2013), leaflet. London: Quaker Life.

Miller, Robert J, ed. (1994) *The complete Gospels: Annotated scholars version*, 4th ed. Salem, Oregon: Polebridge Press.

Moving into membership: Volume 8 of the Eldership and Oversight handbook series (revised ed., 2011). London: Quaker Books.

New expressions of Quaker community (2014), learning pack. London: Quaker Life.

Outreach handbook: Reaching in, reaching out (2012). London: Quaker Books.

Palmer, Parker J. (1977). *A place called community*, (Pendle Hill Pamphlet 212). Wallingford, PA: Pendle Hill.

Palmer, Parker J. (2000). *Let your life speak: Listening for the voice of vocation*. San Francisco: Jossey-Bass. Copyright © 2000 by John Wiley & Sons, Inc. All rights reserved.

Pastoral care of children and young people: Volume 7 of the Eldership and Oversight handbook series (2001). London: Quaker Books.

Patterns of eldership and oversight: Volume 1 of the Eldership and Oversight handbook series (2nd ed., 2008). London: Quaker Books.

Quaker faith & practice: The book of Christian discipline of the Yearly Meeting of the Religious Society of Friends (Quakers) in Britain (5th ed., 2013). Britain Yearly Meeting.

Quaker Life Children and Young People Inclusion Group, final report (September 2008) London: Quaker Life.

Quality and depth of worship and ministry: Volume 5 of the Eldership and Oversight handbook series (new ed., 2013). London: Quaker Books.

Resources and support for children and young people's work (2012). London: Quaker Life.

Rosen, Michael (2011). *The sad book.* London: Walker Books.

Routledge, Jenny (2014), *Living eldership.* London: Quaker Books.

Safeguarding policy (2012). South Wales Area Meeting.

Sawtell, Roger and Susan (2006), *Reflections from a long marriage* (Swarthmore lecture). London: Quaker Books.

Sayers, Margaret (2014). 'Pastoral care of children: Building caring relationships' in PYM e-newsletter, 23 January.

Spiritual reviews: Volume 3 of the Eldership and Oversight handbook series (2012). London: Quaker Books.

Spring into all age worship, leaflet. Quaker Life, October 2012, revised May 2013.

Tabular statement as at 31 xii 2012. Yearly Meeting of the Religious Society of Friends (Quakers) in Britain.

This is who I am: Listening with older Friends. Volume 9 of the Eldership and Oversight handbook series (2003). London: Quaker Books.

Threshing meetings (2011), leaflet. London: Quaker Life.

Wall, Ginny (2012). *Deepening the life of the Spirit.* London: Quaker Books.

Welton, John (2007). *A vulnerable victim? : A report for North Somerset and Wiltshire Monthly Meeting of the Religious Society of Friends* (amended ed.). Quaker Stewardship Committee.

What about the children in our meeting?: Exploring the purposes of children's work (2008). London: Quaker Life.

When the wind changes. (Children and Young People's Committee on Divorce and changing family patterns project, 2001). London: Quaker Home Service.

Wright, Michael (2014), *Faith – What's God got to do with it?*, in *The Friend*, vol. 172 no. 7, 14 February.

Websites referred to in this book

The online resource that accompanies this book: www.quaker.org.uk/tender-hand

Quaker faith & practice: available online at http://qfp.quaker.org.uk

The Quakers in Britain website www.quaker.org.uk includes many leaflets and other resources mentioned in the book. A full list of online resources is on www.quaker.org.uk/tender-hand

Becoming Friends: www.woodbrooke.org.uk/becomingfriends

Being Friends Together, online resource: http://together.woodbrooke.org.uk

Other websites mentioned:

Alzheimer's Society: www.alzheimers.org.uk

'Circles': www.circles-uk.org.uk/about-circles/purpose-and-values.

Jargon buster: www.ealingquakers.org.uk/jargon_buster

Lewes Quakers: www.hitchin.plus.com

Quaker Concern around Dying and Death (QDD): www.quaker.org.uk/quaker-concern-around-dying-and-death

Quaker Disability Equality Group: http://quakerdisabilitygroup.org.uk

Relate: www.relate.org.uk

Wikipedia article 'Blind carbon copy': http://en.wikipedia.org/wiki/Blind_carbon_copy

Winston's Wish: www.winstonswish.org.uk

Woodbrooke Quaker Study Centre, Guidelines for online learning and 'netiquette': http://moodle.woodbrooke.org.uk/mod/page/view.php?id=3486

Index